Vocabulary Workshop
Second Course

- **Words in Context**
- **Analogies**
- **Multiple Meanings**
- **Synonyms, Antonyms**
- **Prefixes, Suffixes, Roots**
- **Word Origins**

HOLT, RINEHART AND WINSTON

A Harcourt Classroom Education Company

Austin · New York · Orlando · Atlanta · San Francisco · Boston · Dallas · Toronto · London

If you have received these materials as examination copies free of charge, Holt, Rinehart and Winston retains title to the materials and they may not be resold. Resale of examination copies is strictly prohibited.

Possession of this publication in print format does not entitle users to convert this publication, or any portion of it, into electronic format.

T 1 2 3 4 5 6   054 09 08 07

Consultant

Norbert Elliot, general editor of *Vocabulary Workshop,* has a Ph.D. in English from The University of Tennessee. He is a professor of English at New Jersey Institute of Technology. A former site director for the National Writing Project, he has directed summer language arts institutes for kindergarten through twelfth-grade teachers in the public schools. A specialist in test development and evaluation of writing, Norbert Elliot has written books and articles on writing assessment, communication, and critical thinking. Dr. Elliot is the father of five children and is married to Lorna Jean Elliot, under whose care, he says, "everything thrives."

CONTENTS

Heritages of the United States

SKILLS AND STRATEGIES
- Context Clues
- Word Structure
- Sound Clues
- Dictionary Definition
- Like and Opposite Meanings

CONTEXT: The First Americans

CONTEXT: Coming to the United States

CONTEXT: Voices of the United States

UNDERSTANDING NEW WORDS AND THEIR USES 123

SKILLS AND STRATEGIES
- Multimeaning
- Word Analysis
    Prefixes
    Suffixes
    Word Origins

CONTEXT: The First Americans

CONTEXT: Coming to North America

CONTEXT: Voices of the United States

CONNECTING NEW WORDS AND PATTERNS 155

SKILLS AND STRATEGIES
- Understanding Analogies
- Types of Analogies
- Solving Analogies

READING NEW WORDS IN CONTEXT 173

SKILLS AND STRATEGIES
- Reading Longer Passages
- Reading Strategically

CONTEXT: The First Americans

CONTEXT: Coming to the United States

CONTEXT: Voices of the United States

The following tables list some common roots, prefixes, and suffixes. Use these tables to help you determine the meaning of a word by examining its structure.

ROOTS		
BASE	**MEANING**	**EXAMPLES**
act	to do, drive	**act**ion, **act**or, re**act**, trans**act**, en**act**
alt	high	**alt**itude, **alt**imeter
ann, enn	year	**ann**ual, per**enn**ial, bicent**enn**ial
aqua	water	**aqua**rium, **aqua**marine, **aqua**naut
aster, astro	star	**astro**nomy, **astro**nomical, **aster**isk
aud	to hear	**aud**ience, **aud**itorium, **aud**ible
biblio, bibli	book	**biblio**grapher, **biblio**mania, **bibli**cal
bio	life	**bio**logy, **bio**chemistry, **bio**degradable
cede	to go; to yield	inter**cede**, super**cede**, con**cede**
cent	one hundred	per**cent**, bi**cent**ennial, **cent**ennial
chrono	time	**chrono**logy, **chrono**meter, **chrono**scope
circ, circum	around	**circum**ference, **circ**le, **circ**ular
cred	to believe, trust	**cred**ibility, in**cred**ible, **cred**it, **cred**ential
dem	people	**dem**ocracy, **dem**agogue, epi**dem**ic
dent	tooth	**dent**ist, **dent**al, **dent**ifrice
dic, dict	to say, to speak; to assert	**dict**ion, **dict**ionary, **dict**ate
dur	hard, lasting	**dur**ation, **dur**able, en**dur**e
fin	end, limit	**fin**ish, **fin**ite, in**fin**ite, **fin**al
gen	race, family, kind	**gen**ealogy, **gen**eral, **gen**eration
geo	earth	**geo**logy, **geo**centric, **geo**dynamics
graph, gram	to write, draw, record	auto**graph**, tele**gram**, para**graph**
hab	to have, hold; to dwell	**hab**it, **hab**itat, in**hab**it
hydro	water	**hydro**gen, **hydro**dynamics, **hydro**plane
hypo	under, below	**hypo**dermic, **hypo**tension, **hypo**thermia
jur, jus, judic	law, right, judgment	**jur**ist, **jus**tify, **judic**ial
leg	law	**leg**al, **leg**islator, **leg**itimate
loc	place	**loc**al, **loc**alize, re**loc**ate, dis**loc**ate

ROOTS (continued)

BASE	MEANING	EXAMPLES
logue, logo	idea, word, speech, reason	dia**logue**, mono**logue**, epi**logue**, **log**ical
manu	hand	**manu**al, **manu**facture
med, medi	middle	**med**iate, **med**ieval, **medi**ocre
meter, metr	measure	dia**meter**, **metr**ic, milli**meter**
morph	form	pseudo**morph**, meso**morph**, meta**morph**osis
micro	small	**micro**scope, **micro**organism
mono	one	**mono**logue, **mono**gamy, **mono**graph
mov, mob, mot	to move	**mob**, **mob**ile, re**mov**e, **mot**ion
noc, nox	night	equi**nox**, **noc**turnal, **noc**turne
ped	foot	**ped**estal, **ped**estrian, **ped**al
peri	around	**peri**meter, **peri**scope, **peri**phery
petr	rock	**petr**ify, **petr**oleum, **petr**oglyph
phon	sound, voice	**phon**etics, **phon**ics, tele**phone**
photo	light	**photo**graphy, **photo**flash, **photo**genic
port	to carry	im**port**, ex**port**, **port**able
pyr	fire	**pyr**omania, **pyr**otechnic
sci	to know	con**sci**ence, **sci**ence, **sci**entist
scope	to see	kaleido**scope**, tele**scope**, micro**scope**
scrib, script	to write	in**scrib**e, sub**script**ion, **script**
sign	mark	**sign**al, **sign**ature, in**sign**ia
spec, spect, spic	to see, look at, behold	in**spect**, re**spect**, **spect**acle, **spec**ies
syn, sym	together	**sym**phony, **syn**thesize
techn	art, skill	**techn**ical, **techn**ology, **techn**ique
temp	time	**temp**orary, **temp**er
therm	heat	**therm**ometer, **therm**onuclear
tract	to pull, draw	at**tract**, re**tract**, **tract**ion
vis, vid	to see, look	re**vis**ion, **vid**eo, **vis**ible
volve	roll	in**volve**, re**volve**, re**volu**tion

PREFIXES

PREFIX	MEANING	EXAMPLES
ab–	from; away from	**ab**normal, **ab**duct, **ab**sent, **ab**hor
ad–	to; motion toward; addition to	**ad**apt, **ad**dict, **ad**here, **ad**mit
aero–	air	**aero**bic, **aero**biology, **aero**space
amphi–	both, around	**amphi**bian, **amphi**theater
an–	not	**an**archy, **an**esthesia, **an**onymous
ante–	before	**ante**bellum, **ante**cede, **ante**date
anti–	against; opposite; reverse	**anti**aircraft, **anti**freeze, **anti**biotics
ap–	to; nearness to	**ap**proximate, **ap**point, **ap**proach
auto–	self	**auto**matic, **auto**graph, **auto**biography
bene–	good	**bene**diction, **bene**factor, **bene**volent
bi–	two	**bi**facial, **bi**focal, **bi**ennial
circum–	around	**circum**navigate, **circum**ference
co–, con–	together	**co**author, **co**operate, **con**front, **con**found
contra–	against	**contra**dict, **contra**distinguish, **contra**ry
de–	opposite of; away from; undo	**de**activate, **de**form, **de**grade, **de**plete, **de**scend
dis–	opposite	**dis**agree, **dis**arm, **dis**continue, **dis**honest
ex–	out; beyond; away from; former	**ex**cel, **ex**clude, **ex**hale, **ex**ile
extra–	outside; beyond; besides	**extra**ordinary, **extra**curricular
for–	not	**for**bid, **for**get, **for**go
fore–	before	**fore**cast, **fore**word, **fore**stall, **fore**thought
hyper–	more than normal; too much	**hyper**active, **hyper**critical, **hyper**tension
il–	not	**il**legal, **il**legible, **il**literate, **il**logical
im–	into	**im**mediate, **im**merse, **im**migrate, **im**port
im–	not	**im**balance, **im**mature, **im**mobilize
in–	not; go into	**in**accurate, **in**active, **in**habit
inter–	among; between	**inter**action, **inter**cede, **inter**change
intra–	within	**intra**mural, **intra**state, **intra**venous
ir–	not	**ir**redeemable, **ir**regular, **ir**responsible
mal–	wrong; bad	**mal**adjusted, **mal**function, **mal**ice
mis–	wrong; bad; no; not	**mis**fire, **mis**behave, **mis**conduct
non–	not; opposite of	**non**committal, **non**conductor, **non**partisan
ob–	against	**ob**stacle, **ob**stinate, **ob**struct, **ob**ject

PREFIXES (continued)		
PREFIX	**MEANING**	**EXAMPLES**
per–	through	**per**colate, **per**ceive
post–	after	**post**glacial, **post**graduate, **post**erior
pre–	before	**pre**amble, **pre**arrange, **pre**caution
pro–	before; for; in support of	**pro**gnosis, **pro**gram, **pro**logue, **pro**phet
pro–	forward	**pro**ceed, **pro**duce, **pro**ficient, **pro**gress
re–	back; again	**re**call, **re**cede, **re**flect, **re**pay
retro–	backward	**retro**active, **retro**spect, **retro**cede
se–	apart	**se**cure, **se**cede, **se**cession
self–	of the self	**self**-taught, **self**-worth, **self**-respect, **self**ish
semi–	half; partly	**semi**circle, **semi**formal, **semi**trailer
sub–	under; beneath	**sub**contract, **sub**ject, **sub**marine, **sub**merge
super–	over	**super**abound, **super**abundant, **super**human
sur–	over; above	**sur**charge, **sur**face, **sur**mount, **sur**pass
trans–	across; over	**trans**atlantic, **trans**cend, **trans**cribe, **trans**fer
ultra–	extremely	**ultra**liberal, **ultra**modern, **ultra**sonic
un–	not	**un**able, **un**comfortable, **un**certain, **un**happy

SUFFIXES

SUFFIX	MEANING	EXAMPLES
–able, ible	able to be; capable of being	intelligible, probable, inevitable
–ade	action or process	blockade, escapade, parade
–age	action or process	marriage, pilgrimage, voyage
–al, –ial	of; like; relating to; suitable for	potential, musical, national
–ance	act; process; quality; state of being	tolerance, alliance, acceptance
–ant	one who	assistant, immigrant, merchant
–ary	of; like; relating to	customary, honorary, obituary
–ate	characteristic of; to become	officiate, consecrate, activate
–cle, –icle	small	corpuscle, cubicle, particle
–cy	fact or state of being	diplomacy, privacy, relevancy
–dom	state or quality of	boredom, freedom, martyrdom
–ence	act or state of being	occurrence, conference
–ent	doing; having; showing	fraudulent, dependent, negligent
–er	one who; that which	boxer, rancher, employer
–ery	place for; act, practice of	surgery, robbery, nursery
–esque	like	picturesque, statuesque
–ess	female	goddess, heiress, princess
–ful	full of	careful, fearful, joyful, thoughtful
–ible	capable of being	collectible, legible, divisible
–ic	relating to; characteristic of	comic, historic, poetic, public
–ify	to make; to cause to be	modify, glorify, beautify, pacify
–ion	act, condition, or result of	calculation, action, confederation
–ish	of or belonging to; characterized by	tallish, amateurish, selfish
–ism	act, practice, or result of; example	barbarism, heroism, cyncism
–ity	condition; state of being	integrity, sincerity, calamity, purity
–ive	of; relating to; belonging to; tending to	inquisitive, active, creative
–ize	make; cause to be; subject to	jeopardize, standardize, computerize
–less	without	ageless, careless, thoughtless, tireless
–let	small	islet, leaflet, owlet, rivulet, starlet
–like	like; characteristic of	childlike, waiflike
–logy	study or theory of	biology, ecology, geology

SUFFIXES (continued)		
SUFFIX	**MEANING**	**EXAMPLES**
–ly	every	daily, weekly, monthly, yearly
–ly	like; characteristic of	fatherly, queenly, deadly
–ly	resembling	officially, sincerely, kindly
–ment	action or process	development, government
–ment	state or quality of	amusement, amazement, predicament
–ment	product or thing	fragment, instrument, ornament
–ness	state or quality of being	kindness, abruptness, happiness
–or	one who	actor, auditor, doctor, donor
–ous	having; full of; characterized by	riotous, courageous, advantageous
–ship	state or quality of being	censorship, ownership, governorship
–some	like; tending to be	meddlesome, bothersome, noisome
–tude	state or quality of being	solitude, multitude, aptitude
–y	characterized by	thrifty, jealousy, frequency, sticky

CONTEXT

The words, phrases, or sentences around an unfamiliar word often provide clues about the word's meaning. In some cases, *signal words* can act as clues. See pp. 173–174 for further discussion of context clues.

Restatement Clues

Look for words and phrases that define an unfamiliar word or restate its meaning in familiar terms.

EXAMPLE The dried rose was as *fragile* as a butterfly's wing. **In other words,** its delicate petals can be damaged easily.

From the context, readers can tell that *fragile* means "damaged easily." The phrase *in other words* signals that the words *easily damaged* restate the meaning of the word *fragile.*

Restatement Signal Words		
in other words	that is	these

Example Clues

Examples sometimes give us hints to a word's meaning. If an unfamiliar word means a certain type of thing, action, or characteristic, examples of the type can be excellent clues to the word's meaning.

EXAMPLE When our neighbors travel, they always look for comfortable *accommodations,* **such as** a beach cottage, hotel suite, or mountain cabin.

From the context, readers can tell that the word *accommodations* means "a place to stay." The words *such as* signal that the list of places to stay provides examples of *accommodations.*

Example Signal Words		
for example	such as	in that
likewise	especially	

Contrast/Antonym Clues

Look for words or phrases that are the opposite of a word's meaning.

EXAMPLE Knowledge is a *remedy* for many environmental problems, **but** knowledge without action cannot cure the ills.

From the context, readers can tell that *remedy* means "cure." The word ***but*** signals that *remedy* contrasts with the phrase "cannot cure."

Contrast/Antonym Signal Words			
but	not	in contrast	on the other hand
however	still	although	some . . . but others

Keyword Clues

Look for words or phrases that modify or are related to the unfamiliar word.

EXAMPLE The two characters in my story believe it is their *destiny* to be enemies. Their elders have taught them that this is **meant to be.**

From the context, readers can tell that *destiny* means "something that necessarily happens to a person." The words *meant to be* signal the meaning of the word.

Definition/Explanation Clues

A sentence may actually define or explain an unfamiliar word.

EXAMPLE Alan will help the woman once she **escapes** and becomes a *fugitive* from her troubled country.

From the context, readers can tell that *fugitive* means "runaway." The word *escapes* signals the meaning of the word.

How We Make New Words Our Own

Use the **Context Structure Sound Dictionary (CSSD)** strategy to improve your vocabulary, to make new words your own. Use one or more of the strategies to determine the meanings of each word you do not know. The exercises that follow will show you how to go about making new words your own.

HOW TO DO EXERCISE 1 *Wordbusting*

In these exercises, you will read the Vocabulary Word in a sentence. You will figure out the word's meaning by looking at its **context,** its **structure,** and its **sound.** Then you will look up the word in a **dictionary** and write its meaning *as it is used in the sentence.*

Here is an example of the Wordbusting strategy, using the word *manuscript.*

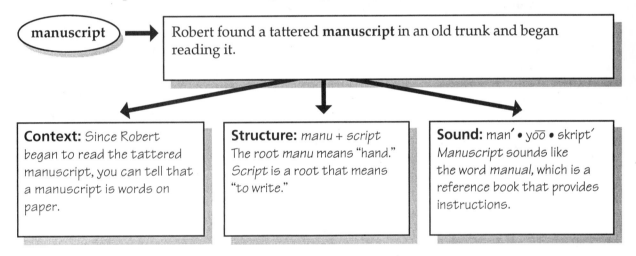

manuscript → Robert found a tattered **manuscript** in an old trunk and began reading it.

Context: *Since Robert began to read the tattered manuscript, you can tell that a manuscript is words on paper.*

Structure: *manu + script The root manu means "hand." Script is a root that means "to write."*

Sound: *man′ • yoo • skript′ Manuscript sounds like the word manual, which is a reference book that provides instructions.*

Dictionary: *"a handwritten or typewritten document or paper, especially a copy of an author's work"*

Hint #1   **Context:** Look for clues to the meaning of the word in the sentence. For example, "reading" is a keyword that helps reveal the meaning of *manuscript.*

Hint #2   **Structure:** Examine the word parts for roots, prefixes, and suffixes that you know. Consult the word-part tables on pages ix–xiv for meanings of parts you do not know.

Hint #3   **Sound:** Say the word aloud and listen for any word parts you know.

Hint #4   **Dictionary:** If you cannot determine a word's meaning from applying context, structure, and sound strategies, look up the unfamiliar word in a dictionary. Read all the definitions, and choose one that best fits the given sentence.

Context Clues ✍

In this exercise, you will again see the new word used in a sentence. This exercise gives you the word's definition, and you must match the word in the sentence with its meaning. The word may be used in the same way as it was used in Wordbusting, or it may be used in a new way.

Here's an example of a Context Clues exercise:

COLUMN A	COLUMN B
_D_ **1.** word: _____*decrease*_____ *v.* to become smaller; to lessen; *n.* a lessening	(D) Recent years have seen a steady rise in the number of cat owners. On the other hand, there has been a **decrease** in the number of dog owners.

Hint #1 First, scan the definitions in Column A. Then, read Column B and look for clues to the meaning of the word. Here, the words "on the other hand" tell us that the sentence containing the word **decrease** contrasts with the sentence containing the words "a steady rise." Thus, the correct definition is probably the opposite of "a steady rise."

Hint #2 Read column A and look for a likely definition of the word. In the example, the student chose the definition that contained the meaning "a lessening," which is most nearly the opposite of "a rise."

Hint #3 Write the word in the blank so that later you can find its definition at a glance.

HOW TO DO EXERCISE 3 *Like and Opposite Meanings* ✍

A synonym is a word that has practically the same meaning as another word. An antonym is a word opposite in meaning to another word. In the Like Meanings part of Exercise 3, you will be asked to find the synonym for (or, in some cases, the phrase that best defines) the Vocabulary Word. In the Opposite Meanings part of Exercise 3, you will be asked to find the antonym for (or, in some cases, the phrase that means the opposite of) the Vocabulary Word.

Here is an example of a Like Meanings item:

21. decrease the shedding of fur
   (A) remove
   (B) make comfortable
   (C) add to
   (D) lessen

Hint #1 Don't be fooled by choices that are closely related to the Vocabulary Word. Choice A may be tempting, but the removal of shedding is more extreme than a **decrease** in shedding.

Hint #2 Don't be fooled by distantly related choices. An animal may be more comfortable when it sheds, but there is no direct link between **decrease** and Choice B.

Hint #3 Don't be fooled by the opposite of the Vocabulary Word. Choice C would be the correct choice if this were an Opposite Meanings exercise, but here you are looking for a similar meaning.

MAKING NEW WORDS YOUR OWN

Lesson 1 CONTEXT: The First Americans
The Peoples and Their Lands

Early explorers of America commented on the excellent health of American Indians. Thriving populations existed throughout the country. However, with Europeans came diseases against which the Indians had no defense. These deadly diseases helped unravel the fabric of American Indian culture. Thousands of people fell to disease, which made the way clear for the settlers.

In the following exercises, you will have the opportunity to expand your vocabulary by reading about American Indian peoples and their lands. Below are ten Vocabulary Words that will be used in these exercises.

appalling   eminent   intentional   picturesque   romantic
contagious   epidemic   myriad   probable   ruthless

EXERCISE 1 *Wordbusting*

Directions. Follow these instructions for this word and the nine words on the next page.
- Figure out the word's meaning by looking at its **context,** its **structure,** and its **sound.** Fill in at least one of the three **CSS** boxes. Alternate which boxes you complete.
- Then, look up the word in a dictionary, read all of its meanings, and write the meaning of the word as it is used in the sentence.
- Follow this same process for each of the Vocabulary Words on the next page. You will need to draw your own map for each word. Use a separate sheet of paper.

1.

(appalling) → One of the most **appalling** results of the Europeans' encounters with American Indians was the spread of disease. The situation was horrifying: Tens of thousands of people died.

Context:	Structure:	Sound:

Dictionary:

2.

(myriad) → Among the **myriad** of diseases that faced American Indians after the Europeans arrived were smallpox, cholera, scarlet fever, and measles.

3.

(contagious) → These **contagious** diseases, which spread from person to person, took hold among the American Indians and quickly spread across the continent.

4.

(epidemic) → Smallpox **epidemics** were surely the worst. Between 1630 and 1650, the populations of the Huron and the Iroquois were reduced by half. In 1781 and again in 1837, the majority of the Blackfoot died.

5.

(eminent) → One **eminent** anthropologist commented that smallpox defeated Mexico. Many people agree with the opinions of this outstanding scholar.

6.

(intentional) → Some American Indians began to think that the attacks of disease were **intentional**. They suspected that European settlers were spreading infectious diseases on purpose.

7.

(ruthless) → These diseases were so destructive that some scholars have wondered which was more **ruthless**—the merciless conquerors of the Americas or the disease they brought with them.

8.

(probable) → Without modern vaccinations, it is **probable** that the diseases that weakened American Indians would continue to kill.

9.

(romantic) → In the meantime, a **romantic** image very different from the reality of the situation was becoming popular in Europe.

10.

(picturesque) → People in Europe were enchanted with the image of American Indians living perfect lives in **picturesque** settings.

EXERCISE 2 Context Clues ✍

Directions. Scan the definitions in Column A. Then, think about how the boldface words are used in the sentences in Column B. To complete the exercise, match each definition in Column A with the correct Vocabulary Word from Column B. Write the letter of your choice on the line provided. Finally, write the Vocabulary Word on the line before the definition.

COLUMN A	COLUMN B
D 11. word: Probable ✓✓ *adj.* likely to be true or to happen	**(A)** In California, the native peoples escaped the worst of the great **epidemics** of 1781 and 1837, which swept from the eastern seaboard to the Rocky Mountains.
G. 12. word: ruthless ✓✓ *adj.* without pity; cruel; hardhearted	**(B)** For the **romantic,** California offered a fanciful, ideal view of American Indians. There, peoples who spoke perhaps twenty different dialects lived mostly in peace.
A. 13. word: epidemics ✓ *n.* a sudden, widespread outbreak, usually of an infectious disease; *adj.* breaking out and spreading quickly	**(C)** A **myriad** of sources fed their needs. Seafood was plentiful, as were game, edible plants, and nuts.
C. 14. word: Myriad ✓✓ *n.* an indefinitely great or vast number; *adj.* countless, innumerable	**(D)** Before the explorers came, it is **probable** that the population of California totalled as many as 350,000 people.
E 15. word: appalling ✓✓ *adj.* causing horror, shock, or dismay	**(E)** Yet, by about 1839, there was an **appalling,** or shocking, decline in the population. By that time, only approximately 20,000 people remained.
B. 16. word: Romantic ✓✓ *adj.* having to do with love or adventure; appealing to the imagination; fanciful and unrealistic; *n.* a person who demonstrates these qualities	**(F)** Despite outbreaks of malaria, a disease that spreads quickly, many of the dead were not victims of **contagious** illnesses.
I 17. word: intentional ✓✓ *adj.* high in rank or reputation; distinguished; outstanding or noteworthy	**(G)** Many American Indians were the victims of the **ruthless,** or hardhearted, greed that swept in with the gold rush.
J. 18. word: Picturesque ✓✓ *adj.* suggesting a picture; strikingly vivid; charming or quaint to look at	**(H)** Gold seekers knowingly killed many. These **intentional** murders allowed the prospectors to claim any lands they wanted.
H. 19. word: intentional ✓ *adj.* done on purpose; deliberate	**(I)** The **eminent** anthropologist Theodora Kroeber wrote a book about Ishi, the last of the Yana people. Many people have read her book *Ishi in Two Worlds.*
F 20. word: contagious *adj.* easily spread from person to person	**(J)** The book is a **picturesque** portrait of a survivor of a lost culture. Scenes from the book linger in one's mind.

Name _Shelby Dudde_ Date _____ Class _____

EXERCISE 3 _Like Meanings and Opposite Meanings_

Directions. For each item below, circle the letter of the choice that means the same, or about the same, as the boldface word.

21. **epidemic** unhappiness
    (A) widespread
    (B) foolish
    (C) youthful
    (D) out-of-date

22. **contagious** ideas
    (A) catching
    (B) brilliant
    (C) impractical
    (D) interesting

23. **romantic** ideas
    (A) musical
    (B) comic
    (C) adventurous
    (D) serious

24. **myriad** stars
    (A) sparkling
    (B) countless
    (C) far away
    (D) brilliant

25. that **picturesque** scene
    (A) country
    (B) charming
    (C) historic
    (D) ancient

Directions. For each item below, circle the letter of the choice that means the opposite, or about the opposite, of the boldface word.

26. **ruthless** attitude
    (A) plentiful
    (B) negative
    (C) hardhearted
    (D) merciful

27. **probable** cause
    (A) chief
    (B) usual
    (C) unlikely
    (D) only

28. their **intentional** act
    (A) cruel
    (B) accidental
    (C) kind
    (D) official

29. the **eminent** historian
    (A) skillful
    (B) young
    (C) unknown
    (D) famous

30. **appalling** news
    (A) surprising
    (B) expected
    (C) sad
    (D) delightful

MAKING NEW WORDS YOUR OWN

| Lesson 2 | **CONTEXT:** The First Americans

Language Without Words

American Indians developed a variety of ways to express information and ideas without written words. For example, in the Northeast the Chippewa recorded events by scratching symbols, or pictographs, on birchbark scrolls. These documents recorded songs, teachings, dreams, and the details of religious ceremonies. The Plains people also used pictographs to make records.

In the following exercises, you will have the opportunity to expand your vocabulary by reading about American Indian language without words. Below are ten Vocabulary Words that will be used in these exercises.

| abuse | barbarism | calamity | folklore | novelty |
| baffle | bewilder | deceive | knoll | sincerity |

EXERCISE 1 *Wordbusting*

Directions. Follow these instructions for this word and the nine words on the next page.
- Figure out the word's meaning by looking at its **context,** its **structure,** and its **sound.** Fill in at least one of the three **CSS** boxes. Alternate which boxes you complete.
- Then, look up the word in a dictionary, read all of its meanings, and write the meaning of the word as it is used in the sentence.
- Follow this same process for each of the Vocabulary Words on the next page. You will need to draw your own map for each word. Use a separate sheet of paper.

1.

(abuse) ➝ Despite the **abuse** American Indians suffered, some aspects of their culture survived. Many place names in the United States come from American Indian names.

| Context: | Structure: | Sound: |

| Dictionary: |

2.

baffle ➡️ Today's place names would probably **baffle** the American Indians who originated them. The Cap Illinewek Indians, for instance, might not recognize their word in the French version, *Illinois*.

3.

barbarism ➡️ Many American Indian words became **barbarisms,** twisted in the mouths of strangers.

4.

bewilder ➡️ Using sign language, various Plains tribes could communicate with each other quite well, although the signs possibly **bewildered** and confused most observers.

5.

calamity ➡️ The Plains people depended on gestures to give and receive important information. With sign language, for example, they could warn one another of approaching danger, and **calamity** could be avoided.

6.

deceive ➡️ Perhaps you have seen some famous sign language gestures. Someone who is lying or language that is meant to **deceive** is signed with a gesture for two tongues.

7.

folklore ➡️ Enough signs existed for people to carry on long conversations or even to tell stories. People who study the **folklore** of American Indians have already recorded much of the tradition of signs.

8.

knoll ➡️ There were signs for time, plants, animals, trading, as well as for geographic features, such as a canyon, a ravine, and a **knoll,** or small hill.

9.

sincerity ➡️ Sign language along with body language could also convey feelings, such as anger, **sincerity,** and happiness.

10.

novelty ➡️ Many people think sign language is interesting as a **novelty,** as something new and unusual, but they may not realize how effective it is.

Name Shelby Duell Date _____ Class _____

EXERCISE 2 Context Clues

Directions. Scan the definitions in Column A. Then, think about how the boldface words are used in the sentences in Column B. To complete the exercise, match each definition in Column A with the correct Vocabulary Word from Column B. Write the letter of your choice on the line provided. Finally, write the Vocabulary Word on the line before the definition.

COLUMN A

H **11.** word: _Knoll_
n. a small, rounded hill; a mound

B **12.** word: _Calamity_
n. a disaster; any happening that causes great distress or misery

E **13.** word: _deceive_
v. to mislead or delude someone, as by lying; to trick

I **14.** word: _Sincerity_
n. the quality or condition of being sincere; honesty; genuineness

15. word: _Bewilder_
v. to perplex; to frustrate, hinder, or interfere with

C **16.** word: _Barbarism_
n. uncivilized, brutal behavior; cruelty; a nonstandard word or expression

G **17.** word: _Abuse_
v. to misuse; to injure or damage through maltreatment; *n.* a misuse; cruel treatment or words

D **18.** word: _Novelties_
n. something new or unusual; an innovation; newness; originality

19. word: _Baffle_
v. to confuse terribly; to puzzle

A **20.** word: _Folklore_
n. unwritten stories, customs, sayings, and traditional beliefs of a culture; the study of these

COLUMN B

(A) Some American Indians used pictographs to record important events as well as the stories and customs that make up their **folklore.**

(B) In pictographs, small pictures or symbols tell a story. Some Indians represented the **calamity** of a smallpox outbreak as a human figure with a red body spotted in black.

(C) Acts of **barbarism** by a brutal enemy might be painted alongside tales of victory.

(D) When something new entered the scene, a symbol would be created. **Novelties** like wagons and trains needed new symbols.

(E) The simplicity of pictographs can **deceive** observers. Actually, these accounts are complex, and only experts can read them now.

(F) Some pictographic writing is no doubt meant to **baffle,** or perplex, would-be readers.

(G) One account of the Battle of the Little Big Horn did not note General Custer's death. One reason may have been fear of revenge or further **abuse** and cruel treatment by the U.S. forces.

(H) Standing on a **knoll,** where the slightly higher ground improved visibility, a person could use smoke to signal people far away.

(I) Face paint or the way a blanket was worn might signal anger or love. The **sincerity** of such emotions would be difficult to doubt since the wearer was purposefully displaying his or her feelings.

(J) These and other ways of communicating may **bewilder** a nonnative speaker. However, American Indians were taught the different signs early and were not confused by them.

EXERCISE 3 *Like Meanings and Opposite Meanings* 👈

Directions. For each item below, circle the letter of the choice that means the same, or about the same, as the boldface word.

21. studying **folklore**
  (A) famous people
  (B) modern history
  (C) manners
  (D) oral tradition

22. **baffle** our enemies
  (A) crush
  (B) confuse
  (C) fight
  (D) plan

23. **deceive** their friends
  (A) invite
  (B) entertain
  (C) mislead
  (D) leave

24. a low **knoll**
  (A) mound
  (B) intelligence
  (C) forehead
  (D) expectation

25. an interesting **novelty**
  (A) type of literature
  (B) new item
  (C) distant star
  (D) large sign

Directions. For each item below, circle the letter of the choice that means the opposite, or about the opposite, of the boldface word.

26. in all **sincerity**
  (A) hopelessness
  (B) haste
  (C) dishonesty
  (D) anger

27. **bewilder** the newcomer
  (A) make clear to
  (B) civilize
  (C) entertain
  (D) seem strange to

28. to **abuse** equipment
  (A) borrow
  (B) damage
  (C) care for
  (D) return

29. a surprising **calamity**
  (A) expense
  (B) disaster
  (C) good fortune
  (D) excitement

30. a recent **barbarism**
  (A) civil gesture
  (B) poem
  (C) quotation
  (D) modern invention

MAKING NEW WORDS YOUR OWN

Lesson 3 | **CONTEXT: The First Americans**

Metacomet's Dream

During the European settlement of New England, the Wampanoags were very helpful to their new neighbors. After Chief Massasoit died, his son Metacomet (Metacom) came to power when he was only twenty-four years old. Metacomet soon became angry at colonists who punished Wampanoags for trespassing. He felt that if the tribes in the area united, they could overpower the settlers. Though Metacomet's forces killed hundreds of people, his dream of a union failed, as did his war.

In the following exercises, you will have the opportunity to expand your vocabulary by reading about Metacomet. Below are ten Vocabulary Words that will be used.

aggressive	ecology	inevitable	motivate	strategy
catastrophe	ferocious	intelligible	sanctuary	valid

EXERCISE 1 *Wordbusting*

Directions. Follow these instructions for this word and the nine words on the next page.
- Figure out the word's meaning by looking at its **context,** its **structure,** and its **sound.** Fill in at least one of the three **CSS** boxes. Alternate which boxes you complete.
- Then, look up the word in a dictionary, read all of its meanings, and write the meaning of the word as it is used in the sentence.
- Follow this same process for each of the Vocabulary Words on the next page. You will need to draw your own map for each word. Use a separate sheet of paper.

1.

(aggressive) → Metacomet felt it was necessary to take **aggressive** action to regain power over the lives of his people. During the years 1675 and 1676, the young leader took arms against the growing population of settlers.

Context:	Structure:	Sound:

Dictionary:

2.

(ecology) ➤ The Wampanoag had survived by their keen knowledge of the **ecology**. Their ability to recognize the relationships between animals or plants and the environment resulted in great skill at agriculture and hunting.

3.

(ferocious) ➤ The feelings between the Wampanoag and the settlers turned from mildly angry to **ferocious** as the Wampanoag found themselves in deep debt to the Europeans.

4.

(inevitable) ➤ Added to this problem was the settlers' insistence that the Wampanoag obey the settlers' laws. It was **inevitable** that the Wampanoag would take fierce action; the only uncertainty was *when* they would rebel.

5.

(intelligible) ➤ Moreover, the sale of land was not always **intelligible** to the Wampanoag. Because their concept of land ownership was different from the Europeans', the Wampanoags sold land that they thought they were simply lending.

6.

(motivate) ➤ These unfair treatments and differences in customs **motivated** Metacomet to attempt to drive the settlers out. He was prompted to fight them to save his people.

7.

(sanctuary) ➤ The colonists called Metacomet "King Philip." During King Philip's War, no colonist could rely on **sanctuary** in New England. No place was safe; Metacomet attacked over fifty of the ninety European settlements.

8.

(catastrophe) ➤ He and his warriors created one **catastrophe** after another for the colonists by attacking and damaging villages throughout New England.

9.

(strategy) ➤ In the end, other American Indians betrayed Metacomet. He was brutally killed by the colonists and their Indian allies. His key **strategy** for victory had failed. Because other tribes considered him an enemy, his plan to unite with them against the colonists did not succeed.

10.

(valid) ➤ Only with the support of other tribes did Metacomet have a **valid** hope for victory. Without the full support of neighboring tribes, he did not have a reasonable chance against the colonists.

EXERCISE 2 *Context Clues* ✍

Directions. Scan the definitions in Column A. Then, think about how the boldface words are used in the sentences in Column B. To complete the exercise, match each definition in Column A with the correct Vocabulary Word from Column B. Write the letter of your choice on the line provided. Finally, write the Vocabulary Word on the line before the definition.

COLUMN A	COLUMN B

_B_ **11.** word: _Strategy_

n. the science or art of war; the careful planning and management of anything; a plan or method of action

_D_ **12.** word: _Inevitable_

adj. unavoidable; certain to happen

_H_ **13.** word: _Catastrophe_

n. a sudden, widespread disaster; a misfortune

_F_ **14.** word: _Aggressive_

adj. quick to attack; inclined to hostile actions; assertive; bold and energetic

_G_ **15.** word: _Motivated_

v. to give one the idea for; to incite; to urge to action

_E_ **16.** word: _ferocious_

adj. savage, fierce, or cruel; intense

_J_ **17.** word: _valid_

adj. having legal force; well-grounded on principles or evidence

_A_ **18.** word: _ecology_

n. the relationships between living things and their environments

_C_ **19.** word: _Sanctuary_

n. a holy place; a place of shelter and protection; a reservation where birds or animals cannot be hunted or trapped.

_I_ **20.** word: _Intelligible_

adj. capable of being understood; clear

(A) After studying the **ecology** of New England, I turned to the history of the area. In fact, the environment and the people's relationship to it have greatly affected history.

(B) I opened my history book and tried to think of a **strategy** for an essay on Metacomet. I needed a really good plan.

(C) I learned how early settlers repaid Metacomet's father's offer of **sanctuary**. Instead of thanking him for his protection, they took his land.

(D) The **inevitable** action took place. The Indians were angered by the settlers' offense and had no choice but to take up arms.

(E) The settlers' lack of gratitude explains the high level of emotion behind Metacomet's **ferocious,** brutal attacks.

(F) Metacomet had reasons for the **aggressive** actions he took against the colonists. He must have attacked them because he felt betrayed.

(G) As I learned the reasons that must have pushed Metacomet to action, I understood what **motivated** him to act as he did.

(H) The settlers had brought **catastrophe** to the Indians, including disease, loss of land, and loss of life. Metacomet's brother had died from a disease he caught from the settlers.

(I) No doubt the settlers thought their own laws and customs were **intelligible** to the Indians. However, the Indians not only did not understand those laws and customs, they had no desire to follow them.

(J) Metacomet's point of view seemed **valid.** It provided convincing evidence for the reasons for King Philip's War. I began my paper.

EXERCISE 3 — *Like Meanings and Opposite Meanings* ✍

Directions. For each item below, circle the letter of the choice that means the same, or about the same, as the boldface word.

21. a private **sanctuary**
    (A) small room
    (B) garden
    (C) place of safety
    (D) cemetery

22. an unexpected **catastrophe**
    (A) disaster
    (B) early American boat
    (C) punctuation mark
    (D) meeting of officials

23. the **ecology** of the planet
    (A) rotation
    (B) future
    (C) layers of atmosphere
    (D) study of the environment

24. their new **strategy**
    (A) government official
    (B) a type of telescope
    (C) plan of action
    (D) financial report

25. to **motivate** a student
    (A) pass
    (B) understand
    (C) encourage
    (D) ignore

Directions. For each item below, circle the letter of the choice that means the opposite, or about the opposite, of the boldface word.

26. his **aggressive** attitude
    (A) peaceful
    (B) unfair
    (C) helpful
    (D) vicious

27. a **valid** argument
    (A) angry
    (B) long
    (C) unconvincing
    (D) useful

28. the **inevitable** result
    (A) enviable
    (B) unfortunate
    (C) avoidable
    (D) correct

29. a **ferocious** animal
    (A) wild
    (B) tame
    (C) hairy
    (D) caged

30. **intelligible** communication
    (A) confusing
    (B) wise
    (C) understandable
    (D) important

MAKING NEW WORDS YOUR OWN

Lesson 4 | CONTEXT: The First Americans
Wisdom Stories

Like stories all over the world, American Indian stories teach children the history, customs, and philosophy of their people. A Blackfoot story explains how the Buffalo Dance began. An Ojibwa legend recounts how maize first grew from the body of a young man who came from the sky. Strange events occur, and the laws of nature may not operate as expected. For these stories do not simply teach practical, everyday knowledge. They also show ways to inner wisdom.

In the following exercises, you will have the opportunity to expand your vocabulary by reading about American Indian wisdom stories. These ten Vocabulary Words will be used.

advent	anthology	integrity	mystical	pacify
alliance	defy	misdeed	nourish	sustain

EXERCISE 1 | Wordbusting

Directions. Follow these instructions for this word and the nine words on the next page.
- Figure out the word's meaning by looking at its **context,** its **structure,** and its **sound.** Fill in at least one of the three **CSS** boxes. Alternate which boxes you complete.
- Then, look up the word in a dictionary, read all of its meanings, and write the meaning of the word as it is used in the sentence.
- Follow this same process for each of the Vocabulary Words on the next page. You will need to draw your own map for each word. Use a separate sheet of paper.

1.

(advent) → A wisdom story may tell how the world began. According to the Cherokee, the **advent** of people on earth resulted when Star Woman fell from the sky.

Context:	Structure:	Sound:

Dictionary:

2.
 → Only the **alliance** of many creatures—turtle, water spider, muskrat, and buzzard all working together—saved her. From her body came all life.

3.
 → The story of Star Woman is included in an **anthology** of Cherokee legends. It is just one of several stories published in this group of tales.

4.
 → Star Woman also bore two sons. One son loved the good. The other chose to **defy** the way of peace and order and follow the way of anger. He is called the Brother of the Dark Face.

5.
 → Yet the Cherokee do not scorn this brother because they believe that the **integrity** of a person cannot be completely lost. They believe that each person contains both good and bad, and these two elements are what make a person whole.

6.
 → For that reason, no matter how bad a person's **misdeed** is, even if it is a serious crime, he or she can always turn toward the good and find a new life.

7.
 → To the Cherokee, each life has **mystical** value; there is something divine in each of us.

8.
 → A person has only to **nourish** the seed of good—to care for it and feed it—and it will grow into strength.

9.
pacify → In the old days, at a special village called Peace Village, anyone—no matter what his or her crimes—could come and learn how to **pacify,** or calm, strong emotions such as fear, anger, and jealousy.

10.
 → In a year's time, the person could be accepted again into society. In this way, the Cherokee sought to **sustain,** or keep up, peace in the community.

EXERCISE 2 *Context Clues*

Directions. Scan the definitions in Column A. Then, think about how the boldface words are used in the sentences in Column B. To complete the exercise, match each definition in Column A with the correct Vocabulary Word from Column B. Write the letter of your choice on the line provided. Finally, write the Vocabulary Word on the line before the definition.

COLUMN A

_B_ **11.** word: _Nourish_
v. to refuse or resist openly; to dare; to withstand successfully

_J_ **12.** word: _Alliance_
n. a bad or illegal act

_F_ **13.** word: _sustain_
adj. having spiritual meaning; mysterious; secret

_E_ **14.** word: _mystical_
n. wholeness; soundness; strength of character; honesty

_A_ **15.** word: _deeds_
n. a formal agreement between nations or people for a particular cause

_H_ **16.** word: _Advent_
n. a collection of stories, poems, etc.

_C_ **17.** word: _Integrity_
v. to bring into submission; to soothe someone who is upset; to quiet or calm

_I_ **18.** word: _defy_
v. to keep up; to provide with food; to support; to encourage; to endure

_G_ **19.** word: _pacified_
n. arrival; the coming of something, especially something long awaited

_D_ **20.** word: _Anthologies_
v. to support; to withstand; to provide for; to keep in existence; to uphold as reasonable; to suffer or undergo

COLUMN B

(A) Many people see modern civilization's **misdeeds** against the planet everywhere. Examples are the pollution of the air and water.

(B) Traditional stories remind us to **nourish,** to develop and strengthen, our ties to the earth.

(C) According to American Indian philosophy, a good relationship with Earth is crucial to one's **integrity,** to one's sense of wholeness.

(D) A good relationship with Earth is a theme that runs through many of the stories collected in American Indian **anthologies**.

(E) People's relationship to Earth has **mystical** meaning to many American Indians. In fact, it is central to their religions.

(F) The Taos people use stories to **sustain** their beliefs. They believe that Earth is the source of all life and that the first people came out of Blue Lake.

(G) When the U.S. government placed Blue Lake inside Kit Carson National Forest, the Taoseños could not be **pacified** into accepting their loss. They protested strongly against being separated from their sacred land.

(H) When they regained their lake in 1971, their victory marked the **advent** of a new respect for the traditions of American Indians.

(I) With the American Indian Freedom of Religion Act in 1978, American Indians no longer needed to **defy** the government to practice their ancient beliefs. They could do so freely.

(J) In addition, American Indians formed a sort of **alliance** with all against any threat to religious freedom. All stood together for a common cause.

EXERCISE 3 *Like Meanings and Opposite Meanings* ✍

Directions. For each item below, circle the letter of the choice that means the same, or about the same, as the boldface word.

21. a person of **integrity**
(A) many interests
(B) another country
(C) honesty
(D) intelligence

22. to address the **alliance**
(A) a small audience
(B) a business-size envelope
(C) persons having a formal agreement
(D) business people

23. an **anthology** of poems
(A) book
(B) assortment
(C) encyclopedia
(D) author

24. to **sustain** life
(A) study about
(B) support
(C) create
(D) seriously injure

25. a violent **misdeed**
(A) accident
(B) argument
(C) plan
(D) wrong

Directions. For each item below, circle the letter of the choice that means the opposite, or about the opposite, of the boldface word.

26. **defy** orders
(A) follow
(B) announce
(C) give
(D) resist

27. a **mystical** experience
(A) spiritual
(B) mysterious
(C) secret
(D) ordinary

28. **pacify** the baby
(A) upset
(B) calm
(C) hold
(D) feed

29. **nourish** our hopes
(A) cherish
(B) raise
(C) starve
(D) protect

30. **advent** of the political movement
(A) adventure
(B) justice
(C) customs
(D) departure

Name _____ Date _____ Class _____

MAKING NEW WORDS YOUR OWN

Lesson 5 | CONTEXT: The First Americans
American Indians and Their Horses

The horse forever changed the lives of American Indians. Hunting became easier. Journeys could now be swift and safe, and longer distances could be covered. Traveling farther also increased trade and contact with other peoples. Territories shifted and were enlarged, and new borders had to be fought for and agreed upon. Yet, in the horse, the native peoples of the West found their destiny. So much so that the name of one tribe, the Cayuse, now also means "horse."

In the following exercises, you will have the opportunity to expand your vocabulary by reading about American Indians and their horses. These ten Vocabulary Words will be used.

| accessory | calculation | convert | gallery | valor |
| badger | complement | customary | intervene | vitality |

EXERCISE 1 *Wordbusting*

Directions. Follow these instructions for this word and the nine words on the next page.
- Figure out the word's meaning by looking at its **context,** its **structure,** and its **sound.** Fill in at least one of the three **CSS** boxes. Alternate which boxes you complete.
- Then, look up the word in a dictionary, read all of its meanings, and write the meaning of the word as it is used in the sentence.
- Follow this same process for each of the Vocabulary Words on the next page. You will need to draw your own map for each word. Use a separate sheet of paper.

1.

(accessory) → When a Spanish explorer came to America, his most important **accessory** was his riding gear. The equipment allowed him to ride his horse. The famous mustangs and the beautiful paint ponies of the West are descended from horses brought by the Spanish.

Context:

Structure:

Sound:

Dictionary:

2.

badger →

The compact, well-balanced Spanish horses traveled deep into the western interior of the continent, the land of such animals as the **badger** and the antelope.

3.

calculation →

Historians can make **calculations** about when the Plains Indians began to use horses—most agree it was around 1600. However, historians may never be able to estimate how much horses changed the Plains Indians' lives.

4.

complement →

Horses were the perfect **complement** to the Plains Indians' needs. They used horses to hunt buffalo and to fight battles more successfully.

5.

convert →

Tribe after tribe became a willing **convert** to the improvements that the horse allowed. They changed their ways of living and eagerly sought more horses.

6.

customary →

Because horses made traveling much easier, trade increased. It became **customary** for the Plains people to trade with peoples in the West. Thus, it became common to see a Nez Perce horse wearing a Crow collar and bridle.

7.

gallery →

The Cayuse, the Shoshone, the Flathead, and the Nez Perce showed their pride in their horses by decorating them with trappings worthy of hanging in any art **gallery**.

8.

intervene →

On magnificent saddle bags, black geometric designs **intervene,** or come between, bands of red. Beaded stirrups, especially on women's mounts, were often hung with pendants.

9.

valor →

War horses were brilliantly draped and masked like steeds of the medieval knights of Europe. A horse might bear colorfully painted images showing its own feats of **valor,** or bravery.

10.

vitality →

A horse might be painted with symbols of **vitality** in the hope that such symbols would add to the horse's strength. It is this image of painted horse and rider dressed in splendor that will charge on through the imaginations of future generations.

EXERCISE 2 *Context Clues*

Directions. Scan the definitions in Column A. Then, think about how the boldface words are used in the sentences in Column B. To complete the exercise, match each definition in Column A with the correct Vocabulary Word from Column B. Write the letter of your choice on the line provided. Finally, write the Vocabulary Word on the line before the definition.

COLUMN A

_B_ **11.** word: _____
n. the process of using mathematics; careful thinking or planning; an estimate

____ **12.** word: _____
n. a long passageway; the cheapest seats in a theater; a place where paintings are displayed

____ **13.** word: _____
adj. according to custom; habitual; usual

____ **14.** word: _____
n. a small burrowing animal with short legs and long claws; *v.* to pester; to nag

____ **15.** word: _____
n. energy; exuberance; vigor

____ **16.** word: _____
v. to come between in order to change a situation; to occur between

____ **17.** word: _____
n. something added for looks or convenience; equipment; one who knowingly aids in a crime

____ **18.** word: _____
n. boldness; courage; bravery

____ **19.** word: _____
n. that which completes; number needed to complete; a complete set; *v.* to complete; to add to

____ **20.** word: _____
v. to change; to change or persuade someone to change to a new belief; *n.* one who has changed, as to a religion

COLUMN B

(A) Stronger and larger than mustangs, the **vitality** of the Appaloosa gave great energy to the Nez Perce culture.

(B) Some families had fifteen hundred horses. Much **calculation,** or careful figuring, must have been needed to provide for such a herd!

(C) The artistry of the Nez Perce provided a means for increasing the herd. Their attractive woven bags were sought far and wide as **accessories**.

(D) These bags and other products were swiftly **converted** into horses, just as today people change cash into cars and other goods.

(E) It is unlikely that a Nez Perce child had to **badger** his or her parents for a horse. Horses were abundant, so a child would not have to pester or make a fuss to get one.

(F) It was **customary,** not at all unusual, for Nez Perce women to hang baby cradles from their saddle horns.

(G) Spectacular trappings, such as beaded bridles, **complemented** their riding equipment, making the picture complete.

(H) In 1877, fate **intervened** and ended the days of glory for the Nez Perce. Their lives were changed forever.

(I) The Nez Perces' **valor,** or bold determination, aided them in their attack on United States troops. However, the troops eventually captured most of the Nez Perces' herd. Their hope of freedom was lost, and their leader, Chief Joseph, surrendered.

(J) A painting of Chief Joseph's surrender is displayed in a **gallery** devoted to American Indian art and history.

EXERCISE 3 *Like Meanings and Opposite Meanings* ☞

Directions. For each item below, circle the letter of the choice that means the same, or about the same, as the boldface word.

21. gallery seats
(A) inexpensive
(B) expensive
(C) box
(D) group

22. accessory to murder
(A) aid
(B) plan of attack
(C) weapon
(D) witness

23. a difficult **calculation**
(A) decision
(B) journey
(C) math problem
(D) group discussion

24. an enthusiastic **convert**
(A) person who has changed beliefs
(B) person who has no beliefs
(C) person who believes anything
(D) person who questions everything

25. intervene without permission
(A) enter
(B) exit
(C) go between
(D) make tape recordings

Directions. For each item below, circle the letter of the choice that means the opposite, or about the opposite, of the boldface word.

26. valor in battle
(A) fearlessness
(B) difficulty
(C) cowardice
(D) stupidity

27. customary practice
(A) unusual
(B) sales method
(C) familiar
(D) sensible

28. a sense of **vitality**
(A) importance
(B) possibility
(C) unimportance
(D) weakness

29. to **complement** the set
(A) sell as a unit
(B) improve on
(C) take away from
(D) make complete

30. to **badger** the chief
(A) refuse to ask
(B) pester
(C) worry greatly
(D) ask repeatedly

Name _____ Date _____ Class _____

MAKING NEW WORDS YOUR OWN

| Lesson 6 | **CONTEXT:** The First Americans

The Meanings of American Indian Art

Magnificent Pueblo pottery and dazzling silver work attract buyers and collectors alike. Today's American Indian artists create works that are modern but that preserve traditional values and character. In museums everywhere, traditional American Indian works can be found. What is often not known about many traditional works is their deep meaning. Few people know that the use of a ceremonial pipe was not simply a custom that had to be observed, but a sacred act.

In the following exercises, you will have the opportunity to expand your vocabulary by reading about American Indian art. These ten Vocabulary Words will be used.

adjacent	attain	fragile	harmonious	multicolored
artisan	deceased	glorify	incomparable	pulverize

EXERCISE 1 — Wordbusting

Directions. Follow these instructions for this word and the nine words on the next page.
- Figure out the word's meaning by looking at its **context,** its **structure,** and its **sound.** Fill in at least one of the three **CSS** boxes. Alternate which boxes you complete.
- Then, look up the word in a dictionary, read all of its meanings, and write the meaning of the word as it is used in the sentence.
- Follow this same process for each of the Vocabulary Words on the next page. You will need to draw your own map for each word. Use a separate sheet of paper.

1.

(adjacent) → **Adjacent** to some empty display cases in the Smithsonian Institution's National Museum of the American Indian, you will see a small white card. The card next to the case states that an object has been removed.

Context:

Structure:

Sound:

Dictionary:

2.
(artisan) → Each of these objects was made by an American Indian **artisan,** a person with a special ability to make that particular object.

3.
(attain) → Out of respect, the museum has removed objects considered sacred by American Indians. The museum is now trying to learn how to show the pieces properly. With this knowledge, the museum will **attain** its goal of respectful display.

4.
(deceased) → These special items are the creations of long-**deceased** people. However, the holy power that the objects represent is still very much alive in the hearts of many American Indians.

5.
(fragile) → Far from being **fragile,** these beliefs have remained strong for countless years. One of the most valued objects is the ceremonial pipe, which you may know as a peace pipe.

6.
(glorify) → For Plains Indians, these pipes are sacred. Some highly decorated pipes especially **glorify,** or honor, centuries-old beliefs.

7.
(harmonious) → Even the simple and agreeable design of an undecorated pipe may represent the **harmonious** communication between human beings and a divine spirit.

8.
(incomparable) → According to ancient belief, to place the stem and bowl of the pipe together is to release an **incomparable** power. To display a pipe this way shows disrespect for that matchless force and the people who honor it.

9.
(multicolored) → In traditional European art, different colors are usually used to create a certain mood or feeling. In American Indian art, **multicolored** designs have more specific meanings.

10.
(pulverize) → The effect of European settlement in the Americas was to **pulverize** many aspects of American Indian culture. Perhaps museums will succeed in protecting them from being crushed further.

MAKING NEW WORDS YOUR OWN

Lesson 7 CONTEXT: The First Americans
Totems

Although the word *totem* has its roots in the Algonquin languages, totems are used or claimed by many peoples. A totem is an animal or event that has a special connection to a person. That connection may be a family one, for totem animals are often considered ancestors. The connection may be spiritual, for a totem can give a person a special power, such as courage. The word *totem* is also used to refer to the object that represents such an animal or event.

In the following exercises, you will have the opportunity to expand your vocabulary by reading about totems. Below are ten Vocabulary Words that will be used in these exercises.

confederation	discord	foresight	menagerie	posterity
delegate	feline	isolation	phenomenon	revelation

EXERCISE 1 Wordbusting ✍

Directions. Follow these instructions for this word and the nine words on the next page.
- Figure out the word's meaning by looking at its **context,** its **structure,** and its **sound.** Fill in at least one of the three **CSS** boxes. Alternate which boxes you complete.
- Then, look up the word in a dictionary, read all of its meanings, and write the meaning of the word as it is used in the sentence.
- Follow this same process for each of the Vocabulary Words on the next page. You will need to draw your own map for each word. Use a separate sheet of paper.

1.

(confederation) ⟶ The Creek Confederacy was a **confederation,** or unified group, of different Creek clans. Each clan had its own totem.

Context:	Structure:	Sound:

Dictionary:

2.

delegate → A **delegate,** or representative, in the village council or local government was often chosen on the basis of clan.

3.

discord → The totem illustrates the lack of **discord** within a Creek clan. In addition, it represents a connection with a clan's ancestors.

4.

feline → A totem is believed to give a person a spiritual gift. For example, a panther totem might give some **feline** characteristic, such as a cat's speed, grace, or cunning.

5.

foresight → An eagle totem might bestow the gift of **foresight,** which allows a person to see into the future. Members of a bear clan might consider strength to be their most valuable characteristic.

6.

isolation → Membership in a clan helps prevent a feeling of **isolation** in individuals. The clan provides a framework within which people can come together.

7.

menagerie → A list of the totems of American Indians can sound like a magnificent **menagerie,** for it includes birds, land animals such as the bear, and sea animals such as the killer whale.

8.

phenomenon → Large, unexplainable events, such as sudden wind, rain, or thunder, are powerful forces in American Indian culture. The **phenomenon** of wind has served as a totem for some clans.

9.

posterity → Totems are used to pass on important qualities, such as courage, intelligence, and vision, to **posterity**—that is, to children, grandchildren, and so on.

10.

revelation → The use of totems was no **revelation** to the Europeans who came to the Americas. Europeans identified their own families with totem-like objects, such as family crests or coats of arms.

EXERCISE 2   *Context Clues*

Directions. Scan the definitions in Column A. Then, think about how the boldface words are used in the sentences in Column B. To complete the exercise, match each definition in Column A with the correct Vocabulary Word from Column B. Write the letter of your choice on the line provided. Finally, write the Vocabulary Word on the line before the definition.

COLUMN A	COLUMN B

COLUMN A

D **11.** word: _Menagerie_
n. an exhibit of caged animals; the enclosure for such a collection

B **12.** word: _isolation_
n. separation from others; aloneness

I **13.** word: _revelation_
n. something made known; a dramatic disclosure of something

F **14.** word: _discord_
n. a lack of harmony; angry disagreement; strife; clashing sounds

E **15.** word: _Posterity_
n. descendants; future generations

H **16.** word: _Forsight_
n. the act or capacity of foreseeing, looking forward; prudence, preparation

J **17.** word: _menagerie_
n. a condition or an event perceived by the senses; a rare or unexplainable occurrence; a marvel; a happening

C **18.** word: _delegte_
n. a representative who has the authority to act for others; *v.* to send as a representative

G **19.** word: _feline_
adj. of cats; catlike; *n.* a cat

A **20.** word: _Confederation_
n. a group, usually of nations or states, united in some shared purpose; a league of states

COLUMN B

(A) No large **confederation** of peoples existed on the Northwest's Queen Charlotte islands. Each group was independent of the others.

(B) Although the Haida were islanders, they did not live in **isolation**. In fact, they often received visitors, and they erected totem poles along the coast to greet them.

(C) Typically, a family would **delegate** the task of carving their pole. The artist to whom they entrusted the job would carve the family's crest.

(D) The poles show a family's pride in their animal ancestors. At one time many of these animals roamed freely across the continent. Today you are likely to see many of them only in a **menagerie**.

(E) According to legend, an animal totem may be displayed only by that animal's **posterity**. The descendants of unrelated clans may not display that animal on their crests.

(F) If someone not of the bear clan displayed a bear, **discord,** or strife, might result.

(G) Many totem poles have vanished over the years. It is as though someone crept in like a **feline,** with the stealth of a cat, and stole them away.

(H) Luckily, the **foresight** of the Haida will prevent the loss of more poles in the future.

(I) The great totem pole Tsimshian yet stands. Visiting the pole can be a **revelation,** a dramatic lesson, for anyone who can read it.

(J) It is still possible to experience the **phenomenon** of coming face to face with a cedar thunderbird towering in the forest. Such an amazing event is not soon forgotten by visitors to the Northwest.

EXERCISE 3   *Like Meanings and Opposite Meanings*

Directions. For each item below, circle the letter of the choice that means the same, or about the same, as the boldface word.

21. an unexplained **phenomenon**
  (A) a type of chemical
  (B) happening
  (C) discovery
  (D) sculpture

22. our first **delegate**
  (A) representative
  (B) a type of door
  (C) legal action
  (D) a special celebration

23. a stone **menagerie**
  (A) cage of animals
  (B) tribal house for men
  (C) tower
  (D) weapon

24. a strong **confederation**
  (A) festive decoration
  (B) large fire
  (C) type of food
  (D) unified group

25. a playful **feline**
  (A) folk dancing
  (B) cat
  (C) conversation
  (D) personality

Directions. For each item below, circle the letter of the choice that means the opposite, or about the opposite, of the boldface word.

26. a surprising **revelation**
  (A) stillness
  (B) secret
  (C) sadness
  (D) decision

27. the value of **foresight**
  (A) looking ahead
  (B) a device for aiming
  (C) telescopes
  (D) looking backwards

28. a period of **isolation**
  (A) safety
  (B) happiness
  (C) argument
  (D) crowding

29. for our **posterity**
  (A) benefit
  (B) audience
  (C) ancestors
  (D) future

30. avoiding **discord**
  (A) disease
  (B) wrapping
  (C) agreement
  (D) hiding

MAKING NEW WORDS YOUR OWN

Lesson 8 | CONTEXT: The First Americans
Coyote, the American Indian Trickster

The Coyote of Navajo legend is one of the most entertaining examples of a trickster. Quite simply, a trickster is one who deceives others. Yet, strangely enough, it is the trickster who is often tricked. Some small, harmless-looking creature eventually beats the trickster at his own game. Thus, Coyote's mishaps teach listeners that lying and cheating do not pay off in the end. The stories remind listeners that the best way to live is honorably.

In the following exercises, you will have the opportunity to expand your vocabulary by reading about Coyote. Below are ten Vocabulary Words that will be used in these exercises.

adequate	descend	gnarled	inflexible	menace
advantageous	enhance	incite	inherit	mutual

EXERCISE 1 | *Wordbusting* ✍

Directions. Follow these instructions for this word and the nine words on the next page.
- Figure out the word's meaning by looking at its **context,** its **structure,** and its **sound.** Fill in at least one of the three **CSS** boxes. Alternate which boxes you complete.
- Then, look up the word in a dictionary, read all of its meanings, and write the meaning of the word as it is used in the sentence.
- Follow this same process for each of the Vocabulary Words on the next page. You will need to draw your own map for each word. Use a separate sheet of paper.

1.

(adequate) → It is difficult to give an **adequate** description of the legendary Trotting Coyote of the Navajo people in the United States' Southwest. He is so changeable and sneaky that he defies complete description.

Context:	Structure:	Sound:

Dictionary:

Name _____ Date _____ Class _____

2.

advantageous → He is determined to make every situation **advantageous** to himself. By using tricks, he is able to arrange things in his favor.

3.

descend → Trotting Coyote, as he is known among the Navajo, will **descend** to almost any depths to gain the upper hand over others. He will even stoop to tricking children.

4.

enhance → To **enhance** his chance of victory, he will lie, trick, and cheat to get his way. Yet, despite his efforts to better his chances, he rarely comes out on top.

5.

gnarled → Perhaps you have known someone with a conscience as **gnarled** as Trotting Coyote's. This person probably has a twisted sense of right and wrong.

6.

incite → Trotting Coyote is a character who can **incite** anger in you. Being tricked by him can really stir up angry feelings.

7.

inflexible → Trotting Coyote might seem as **inflexible,** or stubborn, as a mule to you. He represents the part in all of us that does not want to play by the rules.

8.

inherit → Every person stands to **inherit** a few of Trotting Coyote's qualities. His traits are passed on to each generation, like a family name.

9.

menace → To be fair, Trotting Coyote has his good points, too. All in all, though, he is generally a **menace**. More often than not, he is a threat to society.

10.

mutual → Sometimes Coyote works for the **mutual** benefit of people and himself. Once, he broke the leg of a giant who was killing human beings, an action that helped both himself and the human race.

MAKING NEW WORDS YOUR OWN

Lesson 9 | **CONTEXT:** The First Americans

Games in the Arctic and Subarctic

Whenever people must depend on one another for survival, the community becomes very important. Dealing with conflict and helping people out in times of need can mean the difference between life and death in arctic and subarctic cultures. One way these cultures reinforce their sense of community is through group games played during the long winter months.

In the following exercises, you will have the opportunity to expand your vocabulary by reading about games in the arctic and subarctic regions. Below are ten Vocabulary Words that will be used in these exercises.

adapt	basis	impel	petition	primitive
assumption	controversy	omission	potential	restore

EXERCISE 1 *Wordbusting* 👉

Directions. Follow these instructions for this word and the nine words on the next page.
- Figure out the word's meaning by looking at its **context,** its **structure,** and its **sound.** Fill in at least one of the three **CSS** boxes. Alternate which boxes you complete.
- Then, look up the word in a dictionary, read all of its meanings, and write the meaning of the word as it is used in the sentence.
- Follow this same process for each of the Vocabulary Words on the next page. You will need to draw your own map for each word. Use a separate sheet of paper.

1.

(adapt) ➡️ The survival of the peoples of the arctic and subarctic regions is due to their ability to **adapt** to a harsh environment. They are able to change and adjust to the brutally cold weather.

Context:

Structure:

Sound:

Dictionary:

2.

(assumption) ➡ However, to make the **assumption** that a life surrounded by ice and snow is without fun would be incorrect. This supposed truth is easily proven wrong.

3.

(basis) ➡ Traditionally, the **basis** for native societies of arctic and subarctic Alaska is human warmth and good cheer. With this foundation, the native peoples there have needed no formal court system—fear of being rejected by the village has kept the peace.

4.

(controversy) ➡ When a **controversy,** or disagreement, occurs, it often ends in an insult or singing contest. Each person in the argument takes turns publicly criticizing the other.

5.

(impel) ➡ During the long winter months, the people of the Arctic traditionally gather together to renew friendships and play games. In *nuglugaqtuq,* a spindle with a hole is turned while players try forcefully to **impel** a stick through the hole.

6.

(omission) ➡ Songs are sung, dances are held, and stories are told. If a listener notices the **omission** of a favorite story, she or he can request that the missing tale be told.

7.

(petition) ➡ The disappointed listener will earnestly **petition** the storyteller if the listener's favorite story is left out. Usually, the storyteller is only too happy to answer the request by telling the tale.

8.

(potential) ➡ Aside from being fun, the games help develop the **potential** of young people. That is, they develop young people's capacity to grow and come into their own.

9.

(primitive) ➡ In a land where living conditions can be **primitive,** where modern conveniences are not always available, simple skills and strength are important to survival. The games are a safe way to practice.

10.

(restore) ➡ Most importantly, the games help **restore** a solid family feeling between people. The games allow people to renew community ties.

MAKING NEW WORDS YOUR OWN

Lesson 10 | CONTEXT: The First Americans
American Indian Languages

Just as Italian is similar to Spanish, so Navajo and Apache are related to languages in Alaska and northwestern Canada—the Athapascan family. Language families can be used to trace the migration of a people. Because Cherokee is an Algonquian language, historians believe that the Cherokee traveled south from the land of the Oneida and Mohawk. Over one hundred American Indian languages are still spoken.

In the following exercises, you will have the opportunity to expand your vocabulary by reading about American Indian languages. These ten Vocabulary Words will be used.

consecutive	diction	feasible	immense	insoluble
creative	durable	hilarious	ingenious	ordeal

EXERCISE 1 *Wordbusting*

Directions. Follow these instructions for this word and the nine words on the next page.
- Figure out the word's meaning by looking at its **context,** its **structure,** and its **sound.** Fill in at least one of the three **CSS** boxes. Alternate which boxes you complete.
- Then, look up the word in a dictionary, read all of its meanings, and write the meaning of the word as it is used in the sentence.
- Follow this same process for each of the Vocabulary Words on the next page. You will need to draw your own map for each word. Use a separate sheet of paper.

1.

(consecutive) → "Class," Mrs. Washington smiled, "we will now hear Gene speak for three **consecutive** minutes, that is, three minutes straight, on the languages of American Indians." I took a deep breath and stood up.

Context:	Structure:	Sound:

Dictionary:

2.

(creative) → "Scholars estimate there were more than two hundred languages in North America before Europeans arrived. Each language was a **creative** system of sounds, capable of great expressiveness."

3.

(diction) → "Within each language, however, **diction** most likely varied from person to person. Each speaker would naturally put the words together in a slightly different way."

4.

(durable) → "The ancient languages were **durable,** as they had lasted through the centuries. However, dialects had evolved as different peoples migrated far from their homelands."

5.

(feasible) → "Spoken language was not the only **feasible** form of communication. American Indians who lived on the Great Plains developed sign language as another possible way of communicating."

6.

(hilarious) → "American Indians use different forms of communication—spoken language and sign language to name two—to express different ideas. Sign language, for example, may be more suitable for telling a joke—a story that is supposed to be **hilarious** might draw more laughter if it were signed than if it were spoken."

7.

(immense) → "The vocabulary of the sign language was not **immense**. Because it was limited, few complex ideas could be communicated through signing."

8.

(ingenious) → "Many American Indian languages were never recorded in writing. But a Cherokee named Sequoyah invented an **ingenious** system of symbols for writing. This imaginative system had eighty-six characters."

9.

(insoluble) → "Some American Indian words present almost **insoluble** problems to translators. One Kiowa name meant 'A Warrior Always Fighting Who Had No Time to Even Take the Saddle Blanket from His Horse.'"

10.

(ordeal) → At last, my **ordeal** was finished. It really hadn't been as hard as I'd feared it might be, and I probably learned more about American Indian languages than anyone in the class.

MAKING NEW WORDS YOUR OWN

Lesson 11 **CONTEXT:** Coming to the United States

My Great-Great-Grandparents' Story

People have come to the United States for a variety of reasons. Many have come in search of religious or political freedom. Others have come seeking economic opportunity. All have come with high hopes of building a new life in a new land. For those immigrants who come to the United States through New York Harbor, the first glimpse of the Statue of Liberty is an unforgettable moment of promise.

In the following exercises, you will have the opportunity to expand your vocabulary by reading about the arrival of two immigrants. These ten Vocabulary Words will be used.

aristocrat	decade	emigrate	malnutrition	optimism
censorship	deport	famine	morale	refuge

EXERCISE 1 *Wordbusting*

Directions. Follow these instructions for this word and the nine words on the next page.
- Figure out the word's meaning by looking at its **context,** its **structure,** and its **sound.** Fill in at least one of the three **CSS** boxes.
- Then, look up the word in a dictionary, read all of its meanings, and write the meaning of the word as it is used in the sentence.
- Follow this same process for each of the Vocabulary Words on the next page. You will need to draw your own map for each word. Use a separate sheet of paper.

1.

(aristocrat) → When my great-great-grandmother met my great-great-grandfather on board the ship to the United States, she did not know that he was an **aristocrat** because he was dressed in peasant's clothing.

Context:	Structure:	Sound:

Dictionary:

2.

He was leaving Russia because of **censorship**. The government did not approve of his ideas and had forbidden him to operate his newspaper.

3.

He had struggled to publish his thoughts for a **decade**. After ten years of fighting, however, he was exhausted.

4.
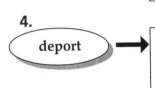

He didn't think the government would **deport** him, but there was always a possibility that he might be forced to leave Russia.

5.

He decided to **emigrate** from Russia to begin a new life in the United States.

6.

My great-great-grandmother was leaving Russia because of a **famine** in her part of the country. Many members of her family had died from lack of food.

7.

She was suffering from **malnutrition;** she had had nothing but bread and water to eat for several months.

8.

She was sick and depressed when she got on the ship, but soon her health and her **morale** began to improve.

9.
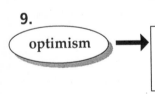

One source of her new **optimism** was her love for my great-great-grandfather. She felt in her heart that their love story would have a happy ending.

10.
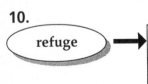

They were holding hands on the deck of the ship when they sailed past the Statue of Liberty. At last they had reached a place of safety, a place of **refuge**.

MAKING NEW WORDS YOUR OWN

Lesson 12 | CONTEXT: Coming to the United States
Dealing with Change

Fitting in with a new culture is extremely difficult for most newcomers to the United States. Moving to a new country can be an exciting experience, but it can also be a frightening and stressful one. Immigrants face many pressures when they arrive in their new home, including the pressures of learning a new language and new customs.

In the following exercises, you will have the opportunity to expand your vocabulary by reading about the experiences of an immigrant attempting to adjust to life in the United States. Below are ten Vocabulary Words that will be used in these exercises.

anxiety	burly	nationality	predicament	resolute
boycott	multitude	naturalization	propaganda	urban

EXERCISE 1 — Wordbusting

Directions. Follow these instructions for this word and the nine words on the next page.
- Figure out the word's meaning by looking at its **context,** its **structure,** and its **sound.** Fill in at least one of the three **CSS** boxes. Alternate which boxes you complete.
- Then, look up the word in a dictionary, read all of its meanings, and write the meaning of the word as it is used in the sentence.
- Follow this same process for each of the Vocabulary Words on the next page. You will need to draw your own map for each word. Use a separate sheet of paper.

1.

(anxiety) → It's probably hard for you to imagine the **anxiety** we felt when we first arrived in the United States. We were nervous and excited, filled with hope, fear, joy, and grief.

Context:	Structure:	Sound:

Dictionary:

2.

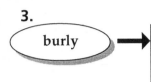

When I first went to work on the docks, I discovered that the dockworkers were engaged in some kind of **boycott**. They refused to handle cargo from certain ships.

3.

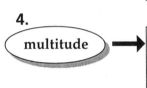

I made a mistake and started to load cargo that I wasn't supposed to move. That made several workers angry, but a big, **burly** dockworker came to my rescue.

4.

This mistake was just the first of a **multitude** of mistakes I made when I first arrived. Of the hundreds of mistakes I made, almost all were a result of not understanding English very well.

5.

At work, I missed having people of my own **nationality** around. I missed being able to communicate in the language of my homeland.

6.

It was important to me that, in time, I could become a citizen of the United States. I began to study the requirements for **naturalization**.

7.

I was in a real **predicament**. I couldn't get a better job because I couldn't speak English well, but I didn't have time to learn the language because of my job.

8.

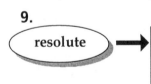

I also realized that I was a victim of **propaganda**. Everything that I had read was designed to make people think that life in the U.S. would bring instant wealth.

9.

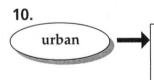

Nevertheless, I remained **resolute** in my will to learn English. I was also firm in my determination to speak as well as someone who was born here.

10.

As I look at the crowds and the factories, I sometimes miss my life on the farm in my homeland, but I've learned to love life in an **urban** setting.

MAKING NEW WORDS YOUR OWN

Lesson 13 | CONTEXT: Coming to the United States
A Day in the City

Life in the city can be very difficult for people who are used to living in small villages or on farms, but it can also be very exciting. Of course, not all people who move to the United States from other countries settle in cities, but millions have. As a result, every large city in the country is rich with a great cultural diversity.

In the following exercises, you will have the opportunity to expand your vocabulary by reading about an immigrant family that lived in the city. Below are ten Vocabulary Words that will be used in these exercises.

accessible	boisterous	fraudulent	impulsive	riotous
bankrupt	dilapidated	hospitable	premiere	transit

EXERCISE 1 *Wordbusting*

Directions _____ these instructions for this word and the nine words on the next page.
- Figure out the _____ ning by looking at its **context,** its **structure,** and its **sound.** Fill in at least one of the thi___ ___s. Alternate which boxes you complete.
- Then, look up the word in a ___ ___ read all of its meanings, and write the meaning of the word as it is used in the senten___
- Follow this same process for each of the ___ ~v Words on the next page. You will need to draw your own map for each word. Use ___ ___heet of paper.

1.

(accessible) ➔ Money certainly was not readily **accessible** in th___ ears. We had to struggle to obtain every dollar.

Context:	Structure:	Sound:

Dictionary:

2.
bankrupt ➤ In fact, during our first few years in the United States, my parents worried that we would become **bankrupt**. They had to work very hard to keep the restaurant in business.

3.
boisterous ➤ My early childhood memories are of **boisterous** children playing on a sidewalk. The noise of our loud and lively games floated through the open windows of the apartment buildings that lined the street.

4.
dilapidated ➤ In reality, our apartment building was **dilapidated** because the owner never kept up with repairs.

5.
fraudulent ➤ Furthermore, the builders had been guilty of about a dozen different **fraudulent** actions when they built it. Two of them later went to jail for their crimes.

6.
hospitable ➤ When I was a child, however, that building and the other run-down buildings in our neighborhood seemed the friendliest, warmest, and most **hospitable** places in the world.

7.
impulsive ➤ My father was a thoughtful man who planned carefully. He rarely did anything **impulsive**.

8.
premiere ➤ One day he took my sister and me downtown on the day of a movie **premiere**. He said that since it was the first showing, the movie's stars would be there in their limousines.

9.
riotous ➤ I was sure that a **riotous** crowd would await us at the theater, as people pushed and shoved to get a glimpse of their favorite stars.

10.
transit ➤ The three of us were in **transit** for about an hour each way, but the movie was worth the long ride across town.

EXERCISE 2 *Context Clues* ✍

Directions. Scan the definitions in Column A. Then, think about how the boldface words are used in the sentences in Column B. To complete the exercise, match each definition in Column A with the correct Vocabulary Word from Column B. Write the letter of your choice on the line provided. Finally, write the Vocabulary Word on the line before the definition.

COLUMN A

____ **11.** word: _____

adj. loud and unruly; rough

____ **12.** word: _____

adj. welcoming guests with fondness and generosity; having an open and receptive mind

____ **13.** word: _____

adj. lacking in some quality; impoverished; destitute; *v.* to impoverish

____ **14.** word: _____

adj. deceitful; dishonest

____ **15.** word: _____

adj. acting on a sudden desire or feeling; hasty; spontaneous

____ **16.** word: _____

adj. easy to approach, enter, obtain

____ **17.** word: _____

adj. falling to pieces; ruined by neglect

____ **18.** word: _____

n. the first public performance; *v.* to exhibit for the first time

____ **19.** word: _____

adj. like a riot; disorderly; disturbing the peace; loud and uproarious

____ **20.** word: _____

n. the act of passing or carrying through or across; a carrying through or across; surveying instrument for measuring horizontal angles; *v.* to pass through or across

COLUMN B

(A) As it turned out, the movie was to **premiere** in several cities at once. However, the stars chose to attend only the opening in Los Angeles, near their homes.

(B) When Father saw my disappointment, he made an **impulsive,** or sudden, decision.

(C) He said, "I guess the price of three tickets won't **bankrupt** me. Would you children like to see this movie?"

(D) My father was as excited as we were. We took the city **transit** system and were carried downtown to the theater.

(E) Actually, the entrance to the theater was very **accessible.** We were dropped off nearby and easily made our way inside.

(F) The crowd in the theater was a **boisterous** one; Father clearly disapproved of their loud, lively behavior.

(G) The movie was a comedy, and the audience did engage in **riotous** laughter. In fact, it was hard to hear the actors because of the uproar.

(H) One of the characters was an old man who decided that his neighbors were engaged in **fraudulent** activities, so he called the police. It turned out that the neighbors had not done anything dishonest.

(I) The movie's hero drove a car like my father's **dilapidated** old station wagon that was always on the verge of breaking down.

(J) My neighborhood might not have been a rich one, but it was a **hospitable** environment for my dreams. They grew and flourished there.

EXERCISE 3 *Like Meanings and Opposite Meanings* 👈

Directions. For each item below, circle the letter of the choice that means the same, or about the same, as the boldface word.

21. an **impulsive** remark
- (A) unplanned
- (B) careful
- (C) painful
- (D) complimentary

22. a **dilapidated** porch
- (A) run-down
- (B) repainted
- (C) attractive
- (D) antique

23. a **hospitable** group
- (A) ill
- (B) concerned
- (C) welcoming
- (D) well-dressed

24. a surveyor's **transit**
- (A) travel
- (B) assignment
- (C) records
- (D) tool

25. a **riotous** crowd
- (A) content
- (B) enormous
- (C) disorderly
- (D) well-behaved

Directions. For each item below, circle the letter of the choice that means the opposite, or about the opposite, of the boldface word.

26. by **fraudulent** means
- (A) dishonest
- (B) understandable
- (C) honest
- (D) confusing

27. a **bankrupt** business
- (A) successful
- (B) poor
- (C) unusual
- (D) ordinary

28. the **accessible** doorway
- (A) hard to reach
- (B) crowded
- (C) large
- (D) easy to reach

29. the **premiere** showing
- (A) first
- (B) last
- (C) most frequent
- (D) least frequent

30. a **boisterous** laugh
- (A) noisy
- (B) quiet
- (C) friendly
- (D) unfriendly

MAKING NEW WORDS YOUR OWN

Lesson 14 | CONTEXT: Coming to the United States

Arriving in a New City

Not everyone who came to the United States in the late 1800s arrived in New York Harbor, although it was the most common route. People entered the United States through many other ports as well. In the mid-1800s, for example, thousands of immigrants arrived at the Port of New Orleans. They added their number to the city's already varied population of African Americans, Creoles, and Cajuns.

In the following exercises, you will have the opportunity to expand your vocabulary by reading about immigrants arriving in various port cities. These ten Vocabulary Words will be used.

acceptance	exaggeration	immigrate	jubilation	prosecute
circulate	grieve	intensity	privilege	thrive

EXERCISE 1 *Wordbusting*

Directions. Follow these instructions for this word and the nine words on the next page.
- Figure out the word's meaning by looking at its **context,** its **structure,** and its **sound.** Fill in at least one of the three **CSS** boxes. Alternate which boxes you complete.
- Then, look up the word in a dictionary, read all of its meanings, and write the meaning of the word as it is used in the sentence.
- Follow this same process for each of the Vocabulary Words on the next page. You will need to draw your own map for each word. Use a separate sheet of paper.

1.

```
( acceptance ) ───►  Newcomers to the United States could find acceptance easily in New York.
                     In fact, New York still seems to welcome people of all cultures.
```

Context:	Structure:	Sound:

Dictionary:

2.

If you **circulate** through all the neighborhoods in Chicago, you will hear many different languages spoken.

3.

You might think it is an **exaggeration** to say that New York is the most interesting city in the United States, but many people would say that this is not stretching the truth at all.

4.

Cuban culture is so alive in Miami that a new arrival from Cuba might not **grieve**, or mourn, the loss of Cuban culture. He or she would feel right at home.

5.

Most people who have chosen to leave their native lands and **immigrate** to New York have been happy with their decision to go there.

6.

Almost everyone who has ever been to Miami loves the city's **intensity.** The air is abuzz with an energy that you can almost touch.

7.

Mardi Gras, carnival time in New Orleans, is a period of celebration and **jubilation.**

8.

The festivities for Mardi Gras last a week, and many people **prosecute** the celebration with vigor until its conclusion on Fat Tuesday.

9.

Many people who live in San Francisco consider it a **privilege.** They feel they are fortunate to live in such a fascinating city.

10.

thrive

Several cultures **thrive** there. Among these flourishing cultures are the Chinese and the Japanese, to name but two.

EXERCISE 2 *Context Clues*

Directions. Scan the definitions in Column A. Then, think about how the boldface words are used in the sentences in Column B. To complete the exercise, match each definition in Column A with the correct Vocabulary Word from Column B. Write the letter of your choice on the line provided. Finally, write the Vocabulary Word on the line before the definition.

COLUMN A	COLUMN B

_____ **11.** word: _____
n. the act of accepting; a condition of being accepted; approval; belief

(A) The **intensity** of the celebration of Mardi Gras is exceptional in New Orleans. No other U.S. city celebrates with such enthusiasm.

_____ **12.** word: _____
v. to cause to feel sorrow; to mourn

(B) Mardi Gras is a time when originality **thrives,** when people allow their imaginations to flourish.

_____ **13.** word: _____
v. to enter and settle in a new country

(C) Many people want to pack up and **immigrate** to New Orleans during Mardi Gras. Others feel just the opposite. They wouldn't want to move to the home of such a wild celebration.

_____ **14.** word: _____
n. degree of strength, force, or feeling; extreme brightness or concentration

(D) True sons and daughters of New Orleans **grieve** if they have to be away from the city during this period of celebration. They ache for what they are missing.

_____ **15.** word: _____
n. an overstatement; the act of making something seem greater than it is

(E) It is not an **exaggeration** to say that some residents of New Orleans live for Mardi Gras.

_____ **16.** word: _____
n. a joyful celebration; gladness

(F) During the summer, as ceiling fans **circulate** the air, moving it around beautiful rooms with tall ceilings, planners prepare for the next year's Mardi Gras.

_____ **17.** word: _____
v. to prosper; to succeed; to flourish; to grow vigorously

(G) New Orleans citizens consider it a **privilege** to participate in a Mardi Gras parade.

_____ **18.** word: _____
v. to follow up or pursue something to a conclusion; to carry on; to take legal action against

(H) Mardi Gras is one big party that lasts for weeks. It has met with **acceptance** because it precedes an important religious occasion.

_____ **19.** word: _____
n. a special advantage or benefit granted to a person or group; a basic legal right; *v.* to grant a privilege to

(I) All the **jubilation,** the energetic partying, is part of the preparation for Lent and Easter.

_____ **20.** word: _____
v. to flow or move in a path that returns to the starting point; to move about freely; to spread widely

(J) Sometimes a few people get carried away during Mardi Gras and are taken to jail and even **prosecuted.** Generally, however, it is not necessary to bring legal action against these overzealous partygoers.

EXERCISE 3 *Like Meanings and Opposite Meanings*

Directions. For each item below, circle the letter of the choice that means the same, or about the same, as the boldface word.

21. a wild **exaggeration**
- (A) explanation
- (B) guess
- (C) place
- (D) overstatement

22. to **immigrate** west
- (A) drive
- (B) fly
- (C) come to
- (D) move away from

23. the **intensity** of his happiness
- (A) discussion
- (B) increase
- (C) results
- (D) power

24. a position of **privilege**
- (A) excitement
- (B) agreement
- (C) honor
- (D) willingness

25. to **prosecute** your studies
- (A) seek assistance with
- (B) be concerned about
- (C) begin
- (D) continue

Directions. For each item below, circle the letter of the choice that means the opposite, or about the opposite, of the boldface word.

26. a sense of **acceptance**
- (A) confusion
- (B) understanding
- (C) disfavor
- (D) welcoming

27. to **circulate** in the room
- (A) move around
- (B) stand still
- (C) draw
- (D) dance

28. to **grieve** for three months
- (A) rejoice
- (B) mourn
- (C) run away
- (D) remain

29. a moment of **jubilation**
- (A) forgiveness
- (B) cooperation
- (C) rejoicing
- (D) sorrow

30. to **thrive** in sandy soil
- (A) live
- (B) plant
- (C) die
- (D) sink

MAKING NEW WORDS YOUR OWN

Lesson 15 | CONTEXT: Coming to the United States
Southeast Asians in Houston, Texas

Houston, Texas, has been the final destination for many immigrants, including thousands who have arrived from the southeast Asian nations of Vietnam, Laos, and Cambodia. Houston is very different from southeast Asia, but the immigrants have worked hard to make a new life in a new land.

In the following exercises, you will have the opportunity to expand your vocabulary by reading about one family that escaped from Vietnam in the 1970s and now lives in Houston. Below are ten Vocabulary Words that will be used in these exercises.

dedicate	dispense	exertion	humidity	restrain
depose	dissect	haven	memento	tumult

EXERCISE 1 · Wordbusting ✍

Directions. Follow these instructions for this word and the nine words on the next page.
- Figure out the word's meaning by looking at its **context,** its **structure,** and its **sound.** Fill in at least one of the three **CSS** boxes. Alternate which boxes you complete.
- Then, look up the word in a dictionary, read all of its meanings, and write the meaning of the word as it is used in the sentence.
- Follow this same process for each of the Vocabulary Words on the next page. You will need to draw your own map for each word. Use a separate sheet of paper.

1.

(dedicate) ➝ Nguyen Truong had intended to **dedicate** his life to farming, but as it turned out, he had to devote his life to something else. He became involved in the civil war that raged in his country, Vietnam.

Context:

Structure:

Sound:

Dictionary:

2.
depose ➔ If he had been able to **depose** the leader in his village, his story might be different, but Nguyen Truong was unable to remove him from office.

3.
dispense ➔ He had to **dispense** with his plan to become a farmer, but he never gave up his dream of a better life for his children.

4.
dissect ➔ He made a plan to escape from Vietnam with his family. He shared the plan with his wife so that she could **dissect** it thoroughly. They wanted to be sure that every single part had been carefully thought out.

5.
exertion ➔ The escape would require all of their mental energy. It would also call for a great deal of physical **exertion**.

6.
haven ➔ On the first night of the journey, the family found a safe **haven** in a cave in the jungle.

7.
humidity ➔ They traveled by night so they could avoid the heat and **humidity**. The high temperature and the dampness would tax their strength.

8.
memento ➔ They could not bring much with them, but each family member carried a **memento,** or keepsake.

9.
restrain ➔ They spent many days on a small boat at sea. Even though they **restrained** their appetites and managed their supplies carefully, they almost ran out of food and water before they were rescued.

10.
tumult ➔ When they reached shore, they were happy to escape the **tumult** and the noise of the large waves crashing into the small boat.

Name _____ Date _____ Class _____

EXERCISE 2 *Context Clues* 👉

Directions. Scan the definitions in Column A. Then, think about how the boldface words are used in the sentences in Column B. To complete the exercise, match each definition in Column A with the correct Vocabulary Word from Column B. Write the letter of your choice on the line provided. Finally, write the Vocabulary Word on the line before the definition.

COLUMN A	COLUMN B
____ **11.** word: _____ *n.* moisture; dampness; the amount of moisture in the air	(A) Eventually the family settled in Houston, where the heat and **humidity** reminded them of the muggy climate of Vietnam.
____ **12.** word: _____ *v.* to devote to a sacred or special purpose; to inscribe a work of art to someone out of affection or respect	(B) Sometimes the noise and commotion of the city was disturbing, especially the **tumult** of the traffic.
____ **13.** word: _____ *n.* a souvenir; a keepsake; anything kept or given to remind one of the past	(C) However, after the hard trip at sea and the months in the refugee camp, the city seemed like a safe **haven**.
____ **14.** word: _____ *v.* to remove from office or high position; to testify or state under oath but out of court.	(D) Nguyen Truong was pleased that they had escaped before the leader of the village tried to force him to **depose,** or swear under oath, that his neighbors had been disloyal.
____ **15.** word: _____ *v.* to hold back from action; to control; to limit or restrict	(E) The family's **mementos** were very dear to them. The keepsakes reminded them of their old home far away.
____ **16.** word: _____ *v.* to cut apart; to analyze closely	(F) Sometimes he had to **restrain** himself from weeping. He held back his tears because he didn't want to upset his grandchildren.
____ **17.** word: _____ *n.* a violent or noisy commotion of a crowd; a disorderly disturbance; a disturbance of mind or feeling	(G) He felt especially sad on Tet, the Vietnamese New Year, when the Vietnamese people traditionally **dedicate** themselves to remembering their past.
____ **18.** word: _____ *v.* to distribute or administer; to do without; to do away with something	(H) During the New Year celebration, neighbors made wonderful treats for one another and **dispensed,** or handed out, gifts of money to the children of the community.
____ **19.** word: _____ *n.* a harbor or port; a place of safe shelter	(I) Preparation for Tet required hours of hard work, but no one minded the **exertion**. It was an opportunity to share time with family.
____ **20.** word: _____ *n.* a strong effort; the act of using	(J) During New Year celebrations, the family members paused to **dissect** their emotions. They found themselves analyzing and evaluating their old lives and their new ones.

EXERCISE 3 *Like Meanings and Opposite Meanings* ✍

Directions. For each item below, circle the letter of the choice that means the same, or about the same, as the boldface word.

21. very low **humidity**
(A) moisture content
(B) heat index
(C) percentages
(D) score

22. in a quiet **haven**
(A) hospital
(B) palace
(C) shelter
(D) heritage

23. a small **memento**
(A) loss
(B) ghost
(C) memory
(D) keepsake

24. to **dedicate** some money
(A) save secretly
(B) borrow
(C) write
(D) set aside

25. to **dissect** his motives
(A) believe
(B) analyze
(C) ignore
(D) understand

Directions. For each item below, circle the letter of the choice that means the opposite, or about the opposite, of the boldface word.

26. to **restrain** strong emotion
(A) train
(B) let go
(C) feel deeply
(D) struggle with

27. the distant **tumult**
(A) memories
(B) friends
(C) calm
(D) noise

28. to **depose** the king
(A) crown
(B) get rid of
(C) argue against
(D) remember

29. a period of **exertion**
(A) work
(B) rest
(C) time
(D) loss

30. to **dispense** with the idea
(A) eliminate
(B) forget
(C) share
(D) keep

MAKING NEW WORDS YOUR OWN

Lesson 16 | **CONTEXT: Coming to the United States**

Remembering the Past

Making the decision to leave home and begin life in a new country was a very difficult one for many immigrants. However, it was just the first in a series of difficult steps. The journey to the United States may have been long and dangerous. And, once there, immigrants faced the gigantic task of adjusting to life in a new country.

In the following exercises, you will have the opportunity to expand your vocabulary by reading about the problems some immigrants faced upon arrival in the United States. Below are ten Vocabulary Words that will be used in these exercises.

hamper	impose	intercept	negligent	recuperate
imperative	inconsiderate	liable	presume	spacious

EXERCISE 1 *Wordbusting*

Directions. Follow these instructions for this word and the nine words on the next page.
- Figure out the word's meaning by looking at its **context,** its **structure,** and its **sound.** Fill in at least one of the three **CSS** boxes. Alternate which boxes you complete.
- Then, look up the word in a dictionary, read all of its meanings, and write the meaning of the word as it is used in the sentence.
- Follow this same process for each of the Vocabulary Words on the next page. You will need to draw your own map for each word. Use a separate sheet of paper.

1.

(hamper) → Many problems might arise in their homelands that could **hamper** immigrants' efforts to come to the United States. Fortunately, these problems didn't hold everyone back.

Context:	Structure:	Sound:

Dictionary:

2.
imperative → It was **imperative** that some people flee to freedom, for their lives were at stake.

3.
impose → Many immigrants still come for the same reason that the first European immigrants came. Their governments **impose** unfair restrictions on them, and they can't live under such forced limitations.

4.
inconsiderate → Immigrants who came in the late 1800s and early 1900s often encountered **inconsiderate** immigration officials who treated them rudely.

5.
intercept → Immigration officials were supposed to **intercept** new arrivals who were ill and send them back to their homelands.

6.
liable → These officials were **liable,** or responsible, for preventing the spread of diseases such as tuberculosis.

7.
negligent → If they were **negligent** in their duty, they could get in trouble. Perhaps that is what made some of them overly cautious.

8.
presume → Unfortunately, sometimes an official would **presume** that an immigrant was seriously ill when in reality he or she was simply exhausted from a difficult voyage.

9.
recuperate → Sometimes an immigrant would be given time to **recuperate** from an illness. When well, the immigrant would be admitted into the country.

10.
spacious → Immigrants were overjoyed to be admitted to the United States. They were sure that this new **spacious** nation would offer them plenty of room to carve out a new life.

EXERCISE 2 *Context Clues*

Directions. Scan the definitions in Column A. Then, think about how the boldface words are used in the sentences in Column B. To complete the exercise, match each definition in Column A with the correct Vocabulary Word from Column B. Write the letter of your choice on the line provided. Finally, write the Vocabulary Word on the line before the definition.

COLUMN A	COLUMN B

COLUMN A

_____ **11.** word: _____

n. a large covered basket or container;
v. to hold back or hinder

_____ **12.** word: _____

adj. absolutely necessary, urgent;
commanding; describing a verb that
expresses a command; *n.* a command

_____ **13.** word: _____

adj. lacking concern for the needs of
others; thoughtless; selfish

_____ **14.** word: _____

v. to take or seize en route; to block

_____ **15.** word: _____

adj. containing much space; vast; roomy

_____ **16.** word: _____

v. to return to health and strength; to
recover from financial losses

_____ **17.** word: _____

v. to take for granted; to suppose to be
true; to take upon oneself with authority

_____ **18.** word: _____

adj. guilty of neglect; failing to show
proper care or caution

_____ **19.** word: _____

adj. likely; subject or susceptible;
legally responsible

_____ **20.** word: _____

v. to place or set on with authority; to
inflict by force; to pass off deceptively;
(with *on* or *upon*) to take advantage of

COLUMN B

(A) I went with my great-grandfather to visit the museum at Ellis Island. Today, the building is open and **spacious,** but when he arrived there as a boy, its halls were crowded with people.

(B) He thinks it is **imperative** that the whole family remember their heritage; that's why he felt it was necessary to take me to Ellis Island.

(C) He worries that he has been **negligent** in keeping us in touch with our past, but he has really done a good job of it.

(D) Things went smoothly for him at Ellis Island except for one **inconsiderate** official who changed the spelling of his name from Wdzieczak to Wechik. The official didn't even ask whether he minded the change.

(E) Although he didn't say so, I **presume** he will be taking my cousins to the museum next summer. He takes some of his great-grand-children every summer.

(F) He has been ill lately, but he is beginning to **recuperate**.

(G) I do want him to tell me more stories about the family history, but I don't want to **impose** on him. Having someone ask you lots of questions can be tiring after a while.

(H) Until recently, he was **liable** to fall asleep in the middle of a tale, but I don't think that will be likely once he is feeling better.

(I) Once we went on a picnic. I will never forget how his eyes twinkled as he pulled the food from the picnic **hamper** and told me stories of crossing the Atlantic.

(J) "As we left Gdansk," he began, "we were **intercepted** by my Aunt Eva, who stopped us and begged to go with us to the United States."

MAKING NEW WORDS YOUR OWN **65**

EXERCISE 3 *Like Meanings and Opposite Meanings* ☞

Directions. For each item below, circle the letter of the choice that means the same, or about the same, as the boldface word.

21. to **recuperate** his losses
(A) count
(B) understand
(C) lose
(D) regain

22. to **presume** to challenge the official
(A) win over
(B) dare
(C) refuse to count on
(D) rely heavily on

23. to **intercept** the message
(A) send
(B) stop
(C) hear
(D) believe

24. to **impose** her views
(A) get
(B) force on others
(C) design
(D) carefully explain

25. to be **liable** for the mistake
(A) forgiven
(B) concerned
(C) sorry
(D) responsible

Directions. For each item below, circle the letter of the choice that means the opposite, or about the opposite, of the boldface word.

26. in **spacious** quarters
(A) roomy
(B) ugly
(C) cramped
(D) beautiful

27. to be **negligent**
(A) stupid
(B) intelligent
(C) careless
(D) careful

28. an **inconsiderate** host
(A) thoughtful
(B) thoughtless
(C) well-dressed
(D) sloppily dressed

29. an **imperative** consideration
(A) essential
(B) minor
(C) rude
(D) polite

30. to **hamper** the efforts
(A) throw out
(B) box
(C) hinder
(D) encourage

MAKING NEW WORDS YOUR OWN

Lesson 17 | **CONTEXT: Coming to the United States**
The Ballad of Mary Margaret Murphy

Each person who has immigrated to the United States has a special story to tell. Some are stories of triumph, and some are stories of tragedy. Most are stories of ordinary people. All of them, however, are stories of hope for a good life in a new country.

In the following exercises, you will have the opportunity to expand your vocabulary by reading about two immigrants. Below are ten Vocabulary Words that will be used in these exercises.

aroma	elegant	gracious	manageable	occupant
capital	frequency	haughty	monopoly	probation

EXERCISE 1   *Wordbusting*

Directions. Follow these instructions for this word and the nine words on the next page.
- Figure out the word's meaning by looking at its **context,** its **structure,** and its **sound.** Fill in at least one of the three **CSS** boxes. Alternate which boxes you complete.
- Then, look up the word in a dictionary, read all of its meanings, and write the meaning of the word as it is used in the sentence.
- Follow this same process for each of the Vocabulary Words on the next page. You will need to draw your own map for each word. Use a separate sheet of paper.

1.

aroma → Every time I smell the fragrant **aroma** of a rich stew bubbling on the stove, I think of my great-grandmother, Mary Margaret Murphy.

Context:

Structure:

Sound:

Dictionary:

2.

capital → She emigrated from County Cork in Ireland and settled in Boston, the **capital** of Massachusetts. She dreamed that someday one of her children would live in the governor's mansion.

3.
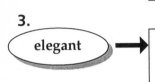
elegant → She found work as a maid in one of those **elegant** townhouses on Beacon Hill, the fancy section of town.

4.
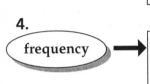
frequency → The kitchen had to be scrubbed with such **frequency** that she felt that was all she ever did.

5.

gracious → Sometimes she felt sad when she compared her hard life to the **gracious** lifestyle of her employers.

6.
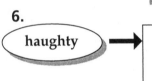
haughty → Her employers could be **haughty** and sometimes treated her as if they were better than she was.

7.

manageable → Although the work was difficult and her schedule was demanding, she found a way to make it **manageable**.

8.
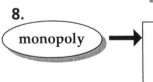
monopoly → Her employers did not have a **monopoly** on all her time. She had some days off, and on those days she rested and dreamed of her future.

9.
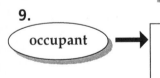
occupant → She had fallen in love with another **occupant** of the boardinghouse where she lived.

10.
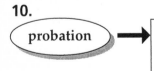
probation → In her heart, she had put him on **probation**. She thought he was handsome and charming, but was he worthy of her love?

EXERCISE 2 *Context Clues* ✍

Directions. Scan the definitions in Column A. Then, think about how the boldface words are used in the sentences in Column B. To complete the exercise, match each definition in Column A with the correct Vocabulary Word from Column B. Write the letter of your choice on the line provided. Finally, write the Vocabulary Word on the line before the definition.

COLUMN A	COLUMN B

COLUMN A

____ **11.** word: _____
n. the official seat of government; the total wealth of a business; wealth available for investment; *adj.* first, foremost; excellent; punishable by death

____ **12.** word: _____
adj. proud and vain to the point of being conceited; scornful of others

____ **13.** word: _____
adj. showing kindness and courtesy; elegant and refined

____ **14.** word: _____
adj. capable of being controlled, directed, or accomplished

____ **15.** word: _____
n. the exclusive control of anything; a company with such control

____ **16.** word: _____
adj. tasteful, beautiful, and luxurious; refined in manner, taste, and style

____ **17.** word: _____
n. one who resides in or occupies a house, land, or a position

____ **18.** word: _____
n. a fragrant or appetizing smell

____ **19.** word: _____
n. a trial period

____ **20.** word: _____
n. the rate or number of times a thing recurs within a given time or group

COLUMN B

(A) Timothy O'Malley was in love with Mary Margaret, but he didn't want to tell her until he had enough **capital** to start his own business. He scrimped and saved to make that dream come true.

(B) He thought Mary Margaret was the most **elegant** woman he had ever seen, despite her lack of education and her hands, which were red and raw from hard work.

(C) Mary Margaret was a warm and **gracious** person, with a quick smile and a loving heart.

(D) The **frequency** with which Timothy looked at her across the supper table had already given her a good clue to his feelings.

(E) He did not know that he had a **monopoly** on her heart; she was interested in no one else.

(F) Other men were also interested in Mary Margaret, including the **occupant** of the small house behind the mansion where she worked.

(G) Another woman might have become conceited, even **haughty,** knowing she had so many admirers, but not Mary Margaret.

(H) She made the situation **manageable** by ignoring most of her would-be boyfriends. She never let the admiration go to her head.

(I) One day Timothy O'Malley finished his period of **probation** at the bank and became a full-time employee. That night, he splashed on his lilac aftershave, dressed in his best clothes, and went to ask Mary Margaret to marry him.

(J) When I smell the **aroma** of lilac aftershave, I always imagine Mary Margaret saying, "I thought you'd never ask!"

EXERCISE 3   *Like Meanings and Opposite Meanings* ✍

Directions. For each item below, circle the letter of the choice that means the same, or about the same, as the boldface word.

21. the **aroma** of stew
    (A) flavor
    (B) love
    (C) smell
    (D) price

22. with some **frequency**
    (A) hurry
    (B) regularity
    (C) hesitation
    (D) friendliness

23. a **monopoly** of the business
    (A) increase
    (B) loss
    (C) game
    (D) control

24. the **occupant** of the palace
    (A) person who lives in
    (B) person who believes in
    (C) person who relies on
    (D) person who loses

25. the end of **probation**
    (A) guesswork
    (B) a month
    (C) a year
    (D) trial period

Directions. For each item below, circle the letter of the choice that means the opposite, or about the opposite, of the boldface word.

26. an **elegant** dress
    (A) beautiful
    (B) shabby
    (C) expensive
    (D) small

27. a **manageable** amount
    (A) easy
    (B) large
    (C) uncontrollable
    (D) questionable

28. a **haughty** manner
    (A) friendly
    (B) cruel
    (C) disorganized
    (D) quick

29. a **capital** idea
    (A) serious
    (B) bad
    (C) excellent
    (D) interesting

30. a **gracious** host
    (A) courteous
    (B) rude
    (C) remarkable
    (D) rich

MAKING NEW WORDS YOUR OWN

Lesson 18 CONTEXT: Coming to the United States
Discovering New Holidays

Adjusting to a new culture means adjusting to its holidays. Of course, many cultures share holidays. Many immigrants to the United States probably already celebrated Christmas, Hanukkah, or Ramadan, as well as the New Year. Most immigrants, however, encounter strictly American holidays—such as Thanksgiving—for the first time.

In the following exercises, you will have the opportunity to expand your vocabulary by reading about Thanksgiving celebrations. Below are ten Vocabulary Words that will be used in these exercises.

baste	dismantle	populate	remote	saturate
diminish	embarrass	prearrange	rigid	sedate

EXERCISE 1 *Wordbusting*

Directions. Follow these instructions for this word and the nine words on the next page.
- Figure out the word's meaning by looking at its **context,** its **structure,** and its **sound.** Fill in at least one of the three **CSS** boxes. Alternate which boxes you complete.
- Then, look up the word in a dictionary, read all of its meanings, and write the meaning of the word as it is used in the sentence.
- Follow this same process for each of the Vocabulary Words on the next page. You will need to draw your own map for each word. Use a separate sheet of paper.

1.

(baste) ➡️ As the students in Ms. Smith's family-living class at Xavier High learn to stuff a Thanksgiving turkey and **baste** it with its own juices, they are discussing family celebrations.

Context:	Structure:	Sound:

Dictionary:

2.

Cooking all week has not **diminished** their enthusiasm for the holiday. In fact, they are as excited as ever.

3.

At one table, students have started to **dismantle** the complicated centerpiece that Ms. Smith made. She wants to take it apart and put it away before the final bell rings for holiday break.

4.

Ms. Smith is talking to a new student, Ezekiel, who recently arrived from Nigeria. "I don't want to **embarrass** you," she says because she is afraid her question might make him feel foolish, "but are you familiar with our Thanksgiving holiday?"

5.

"Yes," says Ezekiel, "I believe its origins are from the time that Europeans first began to settle and **populate** this continent."

6.

"That's right," says Lynda. "It was the Pilgrims who held the first Thanksgiving feast. Ms. Smith, did the Pilgrims **prearrange** the first feast, or did it just sort of happen, without planning?"

7.

"I think William Bradford, the governor of the Pilgrim's settlement in Plymouth, planned it in advance," Alfonso offers. "I have a **remote** memory of discussing all of this in Mr. Dawson's history class, but the class was so long ago that I'm not sure."

8.

"Here's what I think you should know, Ezekiel," says Amber. "In this country, we aren't **rigid** about how we celebrate the holiday. You can do it in any way you see fit."

9.

"I like to **saturate** cheese cloth with melted butter and drape it over the turkey while it roasts," says Elsbeth.

10.

sedate

"It's fun to discuss our family celebrations," says Ms. Smith. "Some dinners are formal, quiet, and **sedate**, but my family's is always casual, noisy, and rowdy."

EXERCISE 2 *Context Clues*

Directions. Scan the definitions in Column A. Then, think about how the boldface words are used in the sentences in Column B. To complete the exercise, match each definition in Column A with the correct Vocabulary Word from Column B. Write the letter of your choice on the line provided. Finally, write the Vocabulary Word on the line before the definition.

COLUMN A	COLUMN B

_____ **11.** word: _____

v. to prepare in advance or beforehand; to plan ahead

_____ **12.** word: _____

v. to tear down; to take apart; to strip of furnishing or equipment

_____ **13.** word: _____

adj. distant; isolated or out of the way; not obvious; slight; cool and aloof

_____ **14.** word: _____

v. to furnish with inhabitants; to inhabit

_____ **15.** word: _____

adj. stiff; firmly fixed; very strict

_____ **16.** word: _____

v. to soak thoroughly; to fill completely; to drench

_____ **17.** word: _____

adj. serious and unemotional; quiet; composed; *v.* to administer a tranquilizer

_____ **18.** word: _____

v. to cause someone to feel ill at ease and self-conscious

_____ **19.** word: _____

v. to sew together with loose, temporary stitches; to moisten food with liquid or oil as it roasts or bakes; to attack verbally

_____ **20.** word: _____

v. to make or become smaller; to decrease; to detract from the authority of

(A) "Learning about the different ways people celebrate Thanksgiving has not **diminished** my enthusiasm for the holiday," says Heather.

(B) Eleni says, "In my family, we **prearrange** our holiday. In fact, we plan weeks in advance."

(C) "In October, my mother was **basting** scraps of material together for a huge holiday quilt. She is still sewing on it," Eleni adds.

(D) "One year my family went to a cabin in a **remote** part of the mountains for Thanksgiving. We wanted to get away from the hustle and bustle of civilization," Karen remarks.

(E) "It was kind of funny because my dad, who is the cook in the family, had to **dismantle** almost our whole kitchen and pack it in the van."

(F) "Personally, I was a little **embarrassed** to be taking a microwave to the wilderness, but Dad isn't self-conscious about anything!"

(G) "At least we didn't take the radio or the television. For once, we were able to avoid all the noise that usually **saturates** the air so that you can't even hear yourself think!"

(H) "My family is like Karen's," Joe remarks. "We're not at all **rigid** about Thanksgiving— except for one strict rule. My mother always makes mashed potatoes."

(I) "At my grandmother's house, the adults sit down to a quiet, **sedate** meal. We kids, however, are anything but well behaved."

(J) "You know," says Ms. Smith, "there may be as many ways to celebrate Thanksgiving as there are families who live in this country, who **populate** our cities and towns."

EXERCISE 3 *Like Meanings and Opposite Meanings* ✍

Directions. For each item below, circle the letter of the choice that means the same, or about the same, as the boldface word.

21. to **baste** your opponent
- (A) attack
- (B) review
- (C) abuse
- (D) thank

22. to **embarrass** the child
- (A) encourage
- (B) ignore
- (C) shame
- (D) talk to

23. to **populate** the city
- (A) leave
- (B) approve of
- (C) live in
- (D) avoid

24. to **prearrange** the trip
- (A) travel
- (B) forget
- (C) plan
- (D) reschedule

25. to **saturate** the sponge
- (A) locate
- (B) wash
- (C) throw out
- (D) soak

Directions. For each item below, circle the letter of the choice that means the opposite, or about the opposite, of the boldface word.

26. to **diminish** the supply
- (A) increase
- (B) make smaller
- (C) hide from
- (D) find

27. to **dismantle** the equipment
- (A) take apart
- (B) put together
- (C) buy
- (D) sell

28. a **remote** spot
- (A) dirty
- (B) unusual
- (C) close
- (D) distant

29. a **rigid** attitude
- (A) good
- (B) terrible
- (C) strict
- (D) flexible

30. to **sedate** the patient
- (A) put to sleep
- (B) wake up
- (C) quiet
- (D) alarm

MAKING NEW WORDS YOUR OWN

Lesson 19 **CONTEXT:** Coming to the United States

Tracing a Heritage

When and how did your family come to the United States? Were they here to greet the Europeans who first landed? Did they arrive with the French in Louisiana? Were they forced to come here in slavery? Did they enter Hawaii from Korea in the late 1800s? Perhaps they fled Vietnam in 1975? Or perhaps they arrived from another place, at another time. Finding out when and how your family first arrived can be a rewarding experience.

In the following exercises, you will have the opportunity to expand your vocabulary by reading about the heritages of several different students. Below are ten Vocabulary Words that will be used in these exercises.

access	circumnavigate	liberate	pleasantry	regime
accommodations	evacuate	notify	provision	remorse

EXERCISE 1 *Wordbusting*

Directions. Follow these instructions for this word and the nine words on the next page.
- Figure out the word's meaning by looking at its **context,** its **structure,** and its **sound.** Fill in at least one of the three **CSS** boxes. Alternate which boxes you complete.
- Then, look up the word in a dictionary, read all of its meanings, and write the meaning of the word as it is used in the sentence.
- Follow this same process for each of the Vocabulary Words on the next page. You will need to draw your own map for each word. Use a separate sheet of paper.

1.

access → "I don't know if you will have **access** to all the information you need to complete this assignment, but I want you to do your best to discover where your family came from and why," says Mr. Whitley.

Context:	Structure:	Sound:

Dictionary:

2.

(accommodations) →

"We may have to make some **accommodations,** or adjustments, to the assignment if you can't find the information," he adds.

3.

(circumnavigate) →

Mr. Whitley briefly reminds his class of the history of people coming to the Americas, including the Europeans' desire to **circumnavigate** the globe—to set out heading west and return from the east. These explorers didn't realize that North America would get in their way.

4.

(evacuate) →

"My parents left Cambodia when they were ordered to leave, or **evacuate,** Phnom Penh," remarks Lo.

5.

(liberate) →

"My family came when Hitler invaded Czechoslovakia. They knew he did not want to **liberate** them but that they would go to prison or die," says April.

6.

(notify) →

"I wish you had decided to **notify** us earlier about this project," says Danny. "My grandparents were here last week, and I could have talked with them if you had told us about it sooner."

7.

(pleasantry) →

"My grandmother came from Japan, and she learned English gradually. For many years all she could do was exchange a few **pleasantries,** such as 'How are you?' and 'Nice weather,'"says Rita.

8.

(provision) →

"Perhaps I should make **provision** to visit my great-aunt this weekend," says Jimmy. "She knows more than anyone else about my dad's family history. I'll call the retirement home."

9.

(regime) →

"My family came to the United States to escape the **regime** that was in power in Guatemala," says Luiz. "That government mistreated members of my family."

10.

(remorse) →

"When my mother left Laos, she had to leave her family behind. That decision filled her with **remorse** because she was very close to them," says Jenny.

EXERCISE 2 *Context Clues* ✍

Directions. Scan the definitions in Column A. Then, think about how the boldface words are used in the sentences in Column B. To complete the exercise, match each definition in Column A with the correct Vocabulary Word from Column B. Write the letter of your choice on the line provided. Finally, write the Vocabulary Word on the line before the definition.

<table>
<tr><td>COLUMN A</td><td>COLUMN B</td></tr>
<tr><td>

____ **11.** word: _____

v. to set free; to release from bondage or enemy occupation

</td><td>

(A) "Later my mother made **provision** for them to come to the United States. Those preparations were difficult to make," Jenny adds.

</td></tr>
<tr><td>

____ **12.** word: _____

v. to give notice; to inform

</td><td>

(B) "Although their **accommodations** here were simple, the new housing was an improvement over the way they had lived in Laos."

</td></tr>
<tr><td>

____ **13.** word: _____

n. the right to enter, make use of, or communicate with; a passage or means of entering, approaching, or using; a sudden outburst; *v.* to gain entrance

</td><td>

(C) "My grandparents just made their first trip back to Russia since the Communist **regime** fell from power. The change in government made them feel safe there," Nadia comments.

</td></tr>
<tr><td>

____ **14.** word: _____

n. a good-natured joke; a polite remark

</td><td>

(D) "My great-grandfather came to the United States after World War II because he admired the U.S. soldiers who **liberated** him from the prison camp," remarks Hayley.

</td></tr>
<tr><td>

____ **15.** word: _____

n. the act of providing; a preparation made for the future; a requirement; [*pl.*] food or supplies for the future

</td><td>

(E) "For a long time, we could not **access** information about our relatives in Argentina," Trina says, "but now we can communicate with them by phone or e-mail."

</td></tr>
<tr><td>

____ **16.** word: _____

v. to travel completely around a thing

</td><td>

(F) "One of my aunts was able to **notify** us that my cousin Roberto was alive and well."

</td></tr>
<tr><td>

____ **17.** word: _____

n. a system or form of government or rule; a political or social system

</td><td>

(G) "My grandparents decided to flee from Cuba after Fidel Castro came to power. They **evacuated** the country in 1961," said Ignacio.

</td></tr>
<tr><td>

____ **18.** word: _____

n. adjustment; convenience; compromise; room and board; lodgings; seating on a public vehicle

</td><td>

(H) "My parents risked their lives to get here. If I complain about my life, I usually feel **remorse** later. I feel guilty when I remember what they have been through."

</td></tr>
<tr><td>

____ **19.** word: _____

n. bitter regret; a sense of guilt

</td><td>

(I) "Yes," says Jenny. "Some of our ancestors practically **circumnavigated** the globe to get here. So I feel kind of silly for complaining about having to walk to school."

</td></tr>
<tr><td>

____ **20.** word: _____

v. to empty; to withdraw; to remove for reasons of safety; to vacate

</td><td>

(J) "I love my grandparents, but we can exchange only a few **pleasantries** since I don't know much German," says Karl.

</td></tr>
</table>

EXERCISE 3 *Like Meanings and Opposite Meanings* ✍

Directions. For each item below, circle the letter of the choice that means the same, or about the same, as the boldface word.

21. to have **access** to the files
 (A) brought things
 (B) avoided using
 (C) the right to use
 (D) forgotten

22. pleasant **accommodations**
 (A) friends
 (B) living quarters
 (C) plans for the future
 (D) thoughts

23. to **circumnavigate** the park
 (A) donate money to
 (B) investigate
 (C) visit
 (D) travel around

24. to make **provision** for
 (A) plans
 (B) friends
 (C) housing
 (D) peace

25. a friendly **regime**
 (A) game
 (B) government
 (C) animal
 (D) boss

Directions. For each item below, circle the letter of the choice that means the opposite, or about the opposite, of the boldface word.

26. to **liberate** the animals
 (A) free
 (B) cage
 (C) purchase
 (D) sell

27. to feel **remorse**
 (A) pride and joy
 (B) bitter regret
 (C) tired
 (D) rested

28. to **notify** the authorities
 (A) recognize
 (B) identify with
 (C) refuse to tell
 (D) inform

29. to **evacuate** the building
 (A) destroy
 (B) rebuild
 (C) empty
 (D) fill up

30. to offer a **pleasantry**
 (A) friendly remark
 (B) rude comment
 (C) snack
 (D) invitation

MAKING NEW WORDS YOUR OWN

Lesson 20 | CONTEXT: Coming to the United States

Coming Soon to a Theater Near You

The immigrant experience has been the subject of many interesting films. Two of the best are *Hester Street* and *Avalon,* but there are many other good ones. Since we are a nation of immigrants, it should come as no surprise that films about immigrants are continually popular.

In the following exercises, you will have the opportunity to expand your vocabulary by reading about two students' plan to make a film about immigrants. Below are ten Vocabulary Words that will be used in these exercises.

adept	disagreeable	jeopardize	persistent	titanic
dingy	humiliate	maroon	thrifty	verify

EXERCISE 1 *Wordbusting*

Directions. Follow these instructions for this word and the nine words on the next page.
- Figure out the word's meaning by looking at its **context,** its **structure,** and its **sound.** Fill in at least one of the three **CSS** boxes. Alternate which boxes you complete.
- Then, look up the word in a dictionary, read all of its meanings, and write the meaning of the word as it is used in the sentence.
- Follow this same process for each of the Vocabulary Words on the next page. You will need to draw your own map for each word. Use a separate sheet of paper.

1.

(adept) ⟶ "I'm **adept** with words, and you're good with cameras, so why don't we make a film?" Carlo asked Eric. "We can use the script I wrote in my drama class as a basis."

Context:	Structure:	Sound:

Dictionary:

2.

 dingy → "We could use that **dingy** old warehouse down at the end of Main Street for our studio. It's so shabby that it would make a great, creepy set," Carlo continued.

3.

maroon → "I agree. We can make the **maroon** walls look like the red brick exterior of the apartment building."

4.

 disagreeable → "We could get Anthony to play the mean old **disagreeable** landlord. You know how good he can be at whining and complaining, don't you, Eric?"

5.

 humiliate → "Do you think it would **humiliate** Anna if we asked her to play the mother?" Carlo asked. "She's certain to want to play the beautiful young daughter, and I don't want to embarrass her."

6.

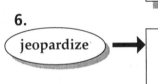 jeopardize → "I don't want to **jeopardize** our friendship. You know how touchy Anna can be. If she gets upset about our casting decisions, our entire relationship could be threatened," he went on.

7.

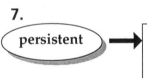 persistent → "But," Carlo continued, "if I go about it right, if I'm **persistent** and don't give up, I'll bet I can get her to play the part."

8.

 thrifty → "It's lucky that my mother is **thrifty**. She saves absolutely everything, so we can get a lot of our props from the trunks in our attic."

9.

 titanic → "She has one **titanic** trunk that must hold a million things. That huge trunk may have all the props we could possibly use."

10.

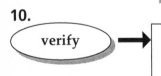 verify → "Before we start, though, I want to **verify** with Ms. Jenkins that we will get as much credit for this project as we could for a research paper. I think we will, but I want to make sure," Carlo concluded.

EXERCISE 2 *Context Clues*

Directions. Scan the definitions in Column A. Then, think about how the boldface words are used in the sentences in Column B. To complete the exercise, match each definition in Column A with the correct Vocabulary Word from Column B. Write the letter of your choice on the line provided. Finally, write the Vocabulary Word on the line before the definition.

COLUMN A	COLUMN B

COLUMN A

_____ **11.** word: _____
adj. unpleasant; offensive; quarrelsome and bad-tempered

_____ **12.** word: _____
adj. economical; frugal; careful about expenses

_____ **13.** word: _____
v. to offend someone's pride or dignity; to reduce someone in position or in esteem; to embarrass

_____ **14.** word: _____
v. to prove to be true; to check the truth of something; to confirm

_____ **15.** word: _____
v. to imperil; to risk injury or loss

_____ **16.** word: _____
adj. skillful; expert

_____ **17.** word: _____
adj. dirty-looking; grimy; shabby

_____ **18.** word: _____
adj. continuing; enduring; refusing to give up

_____ **19.** word: _____
adj. of great size, strength, or power

_____ **20.** word: _____
v. to strand a person on a desolate coast or island; to abandon; *n.* a dark reddish brown or purplish red color

COLUMN B

(A) "You're certainly **adept** at talking, Carlo. You haven't let me get a word in edgewise," Eric said.

(B) "I agree that Anna is the best person to play the mother. She can bring a **titanic** dimension to the role, a force that we need."

(C) "I'll work on getting Zack to play her **disagreeable** boss. It should be easy since he prefers playing nasty people anyway."

(D) "Where do we get furniture that looks old enough and **dingy** enough to be the furniture in the apartment set? I seem to remember a worn-out sofa in the teachers' lounge."

(E) "I want Courtney to play the **thrifty** next-door neighbor who works hard and saves her money to bring her father to the United States."

(F) "I like the idea that she is **persistent** in achieving her dream. Actually, the character reminds me of Courtney—she can be pretty determined herself."

(G) "We'll get Max to play the landlord who tries to **humiliate** the young mother when she needs more time to pay the rent. I love the way you wrote that scene where she refuses to become embarrassed about her money problems."

(H) "I think it really helps the audience to see what it is like to feel **marooned,** to feel alone and abandoned, in a strange city."

(I) "I let my grandmother read the script, and she **verified** that that was the way she felt when she first came to this country. She thought our script was right on target."

(J) "I think we need to do some more research, though. I don't want to **jeopardize** our grade by making mistakes in the script."

MAKING NEW WORDS YOUR OWN **81**

EXERCISE 3 *Like Meanings and Opposite Meanings* ✍

Directions. For each item below, circle the letter of the choice that means the same, or about the same, as the boldface word.

21. to become an **adept** artist
   (A) interesting
   (B) starving
   (C) forgotten
   (D) skillful

22. to **maroon** the boat
   (A) purchase
   (B) sell
   (C) sail
   (D) abandon

23. a **titanic** mistake
   (A) large
   (B) unfortunate
   (C) small
   (D) unlucky

24. a **persistent** problem
   (A) constantly occurring
   (B) seriously threatening
   (C) very minor
   (D) highly unusual

25. a **thrifty** purchase
   (A) economical
   (B) expensive
   (C) unjustified
   (D) unfortunate

Directions. For each item below, circle the letter of the choice that means the opposite, or about the opposite, of the boldface word.

26. in a **disagreeable** situation
   (A) unusual
   (B) uncomfortable
   (C) pleasant
   (D) common

27. to **humiliate** the shopkeeper
   (A) praise
   (B) shame
   (C) pay
   (D) advise

28. to **jeopardize** the plan
   (A) endanger
   (B) rescue
   (C) create
   (D) destroy

29. to **verify** the story
   (A) hear
   (B) tell
   (C) support
   (D) deny

30. a **dingy** window
   (A) clean
   (B) dirty
   (C) broken
   (D) whole

MAKING NEW WORDS YOUR OWN

Lesson 21 | CONTEXT: Voices of the United States

Dreaming of the Future

The United States of America is made up of millions of individuals from hundreds of different heritages. Each of these heritages has its own special voice, just as each individual does. This chorus of many voices is what makes our country unlike any other in the world. For, although each voice is different, together they sing of freedom and possibility.

In the following exercises, you will have the opportunity to expand your vocabulary by reading about the dream of one teenager to be a voice for the United States. Below are ten Vocabulary Words that will be used in these exercises.

aspiration	foreword	premier	sable	satire
diplomat	obituary	pun	salutation	tariff

EXERCISE 1 Wordbusting ✍

Directions. Follow these instructions for this word and the nine words on the next page.
- Figure out the word's meaning by looking at its **context,** its **structure,** and its **sound.** Fill in at least one of the three **CSS** boxes. Alternate which boxes you complete.
- Then, look up the word in a dictionary, read all of its meanings, and write the meaning of the word as it is used in the sentence.
- Follow this same process for each of the Vocabulary Words on the next page. You will need to draw your own map for each word. Use a separate sheet of paper.

1.

(aspiration) → My **aspiration** is to be a voice for the United States overseas. I have had this dream for a long time.

Context:	Structure:	Sound:

Dictionary:

2.
diplomat → I want to be a **diplomat;** I want to represent my country's interests when meeting with representatives from other governments.

3.
foreword → I want to be the person that publishers ask to write the **foreword,** or introduction, to books about other lands.

4.
obituary → When I die, I want my **obituary** in the newspaper to say, "She served her country well."

5.
premier → I want to meet with presidents, kings, **premiers,** and other heads of state.

6.
pun → In other words—to make an awful **pun**—when I collect articles about my career, I want my bulletin board to be "tactful." (Get it? "Tacked full!")

7.
sable → I can see myself now, walking up the steps to the White House in my **sable**-colored coat, the dark contrasting with the white pillars.

8.
salutation → Of course, I'll have to learn all the proper forms of greetings, the **salutations,** for addressing heads of state.

9.
satire → I don't want to make myself or my country the object of **satire,** or ridicule.

10.
tariff → I want to deal with important issues, like **tariff** agreements, which deal with taxes on imports and exports.

EXERCISE 2 *Context Clues* ✍

Directions. Scan the definitions in Column A. Then, think about how the boldface words are used in the sentences in Column B. To complete the exercise, match each definition in Column A with the correct Vocabulary Word from Column B. Write the letter of your choice on the line provided. Finally, write the Vocabulary Word on the line before the definition.

COLUMN A	COLUMN B

COLUMN A

_____ **11.** word: _____
n. a tax or list of taxes on trade goods

_____ **12.** word: _____
n. the use of irony, sarcasm, ridicule, or wit to expose foolishness or vice; a literary work that uses such devices

_____ **13.** word: _____
n. a gesture of greeting; the opening greeting in a letter

_____ **14.** word: _____
n. a small, dark mammal sometimes bred for its fur; *adj.* black or dark brown

_____ **15.** word: _____
n. a play on words; *v.* to play on words

_____ **16.** word: _____
n. a prime minister; a chief executive; *adj.* most important; supreme

_____ **17.** word: _____
n. a published notice of a person's death, usually with a brief biography

_____ **18.** word: _____
n. a book's introduction, a preface

_____ **19.** word: _____
n. a government representative; a person skillful in dealing with others

_____ **20.** word: _____
n. a great ambition; a breathing in; in medicine, the removal of fluids; the act of pronouncing a sound that begins with a puff of breath, such as an *h*

COLUMN B

(A) My older sister is usually the **diplomat** in our family. She smooths out all our disagreements. Last night was different; she went out of her way to annoy me.

(B) Last night she reminded me that my first **aspiration**—that is, my first great ambition—had been to be a big bird.

(C) "Imagine reading your **obituary,** or death notice, in the newspaper if you had succeeded," she joked.

(D) Then she made a terrible **pun:** "The big bird is dead. Her goose is cooked."

(E) I told her that when I became successful, I'd make her use a formal **salutation,** or greeting, when addressing me—maybe something like "the Most Honorable and Admired Lacy Wescott."

(F) She said that if I did become famous, she wanted to write the **foreword** to my autobiography. "Your sister is best suited to introducing you to your readers," she said.

(G) She says that she may just go with me to Washington and New Delhi and Tokyo. The **premier** reason she gives is "to see the world," but she admits that a secondary reason is "just to annoy you."

(H) I can just see myself discussing a **tariff,** or trade-tax, agreement with an important official while my big sister stands around.

(I) She'd say things like "I always said **sable** was a terrible color for you. You just don't look good in black."

(J) My sister can ridicule me all she wants, but being the object of her **satire** will not keep me from my dreams.

EXERCISE 3 *Like Meanings and Opposite Meanings* ✍

Directions. For each item below, circle the letter of the choice that means the same, or about the same, as the boldface word.

21. a high-ranking **diplomat**

(A) movie star
(B) writer
(C) government official
(D) classical musician

22. a silly **pun**

(A) play on words
(B) childish story
(C) prank
(D) rabbit

23. a beautiful **sable**

(A) race horse
(B) dog with a thick coat
(C) cat with no tail
(D) small animal with dark fur

24. the art of **satire**

(A) diplomacy
(B) ridicule
(C) escaping
(D) conversation

25. a high **tariff**

(A) tax on imports
(B) government official
(C) cost of living
(D) art form

Directions. For each item below, circle the letter of the choice that means the opposite, or about the opposite, of the boldface word.

26. a **premier** reason

(A) major
(B) minor
(C) clear
(D) unclear

27. a friendly **salutation**

(A) military maneuver
(B) greeting
(C) farewell
(D) telephone call

28. the **foreword** to the work

(A) understanding
(B) explanation
(C) introduction
(D) conclusion

29. to read his **obituary**

(A) birth notice
(B) death notice
(C) last name
(D) first name

30. her painful **aspiration**

(A) friendship
(B) breathing in
(C) headache
(D) breathing out

MAKING NEW WORDS YOUR OWN

Lesson 22 **CONTEXT: Voices of the United States**

The Founders

The United States of America first began to find its voice as a nation when it was still a collection of colonies dependent on England. Many of the people who first spoke of the ideals of freedom and democracy would become the founders of the United States and the authors of its Constitution.

In the following exercises, you will have the opportunity to expand your vocabulary by reading about that early period in U.S. history. These ten Vocabulary Words will be used.

| blockade | generate | neutral | pewter | quench |
| confiscate | indelible | obscure | quaint | urgent |

EXERCISE 1 *Wordbusting*

Directions. Follow these instructions for this word and the nine words on the next page.
- Figure out the word's meaning by looking at its **context,** its **structure,** and its **sound.** Fill in at least one of the three **CSS** boxes. Alternate which boxes you complete.
- Then, look up the word in a dictionary, read all of its meanings, and write the meaning of the word as it is used in the sentence.
- Follow this same process for each of the Vocabulary Words on the next page. You will need to draw your own map for each word. Use a separate sheet of paper.

1.

(blockade) → Some colonists had begun to speak out even before the British dared to **blockade** Boston Harbor. However, after the British forcefully closed the port, the colonists took action. They formed the First Continental Congress, paving the way for armed rebellion.

Context:	Structure:	Sound:

Dictionary:

2.
(confiscate) ➡ The act that led to the closing of the port was the Boston Tea Party. On December 16, 1773, to protest a high tax, a group of colonists **confiscated** the tea that was on some ships in the harbor. After they took it, they threw it overboard.

3.
(generate) ➡ The colonists were reacting to the British efforts to **generate,** or produce, wealth through unfair taxation.

4.
(indelible) ➡ The colonists who protested British taxes made an **indelible** mark on the nation's mind. The phrase "no taxation without representation" is imprinted forever in our minds.

5.
(neutral) ➡ Not all the colonists opposed the British. Some actually supported them, while others, remaining **neutral,** joined neither side.

6.
(obscure) ➡ We know well the names of the leaders of the American Revolution, but time tends to **obscure** the names of other heroes—the ordinary people who fought the battles and supported the armies.

7.
(pewter) ➡ Paul Revere was a metalsmith who put aside his silver trays and **pewter** candlesticks to make his famous ride. His riding partners, however, are not as well remembered as he is.

8.
(quaint) ➡ These heroes of the Revolutionary War may seem like **quaint** figures in some old-fashioned story, but they played a real role in history.

9.
(quench) ➡ Once the desire for liberty flamed in the hearts of these men and women, it was impossible to **quench** the fire of revolution.

10.
(urgent) ➡ They came to see independence as an **urgent** need, something to be demanded immediately.

EXERCISE 2 *Context Clues* ☞

Directions. Scan the definitions in Column A. Then, think about how the boldface words are used in the sentences in Column B. To complete the exercise, match each definition in Column A with the correct Vocabulary Word from Column B. Write the letter of your choice on the line provided. Finally, write the Vocabulary Word on the line before the definition.

COLUMN A	COLUMN B
____ **11.** word: _____ *adj.* attractively old-fashioned; unusual, curious, fanciful	(A) The American Revolution made an **indelible** impression on the world. Its importance to world history cannot be erased.
____ **12.** word: _____ *v.* to put out (a fire or light); to end or destroy by satisfying or cooling; to cool hot metal by thrusting into water	(B) Actually, some of the founders' ideas once created debate, but now they **generate** little controversy.
____ **13.** word: _____ *adj.* calling for haste or immediate action; pressing or insistent	(C) People who feel strongly about democracy often cannot understand how anyone could have remained **neutral** during the conflict.
____ **14.** word: _____ *n.* the closing off of an area by enemy ships or troops; any obstruction or hindrance; *v.* to obstruct or hinder	(D) The motives of those colonists who supported the British now seem **obscure** to many people. To historians, however, those motives are clear.
____ **15.** word: _____ *adj.* taking no sides; belonging to neither extreme in type, kind, etc.; having little color; *n.* a nation that takes no sides; a disengaged position of gears	(E) Today, we may think of the founders as pleasantly old-fashioned people in powdered wigs and knee breeches or flowing gowns. In fact, they were much more than **quaint** historical figures.
____ **16.** word: _____ *v.* to seize by authority	(F) Their likenesses appear on china cups and **pewter** plates from souvenir stands, but this does not make them trivial.
____ **17.** word: _____ *v.* to produce or bring into being	(G) They were human beings who felt an **urgent** need for liberty and a pressing desire for justice.
____ **18.** word: _____ *adj.* unerasable; permanent	(H) Once they took up the cause of liberty, nothing could **quench** their campaign. The founders were not satisfied until they had established independence.
____ **19.** word: _____ *adj.* not clear; not well known; hidden; dark; *v.* to make dim; to conceal	(I) Early patriots fought bravely against the British, who tried to **confiscate** their private property and take away their freedom.
____ **20.** word: _____ *n.* a dull gray alloy of tin with lead, copper, and other metals	(J) They would let no **blockade** close their ports, nor would they let any obstacle stand in the way of their freedom.

EXERCISE 3 *Like Meanings and Opposite Meanings* 👆

Directions. For each item below, circle the letter of the choice that means the same, or about the same, as the boldface word.

21. to run through the **blockade**
    (A) line
    (B) harbor
    (C) ship
    (D) barrier

22. an observer who is **neutral**
    (A) siding with rebels
    (B) taking neither side
    (C) siding with royalty
    (D) siding with the French

23. a **pewter** tray
    (A) gray metal
    (B) old-fashioned
    (C) expensive
    (D) elegant

24. a **quaint** village
    (A) modern
    (B) small
    (C) old-fashioned
    (D) run-down

25. an **urgent** message
    (A) late
    (B) loud
    (C) important
    (D) secret

Directions. For each item below, circle the letter of the choice that means the opposite, or about the opposite, of the boldface word.

26. to **confiscate** the evidence
    (A) give back
    (B) take away
    (C) forget
    (D) remember

27. to **generate** hope
    (A) cause
    (B) prevent
    (C) consider
    (D) remember

28. an **indelible** mark
    (A) black
    (B) interesting
    (C) erasable
    (D) memorable

29. an **obscure** individual
    (A) famous
    (B) forgotten
    (C) intelligent
    (D) dull

30. to **quench** your thirst
    (A) delight
    (B) satisfy
    (C) end
    (D) worsen

MAKING NEW WORDS YOUR OWN

Lesson 23 | CONTEXT: Voices of the United States

Music of the United States

Music reflects many different heritages. Popular music particularly shows the influence of all the peoples who have built this nation. From be-bop to bluegrass, from swing to salsa, musical styles that were once the property of a particular cultural group have become the standard fare for people of all ages and backgrounds.

In the following exercises, you will have the opportunity to expand your vocabulary by reading about popular music and musicians in the United States. Below are ten Vocabulary Words that will be used in these exercises.

activate	colossal	eccentric	invariable	pious
charitable	confide	intolerance	petty	tarnish

EXERCISE 1 *Wordbusting*

Directions. Follow these instructions for this word and the nine words on the next page.
- Figure out the word's meaning by looking at its **context**, its **structure**, and its **sound**. Fill in at least one of the three **CSS** boxes. Alternate which boxes you complete.
- Then, look up the word in a dictionary, read all of its meanings, and write the meaning of the word as it is used in the sentence.
- Follow this same process for each of the Vocabulary Words on the next page. You will need to draw your own map for each word. Use a separate sheet of paper.

1.

(activate) → If you would like to **activate** a lively discussion, just ask members of two different generations to discuss what they think good music is.

Context:

Structure:

Sound:

Dictionary:

2.
(charitable) →
When people want to be **charitable,** they will admit that another generation's music has value. Still, deep down most of us are convinced that the music we like is the best music.

3.
(colossal) →
However, we would be making a big mistake, a **colossal** blunder, to think that one form of music is better than another.

4.
(confide) →
No matter what people say in public, in private many will **confide** the realization that different kinds of music can enrich us all.

5.
(eccentric) →
People who enjoy unusual music often don't take part in the debate. They feel it is useless to defend their **eccentric** tastes.

6.
(intolerance) →
They know, from past experience, that many people show an **intolerance** for unusual music. Sometimes, people are just unwilling to hear music that differs from the kind they prefer.

7.
(invariable) →
The older generation's opposition to the younger generation's music seems to be an **invariable** truth of any society. The objections are as changeless as the hills—and almost as old.

8.
(petty) →
Arguing about whether country music is better than classical and jazz is a rather **petty** activity. There is room for all kinds of music, and it seems narrow-minded to try to prove that one form of music is better than another.

9.
(pious) →
Most of us are annoyed by people who are **pious** about, or devoted to, their personal taste in music and exclude all other types of music.

10.
(tarnish) →
You could **tarnish** your reputation as an intelligent person by getting into a silly discussion over whether swing is better than rock.

EXERCISE 2 *Context Clues*

Directions. Scan the definitions in Column A. Then, think about how the boldface words are used in the sentences in Column B. To complete the exercise, match each definition in Column A with the correct Vocabulary Word from Column B. Write the letter of your choice on the line provided. Finally, write the Vocabulary Word on the line before the definition.

COLUMN A	COLUMN B

COLUMN A

____ **11.** word: _____

n. unwilling to accept beliefs that are different from one's own; sensitivity to a food or medicine

____ **12.** word: _____

v. to make active; to set in motion; to start

____ **13.** word: _____

adj. trivial or unimportant; spiteful; narrow-minded

____ **14.** word: _____

adj. generous in giving gifts or helping with the needy; lenient when judging others

____ **15.** word: _____

adj. suggesting real or affected devotion to religious beliefs; devout

____ **16.** word: _____

adj. huge; gigantic; vast; extraordinary

____ **17.** word: _____

v. to dull or detract from the brightness of; to stain or disgrace; *n.* a film of chemically altered metal that dulls the surface

____ **18.** word: _____

adj. not changing; without exception

____ **19.** word: _____

adj. very odd in dress or behavior; unconventional; *n.* a person with these qualities

____ **20.** word: _____

v. to tell in confidence; to hand over for safekeeping; to entrust with

COLUMN B

(A) Many popular recording artists do **charitable** work by contributing time and money to important causes.

(B) Some musicians are **invariable** in their support of specific humanitarian causes. They appear at every major benefit.

(C) Their presence seems to **activate** something deep within us. It makes us remember that people have always believed in helping those who are in need.

(D) Songs such as "We Are the World" have been **colossal** successes, helping to raise huge sums of money for worthy causes.

(E) Musical styles are not religions that require **pious** devotion. Instead, they are interesting reflections of our different heritages.

(F) Only a **petty,** or small-minded, person would argue that people should listen to only one kind of music.

(G) It would certainly **tarnish** my enthusiasm for music if I could only listen to one kind. My interest would become dulled very rapidly.

(H) However, I haven't always **confided** in my friends when it comes to music. I don't tell them, for example, of my interest in recordings of traditional Norwegian cow calls, because they might not understand.

(I) They might think I am an **eccentric** because I listen to a pretty odd assortment of music, from North Carolina sea chanteys to old recordings of Appalachian folk music.

(J) Everyone has the ability to appreciate many kinds of music. Few people have a true **intolerance** for a variety of music.

EXERCISE 3   *Like Meanings and Opposite Meanings* ✍

Directions. For each item below, circle the letter of the choice that means the same, or about the same, as the boldface word.

21. to **confide** to a friend
(A) regret telling
(B) entrust a secret
(C) refuse to speak
(D) listen carefully

22. an **intolerance** for penicillin
(A) inability to find
(B) dislike
(C) inability to take
(D) opposition

23. a **petty** mind
(A) small
(B) large
(C) unusual
(D) ordinary

24. a **pious** believer
(A) devout
(B) confused
(C) insincere
(D) new

25. to remove the **tarnish**
(A) cover
(B) paint
(C) dullness
(D) dirt

Directions. For each item below, circle the letter of the choice that means the opposite, or about the opposite, of the boldface word.

26. to **activate** the machine
(A) start
(B) stop
(C) repair
(D) watch

27. a **charitable** act
(A) forgivable
(B) generous
(C) selfish
(D) unforgiven

28. a **colossal** building
(A) elegant
(B) run-down
(C) tiny
(D) huge

29. an **eccentric** musician
(A) talented
(B) worthy
(C) strange
(D) typical

30. an **invariable** attitude
(A) changeable
(B) unchangeable
(C) confusing
(D) clear

MAKING NEW WORDS YOUR OWN

Lesson 24 | CONTEXT: Voices of the United States
A History of Humor in the United States

Humor and laughter have always been important, and the voice of the United States is as much the voice of its humorists as it is the voice of its serious scholars.

In the following exercises, you will have the opportunity to expand your vocabulary by reading about humor in the United States. Below are ten Vocabulary Words that will be used in these exercises.

apt	deduction	irk	sarcasm	summit
clarify	essay	proposal	successor	temperament

EXERCISE 1 Wordbusting ✍

Directions. Follow these instructions for this word and the nine words on the next page.
- Figure out the word's meaning by looking at its **context,** its **structure,** and its **sound.** Fill in at least one of the three **CSS** boxes. Alternate which boxes you complete.
- Then, look up the word in a dictionary, read all of its meanings, and write the meaning of the word as it is used in the sentence.
- Follow this same process for each of the Vocabulary Words on the next page. You will need to draw your own map for each word. Use a separate sheet of paper.

1.

(apt) → A sense of humor is important, even vital. In fact, studies have shown that laughter is an **apt** aid in overcoming cancer. It is a helpful tool in fighting many serious diseases.

Context:

Structure:

Sound:

Dictionary:

2.
clarify ➤ Humor can help **clarify** what is truly important. For when we can laugh about something, we can see clearly that what we thought was a grave problem is actually not so serious after all.

3.
deduction ➤ I arrived at this **deduction**, or conclusion, while reading my American history book.

4.
essay ➤ American writers are famous for the humorous **essay**. Benjamin Franklin, Mark Twain, James Thurber, E. B. White, Erma Bombeck, and Nora Ephron are just a few of the writers known for their funny compositions.

5.
irk ➤ These writers have learned to take annoying everyday things that **irk** most of us and show the humor in them.

6.
proposal ➤ When our teacher asked us for **proposals** for our research papers, I suggested that I write about humor in America.

7.
sarcasm ➤ My early research shows that U.S. citizens have always enjoyed a wide range of humor—everything from gentle ribbing to biting **sarcasm**.

8.
successor ➤ The humorists of each generation have had **successors** who have followed them and built on their work.

9.
summit ➤ Some people resent political humor, but most agree that anything can be viewed with humor, even an important **summit**, or meeting between world leaders.

10.
temperament ➤ Basically, people in the U.S. have a **temperament** that allows them to laugh at themselves. Perhaps the ability to poke fun at our own follies is part of human nature.

EXERCISE 2 *Context Clues* ✍

Directions. Scan the definitions in Column A. Then, think about how the boldface words are used in the sentences in Column B. To complete the exercise, match each definition in Column A with the correct Vocabulary Word from Column B. Write the letter of your choice on the line provided. Finally, write the Vocabulary Word on the line before the definition.

COLUMN A	COLUMN B

____ **11.** word: _____

v. to make clear by removing impurities; to make understandable by explaining

____ **12.** word: _____

v. to irritate; to tire out; to trouble

____ **13.** word: _____

n. a short, often personal, composition on a single topic; an attempt; *v.* to try; to attempt; to test the quality of

____ **14.** word: _____

n. a plan that is put forward for consideration; a suggestion; an offer of marriage

____ **15.** word: _____

n. a sharp remark uttered to mock or make fun of something or someone; the use of such remarks

____ **16.** word: _____

n. one who succeeds or follows another in an office or position; an heir

____ **17.** word: _____

adj. fitting; likely; clever

____ **18.** word: _____

n. the highest point; a peak; a meeting of heads of state

____ **19.** word: _____

n. disposition; the manner in which a person thinks and responds

____ **20.** word: _____

n. a conclusion based on reasoning; a subtraction; the amount subtracted

(A) **Essays** by American humorists cover a variety of subjects. These short prose pieces may be about anything from basketball to politics.

(B) Styles of humor also vary and include everything from humorous observations to pointed **sarcasm,** a form of humor that sharply mocks its subject.

(C) Some humorists are more **apt** with certain styles of humor than others. Some might be more clever at using irony, for example.

(D) On the other hand, not every humorist will suit your **temperament**. For example, humor that is very physical might not appeal to you.

(E) Humorists like today's stand-up comics actually help us to **clarify** our values by poking fun at society. They help explain what is important to us and what is not.

(F) Some humor relies on the process of **deduction**. The joke depends on the audience being able to reason logically.

(G) Each generation seems to think that comedy has reached its **summit**. In fact, as time goes on, popular humor gets more and more daring but never peaks.

(H) Many of the things that might **irk** us and provide humor in this day would not have been funny 100 years ago. Modern inventions like the cell phone are the basis for jokes now that would not have been understood in the past.

(I) However, each new humorist is, in a way, a **successor** to the last generation of comics, an heir to a great American tradition.

(J) Humor is so important that I have a **proposal** for your consideration: Let's have special schools or colleges where people can earn degrees in humor!

Name _____ Date _____ Class _____

EXERCISE 3 *Like Meanings and Opposite Meanings* ✍

Directions. For each item below, circle the letter of the choice that means the same, or about the same, as the boldface word.

21. apt to cause mildew
   (A) never
   (B) attempt
   (C) likely
   (D) possible

22. to **essay** the mountain peak
   (A) avoid
   (B) announce
   (C) try
   (D) remember

23. an unusual **proposal**
   (A) suggestion
   (B) indication
   (C) problem
   (D) result

24. with **sarcasm** in her voice
   (A) enthusiasm
   (B) tiredness
   (C) good humor
   (D) mockery

25. a gentle **temperament**
   (A) person
   (B) manner
   (C) remark
   (D) type of anger

Directions. For each item below, circle the letter of the choice that means the opposite, or about the opposite, of the boldface word.

26. to **clarify** the situation
   (A) create
   (B) destroy
   (C) explain
   (D) confuse

27. a small **deduction**
   (A) amount added
   (B) amount taken away
   (C) problem created
   (D) problem stated

28. the **summit** of the mountain
   (A) price
   (B) top
   (C) base
   (D) snow

29. a worthy **successor**
   (A) one who comes after
   (B) one who comes before
   (C) one who is lost
   (D) one who is found

30. to **irk** someone
   (A) bother
   (B) annoy
   (C) please
   (D) disgust

MAKING NEW WORDS YOUR OWN

Lesson 25 | CONTEXT: Voices of the United States

Writers of the United States

All nations have their writers and storytellers. The United States is no different. We have many writers whose different voices tell us stories, inform us about our world, and help us understand our past.

In the following exercises, you will have the opportunity to expand your vocabulary by reading about the role of writers in the United States. Below are ten Vocabulary Words that will be used in these exercises.

anonymous	climax	famished	fragment	occurrence
casual	contemporary	fictitious	literal	therapy

EXERCISE 1 *Wordbusting*

Directions. Follow these instructions for this word and the nine words on the next page.
- Figure out the word's meaning by looking at its **context**, its **structure**, and its **sound**. Fill in at least one of the three **CSS** boxes. Alternate which boxes you complete.
- Then, look up the word in a dictionary, read all of its meanings, and write the meaning of the word as it is used in the sentence.
- Follow this same process for each of the Vocabulary Words on the next page. You will need to draw your own map for each word. Use a separate sheet of paper.

1.

anonymous → Some authors remain **anonymous**. We do not know the names of those who wrote many favorite stories and ballads.

Context:

Structure:

Sound:

Dictionary:

2.

casual → It is incorrect to believe that people in the United States have only a **casual** interest in literature. Judging from the millions of books sold each year, it is clear that we have a serious interest in reading.

3.

climax → American literature has not yet reached its peak, or **climax**. In many ways, it continues to reach for new ways to express ideas.

4.

contemporary → **Contemporary** life is a great source of material for writers. The modern U.S. experience is interesting to readers as well.

5.

famished → There is no reason for any person to be **famished** for good writing. Readers can go to any library to get their fill of classic U.S. literature.

6.

fictitious → Many writers create **fictitious** voices to tell their stories. To readers, however, they often seem real.

7.

fragment → In the past, some voices went unheard. For example, only a small **fragment** of Emily Dickinson's work was published in her lifetime. Of course, now we have access to her complete works.

8.

literal → Even nonfiction writers do not always stick to the **literal** truth. They enjoy exaggerating and stretching the facts.

9.

occurrence → U.S. writers examine important happenings—an **occurrence** such as a political scandal or the presidential election, for example.

10.

therapy → Writers also give advice on our daily lives. There are books on **therapy,** or the treatment of emotional stress; books on money; and books on how to play golf.

EXERCISE 2 *Context Clues*

Directions. Scan the definitions in Column A. Then, think about how the boldface words are used in the sentences in Column B. To complete the exercise, match each definition in Column A with the correct Vocabulary Word from Column B. Write the letter of your choice on the line provided. Finally, write the Vocabulary Word on the line before the definition.

COLUMN A	COLUMN B

COLUMN A

_____ **11.** word: _____

adj. living at the same time or period; modern; *n.* a person living in the same time period as another

_____ **12.** word: _____

n. the point of greatest intensity in any series of events; the most exciting part; the final, most forceful statement

_____ **13.** word: _____

adj. informal, relaxed; chance, unplanned; occasional; slight, superficial

_____ **14.** word: _____

adj. by or of an unidentified person

_____ **15.** word: _____

adj. restricted to the exact meaning; not figurative; word-for-word, as a translation; concerned chiefly with fact

_____ **16.** word: _____

n. something that takes place; an incident; the action or process of happening

_____ **17.** word: _____

n. treatment to soothe the body or mind; a method of healing

_____ **18.** word: _____

adj. extremely hungry; starving

_____ **19.** word: _____

n. a part of a whole; portion of an incomplete manuscript; *v.* to break into bits

_____ **20.** word: _____

adj. imaginary; false; not genuine

COLUMN B

(A) I told my parents that I was going to write a book about my **contemporaries,** or fellow teenagers. I planned to use myself and my friends as examples of today's typical teens.

(B) My mother said that, if I did, I had better decide to remain **anonymous**. She didn't want anyone to know my name.

(C) Dad said I might use a **fictitious** name, something like E. A. Twiddlethorpe.

(D) Then my mom said, very seriously, that she thought writing a book would be good **therapy** for me, that it would help me work out all my teenage anxiety. I burst out laughing.

(E) Actually, all I had done was make a **casual** remark while setting the table for dinner. I didn't mean for them to take me seriously.

(F) I don't know why I became so irritable about the whole thing. It was probably because I was **famished**. I didn't get to eat lunch that day.

(G) Honestly, my parents have such **literal** minds sometimes. They think I actually mean everything I say.

(H) Still, if you had heard even a tiny **fragment** of the conversation, you'd realize that my parents love to joke.

(I) "And what would be the **climax** of this book?" Mom asked. "The time you locked yourself in the basement or the day you accidentally dyed your hair green? I know those were high points in my life."

(J) My mom doesn't forget anything that happens to me, and Dad is almost as bad. I think they remember every embarrassing **occurrence** in my life.

EXERCISE 3 Like Meanings and Opposite Meanings ✍

Directions. For each item below, circle the letter of the choice that means the same, or about the same, as the boldface word.

21. the **climax** of the story
    (A) end
    (B) high point
    (C) beginning
    (D) story

22. the **fragment** of the poem
    (A) piece
    (B) vision
    (C) purpose
    (D) memory

23. a **literal** translation
    (A) loose
    (B) strange
    (C) exact
    (D) original

24. a strange **occurrence**
    (A) presentation
    (B) evening
    (C) person
    (D) happening

25. **therapy** for the injury
    (A) payment
    (B) judgment
    (C) treatment
    (D) dependent

Directions. For each item below, circle the letter of the choice that means the opposite, or about the opposite, of the boldface word.

26. an **anonymous** donor
    (A) generous
    (B) selfish
    (C) famous
    (D) unknown

27. a **casual** dinner
    (A) informal
    (B) formal
    (C) delicious
    (D) unpleasant

28. a **contemporary** figure
    (A) modern
    (B) important
    (C) unimportant
    (D) historical

29. a **fictitious** tale
    (A) made-up
    (B) true
    (C) ordinary
    (D) unusual

30. the **famished** animal
    (A) starving
    (B) well-fed
    (C) well-known
    (D) unimportant

Name _____ Date _____ Class _____

MAKING NEW WORDS YOUR OWN

Lesson 26 | CONTEXT: Voices of the United States

The Voice of the Press

An important voice in the United States is the voice of the free press. People sometimes get irritated with reporters and with news coverage. If no one gets upset, however, then the reporters are probably not doing their job. The founders of the United States knew this and made a free press part of the foundation of our Constitution.

In the following exercises, you will have the opportunity to expand your vocabulary by reading about news and reporters. Below are ten Vocabulary Words that will be used in these exercises.

condemn	dilute	emphasize	falter	intrigue
dictate	dispatch	endorse	improvise	modify

EXERCISE 1 | Wordbusting ✍

Directions. Follow these instructions for this word and the nine words on the next page.
- Figure out the word's meaning by looking at its **context,** its **structure,** and its **sound.** Fill in at least one of the three **CSS** boxes. Alternate which boxes you complete.
- Then, look up the word in a dictionary, read all of its meanings, and write the meaning of the word as it is used in the sentence.
- Follow this same process for each of the Vocabulary Words on the next page. You will need to draw your own map for each word. Use a separate sheet of paper.

1.

condemn → Although we may criticize the actions of a particular reporter or newspaper, few people in the United States will ever **condemn** the idea of a free press.

Context:

Structure:

Sound:

Dictionary:

2.

(dictate) → People know how important it is that the government not **dictate** what news can be printed or broadcast. A government that has total control over the news is a dangerous government indeed.

3.

(dilute) → A government that controls the press can **dilute,** or weaken, the people's confidence in the press. Few readers believe what is written in newspapers controlled by the government.

4.

(dispatch) → Reporters have serious responsibilities. When they send a **dispatch** to their newspapers, the facts contained in that report must be accurate and up-to-date.

5.

(emphasize) → On the editorial page, the editors are free to **emphasize,** or stress, a certain point of view. However, the opposite point of view should also be addressed.

6.

(endorse) → Newspapers do **endorse** particular political candidates. They show their support by printing favorable letters and editorials.

7.

(falter) → Lack of support by a newspaper can cause a politician's campaign to **falter**. Moreover, once a candidate stumbles, the political race may be lost.

8.

(improvise) → Good reporters go to an interview with prepared questions. They do not like to have to **improvise** their questions on the spot.

9.

(intrigue) → People think reporters' lives are filled with **intrigue,** that they have inside knowledge of plots and schemes. Yet, most reporters wind up covering everyday stories, such as the opening of a new shopping mall or a city council meeting.

10.

(modify) → Good editors do not tamper with the facts of a story; however, they may **modify** a story by changing some words or by cutting it to a certain length.

EXERCISE 2 *Context Clues* ✍

Directions. Scan the definitions in Column A. Then, think about how the boldface words are used in the sentences in Column B. To complete the exercise, match each definition in Column A with the correct Vocabulary Word from Column B. Write the letter of your choice on the line provided. Finally, write the Vocabulary Word on the line before the definition.

COLUMN A	COLUMN B
____ **11.** word: _____ *v.* to give support or approval to; to sign one's name on the back of a check or similar document for validation	(A) Editors usually make the assignments. They may **dispatch** a reporter to a crime scene or send the reporter to the city council meeting.
____ **12.** word: _____ *v.* to criticize or pass judgment against; to find guilty; to find unfit or unsafe	(B) Wanting to be certain that reporters get all the facts, editors will **condemn** any reporting that is sloppy or inaccurate.
____ **13.** word: _____ *v.* to hesitate; to stumble; to stammer	(C) Usually a reporter's talents **dictate** what assignment he or she will get. One story may require a reporter with a science background, while another may require a reporter with Spanish-speaking skills.
____ **14.** word: _____ *v.* to recite something to be recorded; to require or order authoritatively	(D) Editors **emphasize** that it is a reporter's duty to report accurately. They also stress thoroughness and good writing.
____ **15.** word: _____ *v.* to compose or perform without preparation; to make something from whatever materials are available	(E) Reporters frequently hit stumbling blocks that cause them to **falter** when reporting stories. However, a good reporter always charges on and follows a story to the end.
____ **16.** word: _____ *n.* a message; quickness; efficiency; *v.* to send; to finish quickly; to kill	(F) The job of a reporter **intrigues** many people. They think it is fascinating work.
____ **17.** word: _____ *n.* sly or secret scheming; a conspiracy; *v.* to plot or scheme; to excite interest	(G) Even after having written their stories, reporters may **modify** them, or make changes to them, based on new information.
____ **18.** word: _____ *v.* to alter in form or character; in grammar, to qualify the meaning of	(H) Like all other writers, reporters **endorse** the practice of revision. They strongly believe that good writers must rewrite.
____ **19.** word: _____ *v.* to denote as important; to stress	(I) Good reporters know that too many words can **dilute** the impact of a story, so they edit to strengthen their work.
____ **20.** word: _____ *v.* to thin or weaken by adding liquid; to lessen intensity, purity, strength	(J) While it is sometimes tempting to **improvise** a story—to throw it together with few real facts or quotations to back it up—a good reporter always tries to be truthful, accurate, and thorough.

EXERCISE 3 *Like Meanings and Opposite Meanings* ✍

Directions. For each item below, circle the letter of the choice that means the same, or about the same, as the boldface word.

21. to **dictate** the letter
    (A) read for another to record
    (B) record for another to read
    (C) write for another to read
    (D) be unable to read

22. to **dilute** the solution
    (A) strengthen
    (B) boil
    (C) weaken
    (D) analyze

23. to **endorse** the check
    (A) write something on
    (B) handle carefully
    (C) sign the back of
    (D) give away

24. to **falter** on the path
    (A) run
    (B) stumble
    (C) follow
    (D) hurry

25. to **modify** the report
    (A) write
    (B) change
    (C) continue
    (D) ignore

Directions. For each item below, circle the letter of the choice that means the opposite, or about the opposite, as the boldface word.

26. to **condemn** the action
    (A) discuss
    (B) criticize
    (C) praise
    (D) remember

27. to **emphasize** the point
    (A) ignore
    (B) stress
    (C) make
    (D) hurry

28. an **improvised** performance
    (A) rehearsed
    (B) special
    (C) unusual
    (D) offhand

29. to **intrigue** the audience
    (A) entertain
    (B) bore
    (C) interest
    (D) anger

30. to work with **dispatch**
    (A) speed
    (B) slowness
    (C) hope
    (D) unhappiness

MAKING NEW WORDS YOUR OWN

Lesson 27 | **CONTEXT:** Voices of the United States
The Voice of Justice

The founders of this country understood the importance of a strong and fair system of courts. One basic principle of justice is that the accused is innocent until proven guilty. Another is that those accused shall have the opportunity to defend themselves in court. Such principles have made the U.S. system of justice a voice that speaks of democracy.

In the following exercises, you will have the opportunity to expand your vocabulary by reading about the U.S. legal system. Below are ten Vocabulary Words that will be used in these exercises.

articulate	demolish	detach	illuminate	testify
category	denial	distraction	inclination	upbraid

EXERCISE 1 *Wordbusting* 🖎

Directions. Follow these instructions for this word and the nine words on the next page.
- Figure out the word's meaning by looking at its **context,** its **structure,** and its **sound.** Fill in at least one of the three **CSS** boxes. Alternate which boxes you complete.
- Then, look up the word in a dictionary, read all of its meanings, and write the meaning of the word as it is used in the sentence.
- Follow this same process for each of the Vocabulary Words on the next page. You will need to draw your own map for each word. Use a separate sheet of paper.

1.

(articulate) ➡ The voices in our justice system must be **articulate**. They must speak clearly for both the accuser and the accused.

Context:	Structure:	Sound:

Dictionary:

2.

(category) ➔ Lawyers may choose from several different kinds of law in which to specialize. One **category** is criminal law.

3.

(demolish) ➔ Often, lawyers have to **demolish,** or destroy, the statements made by witnesses against their clients.

4.

(denial) ➔ The courts are designed to give everyone a fair hearing. **Denial** of this basic right is dangerous to society—even when it is a guilty person who is refused the right.

5.

(detach) ➔ Judges are supposed to be fair and objective. Therefore, they try to **detach** themselves from the emotions of a situation and listen to the facts.

6.

(distraction) ➔ Some lawyers use **distraction** as a technique in court. If the facts are not in a client's favor, the lawyer tries to draw the jury's attention away from the facts.

7.

(illuminate) ➔ One purpose of a trial is to **illuminate** the truth surrounding the case. Ideally, all the facts are brought to light.

8.

(inclination) ➔ It may be against a lawyer's **inclination** to defend a client who appears to be guilty. But most lawyers are able to overcome this leaning.

9.

(testify) ➔ The lawyer is responsible for calling witnesses to **testify,** or give evidence, on behalf of the client.

10.

(upbraid) ➔ Sometimes lawyers must **upbraid,** or reproach, their clients for not telling them the complete truth. In order to defend clients properly, lawyers have to know all the facts before they enter the courtroom.

EXERCISE 2 *Context Clues* ✍

Directions. Scan the definitions in Column A. Then, think about how the boldface words are used in the sentences in Column B. To complete the exercise, match each definition in Column A with the correct Vocabulary Word from Column B. Write the letter of your choice on the line provided. Finally, write the Vocabulary Word on the line before the definition.

COLUMN A	COLUMN B
____ **11.** word: _____ *n.* a division or group in any classification system; a class	(A) Because I can express myself so clearly, I think I would be a good lawyer. I would not be afraid to **articulate** my ideas in court.
____ **12.** word: _____ *v.* to provide with light; to make understandable; to clarify; to decorate a manuscript with colorful designs	(B) Because I want to be a lawyer, I study hard and avoid any **distraction** that might take my mind off my studies.
____ **13.** word: _____ *v.* to bear witness to, especially in court; to give evidence	(C) When I study at night, I use an old-fashioned desk lamp to **illuminate** my books and papers.
____ **14.** word: _____ *v.* to unfasten; to disconnect	(D) I study hard for every test, although sometimes that means fighting my **inclination** to go outside and play basketball.
____ **15.** word: _____ *n.* a tendency; a personal preference or liking; a slant or slope	(E) I admit that my attention often wanders, and that irritates me. Sometimes, I am forced to **upbraid** myself for not paying attention.
____ **16.** word: _____ *v.* to tear down; to wreck; to ruin	(F) My brother can **testify** that he has caught me shooting long shots into the wastepaper basket.
____ **17.** word: _____ *n.* something that diverts or draws attention away; the act of diverting attention; a condition of mental distress	(G) I had better become a lawyer—because when I play basketball with my brother, he **demolishes** me. He has destroyed my dream of a basketball career.
____ **18.** word: _____ *n.* a statement that something is false; a refusal of a request or a right; a rejection of a belief	(H) Of course, a dream of a basketball career means a **denial** of my 5'2" height. Lawyers, though, don't have to worry about refusing to accept the truth that they are short.
____ **19.** word: _____ *adj.* using distinct syllables or words; able to speak clearly; *v.* to speak clearly and distinctly; to express in words	(I) Sometimes I try to figure out which **category** of law I might enjoy. Instead of working as a criminal lawyer in the courts, I could work in real estate law or tax law for the government.
____ **20.** word: _____ *v.* to scold or criticize sharply	(J) However, when I stay in my fantasy world too long, my brother reminds me that I have **detached** myself from reality again.

EXERCISE 3 | *Like Meanings and Opposite Meanings* 👈

Directions. For each item below, circle the letter of the choice that means the same, or about the same, as the boldface word.

21. a **category** of books
   (A) hatred
   (B) love
   (C) study
   (D) grouping

22. an interesting **distraction**
   (A) something that draws away attention
   (B) something that improves attention
   (C) something that is boring
   (D) something that destroys

23. the **inclination** of the cliff
   (A) height
   (B) trend
   (C) difficulty
   (D) slope

24. to **upbraid** the person
   (A) feed
   (B) jail
   (C) scold
   (D) ignore

25. to **testify** honestly
   (A) reward
   (B) listen
   (C) declare
   (D) ignore

Directions. For each item below, circle the letter of the choice that means the opposite, or about the opposite, of the boldface word.

26. to **detach** the pieces
   (A) take off
   (B) connect
   (C) examine
   (D) tape together

27. to **illuminate** the room
   (A) discover
   (B) paint
   (C) brighten
   (D) darken

28. to **demolish** the work
   (A) create
   (B) destroy
   (C) remember
   (D) finish

29. to **articulate** her wishes
   (A) speak
   (B) remain silent about
   (C) read about
   (D) agree with

30. a **denial** of his words
   (A) description
   (B) understanding
   (C) support
   (D) contradiction

Name _____ Date _____ Class _____

MAKING NEW WORDS YOUR OWN

Lesson 28 | CONTEXT: Voices of the United States

Super Voices: The World of Comics

For several generations now, people in the United States have delighted in comic books. Superheroes have been especially popular, perhaps because they support many U.S. values. Superman, for example, believes in truth, justice, and the "American way."

In the following exercises, you will have the opportunity to expand your vocabulary by reading about comic books from the point of view of a collector. Below are ten Vocabulary Words that will be used in these exercises.

braggart	eligible	imply	secluded	tangible
derive	extensive	miscellaneous	superficial	unique

EXERCISE 1   Wordbusting ✍

Directions. Follow these instructions for this word and the nine words on the next page.
- Figure out the word's meaning by looking at its **context,** its **structure,** and its **sound.** Fill in at least one of the three **CSS** boxes. Alternate which boxes you complete.
- Then, look up the word in a dictionary, read all of its meanings, and write the meaning of the word as it is used in the sentence.
- Follow this same process for each of the Vocabulary Words on the next page. You will need to draw your own map for each word. Use a separate sheet of paper.

1.

(braggart) → I have become quite the **braggart**. I now own about 500 comic books and love to boast about my varied collection.

Context:	Structure:	Sound:

Dictionary:

2.

I **derive** a great deal of pleasure from my comic books. They are a good source of entertainment.

3.

eligible

Few, if any, comic books are **eligible** to be called great literature, but many meet the requirements of good popular literature.

4.

extensive

I have an **extensive** collection of comics. I have old comics, brand-new comics, and even some comics from other parts of the world.

5.

I don't want to **imply,** or suggest, that comics are all I read, but I do spend a lot of time with my favorite superheroes.

6.

miscellaneous

When I began to collect comics, I also started collecting **miscellaneous** items associated with superheroes, anything from buttons to posters to action figures.

7.

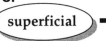

I like to read my comics in a **secluded** spot, a place where no one will bother me.

8.

superficial

Not all comics are **superficial** entertainment. Some address serious issues that can touch readers at a deep level.

9.

Many offer **tangible** support for important values. For example, they make the concepts of equality and justice more concrete by bringing those ideas to life on the page.

10.

One **unique** comic book hero is Flaming Carrot. There is no one else like him!

EXERCISE 2 *Context Clues*

Directions. Scan the definitions in Column A. Then, think about how the boldface words are used in the sentences in Column B. To complete the exercise, match each definition in Column A with the correct Vocabulary Word from Column B. Write the letter of your choice on the line provided. Finally, write the Vocabulary Word on the line before the definition.

COLUMN A	COLUMN B

COLUMN A

_____ **11.** word: _____
adj. cut off; remote; isolated; private

_____ **12.** word: _____
adj. at the surface; shallow, not deep

_____ **13.** word: _____
adj. capable of being touched; concrete; that can be understood; definite

_____ **14.** word: _____
n. someone who brags excessively; a know-it-all; *adj.* boastful

_____ **15.** word: _____
adj. being the only one of its kind; rare

_____ **16.** word: _____
v. to receive or trace, as from a source; to arrive at by logic; to come (from)

_____ **17.** word: _____
adj. fit or worthy to be chosen; qualified; suitable or desirable

_____ **18.** word: _____
adj. far-reaching; vast; of wide scope

_____ **19.** word: _____
v. to suggest without actually stating; to hint; to involve as necessary circumstance or logical necessity

_____ **20.** word: _____
adj. made up of varied parts; possessing a variety of characteristics or abilities; varied; assorted

COLUMN B

(A) A character doesn't have to have fantastic powers to be **eligible** to be a superhero. Batman has no powers other than those of an ordinary human, yet he is worthy of the title superhero.

(B) The name X-Men seems to **imply** all male characters, but this group of comic-book heroes includes many females.

(C) Many superhero groups have **extensive** casts of characters. For example, there are too many X-Men for me to remember them all.

(D) Some heroes **derive** their names from characters in mythology. For example, Thor gets his name from a Scandinavian god.

(E) Generally, superheroes are not **braggarts**. Many of them have special powers but use them without boasting about them.

(F) Phoenix has the power to move objects. In fact, she can move any **tangible,** or solid, object with her mind.

(G) Superman operates from a **secluded** fortress in a freezing arctic region where no one can reach him.

(H) Many superheroes have had only **superficial** appeal, but others have had a deep and enduring appeal to generations of readers.

(I) Comic-book writers try to make their characters interesting. They give each character a **unique** personality. No two are alike.

(J) There are so many **miscellaneous** titles, so many varied heroes, that almost all of us can find a comic that suits our tastes.

EXERCISE 3   *Like Meanings and Opposite Meanings*

Directions. For each item below, circle the letter of the choice that means the same, or about the same, as the boldface word.

21. to **derive** pleasure
(A) get
(B) spend
(C) lose
(D) save

22. to **imply** otherwise
(A) announce
(B) suggest
(C) pretend
(D) look

23. a **miscellaneous** collection
(A) large
(B) valuable
(C) varied
(D) organized

24. **tangible** proof
(A) believed
(B) mysterious
(C) unusual
(D) concrete

25. a **braggart** attitude
(A) boastful
(B) rude
(C) brave
(D) hostile

Directions. For each item below, circle the letter of the choice that means the opposite, or about the opposite, of the boldface word.

26. an **eligible** candidate
(A) likely
(B) unsuitable
(C) available
(D) interested

27. an **extensive** list
(A) unusual
(B) uninteresting
(C) lengthy
(D) limited

28. a **secluded** street
(A) empty
(B) busy
(C) wide
(D) narrow

29. a **superficial** interest
(A) business
(B) personal
(C) shallow
(D) deep

30. a **unique** characteristic
(A) unusual
(B) common
(C) important
(D) unimportant

MAKING NEW WORDS YOUR OWN

Lesson 29 CONTEXT: Voices of the United States

Listening to the Radio

Long before television came into our homes, there was radio. People probably relied on it for music and news and entertainment. Once, radio was the voice of the United States, and today, in some ways, it still is.

In the following exercises, you will have the opportunity to expand your vocabulary by reading about radio. Below are ten Vocabulary Words that will be used in these exercises.

| arrogant | congest | hypothesis | rebate | technology |
| commute | considerate | malfunction | synthetic | warranty |

EXERCISE 1 *Wordbusting*

Directions. Follow these instructions for this word and the nine words on the next page.
- Figure out the word's meaning by looking at its **context,** its **structure,** and its **sound.** Fill in at least one of the three **CSS** boxes. Alternate which boxes you complete.
- Then, look up the word in a dictionary, read all of its meanings, and write the meaning of the word as it is used in the sentence.
- Follow this same process for each of the Vocabulary Words on the next page. You will need to draw your own map for each word. Use a separate sheet of paper.

1.

arrogant → Sometimes I can be **arrogant** about the radio programs I like. I definitely think that my favorite music stations are better than the talk radio Dad listens to.

| Context: | Structure: | Sound: |

Dictionary:

2.
commute → My sister listens to the radio as she **commutes** back and forth to work. It's a two-hour round trip, so she knows every radio station in range.

3.
congest → When traffic **congests** the freeway, she doesn't complain too much about the horns and the slow pace. She just cranks up the volume and sings along with the golden oldies station.

4.
considerate → I try to be **considerate** of my parents and not play my radio too loud since I know they don't like it.

5.
hypothesis → I have a **hypothesis** about hearing, but I haven't tested my theory. I suspect that at twenty-five years of age people grow new nerve endings in their ears. After that, they think everything is too loud.

6.
malfunction → My mom teases me when she hears some of the music I listen to. She claims that my radio is making strange noises and that it must have a **malfunction**.

7.
rebate → Dad listens to the radio, too. That's how he heard about the **rebate,** or cash-back offer, on a state-of-the-art radio. Naturally, he bought one.

8.
warranty → The radio came with a **warranty,** but Dad didn't save it; he believes that nothing can go wrong with this radio.

9.
technology → **Technology** has improved the quality of radio. Scientific discoveries have allowed for clearer broadcasting and reception.

10.
synthetic → He hates music that sounds fake, or **synthetic,** like the mellow stuff played in grocery stores.

EXERCISE 2 *Context Clues*

Directions. Scan the definitions in Column A. Then, think about how the boldface words are used in the sentences in Column B. To complete the exercise, match each definition in Column A with the correct Vocabulary Word from Column B. Write the letter of your choice on the line provided. Finally, write the Vocabulary Word on the line before the definition.

COLUMN A	COLUMN B

COLUMN A

_____ **11.** word: _____

v. to fail to function or act as expected; *n.* a failure to work as expected

_____ **12.** word: _____

n. the technical methods of applying scientific and industrial skills to practical uses; applied science

_____ **13.** word: _____

n. an unproven theory

_____ **14.** word: _____

n. a guarantee by the seller that a product will maintain a certain standard or be replaced or repaired

_____ **15.** word: _____

n. a partial refund; *v.* to give back part of an original payment

_____ **16.** word: _____

adj. artificial; made by chemical process to imitate a natural product

_____ **17.** word: _____

adj. to be full of undue self-importance or feelings of superiority

_____ **18.** word: _____

v. to change; to change a penalty to a less severe one; to travel back and forth

_____ **19.** word: _____

v. to overcrowd; to clog, as with mucus

_____ **20.** word: _____

adj. thoughtful; kind; taking the needs of others into account

COLUMN B

(A) To be **considerate,** I agreed to listen to some tapes my granddad has of old radio shows. I didn't want to hurt his feelings.

(B) My **hypothesis** was that anything recorded before I was born was dull and boring. My theory was wrong.

(C) Granddad told me that his father's family used to have a big radio encased in maple wood. He dislikes the **synthetic,** plastic radios we have today.

(D) "No wonder they come with a **rebate,**" he says. "They'd definitely have to pay me to buy one."

(E) I don't want to sound **arrogant,** or overbearing, but I keep trying to convince Granddad that he would find the sound of those old radios intolerable today.

(F) I remind him that **technology** has improved radio a great deal. Because of applied sciences, sound is much better today.

(G) Granddad keeps expecting mine to **malfunction,** but it works fine.

(H) I also remind him that it came with a **warranty**. If it were to fail to work, the company would just give me another one.

(I) When I had a sore throat and a **congested** chest, I stayed in bed. To entertain myself, I listened to Granddad's tapes.

(J) At first, Mom said that I had to stay in all weekend because I was sick. However, on Sunday afternoon, she decided to **commute** my sentence to time already served, so I went to Granddad's house to borrow more tapes.

EXERCISE 3 *Like Meanings and Opposite Meanings* ✍

Directions. For each item below, circle the letter of the choice that means the same, or about the same, as the boldface word.

21. to **commute** the penalty
(A) change
(B) borrow
(C) recognize
(D) review

22. a strange **hypothesis**
(A) individual
(B) animal
(C) medicine
(D) theory

23. a new **technology**
(A) type of business
(B) application of science
(C) guarantee
(D) machine

24. a six-month **warranty**
(A) school term
(B) guarantee
(C) vacation
(D) return trip

25. to **malfunction** often
(A) prevent
(B) break down
(C) attend
(D) throw away

Directions. For each item below, circle the letter of the choice that means the opposite, or about the opposite, of the boldface word.

26. to **congest** the tunnel
(A) enter
(B) build
(C) crowd
(D) clear

27. a **considerate** person
(A) wealthy
(B) poor
(C) rude
(D) thoughtful

28. a **synthetic** rose
(A) artificial
(B) real
(C) lovely
(D) ugly

29. an **arrogant** attitude
(A) haughty
(B) rude
(C) pleasant
(D) sneering

30. to **rebate** the money
(A) give back
(B) divide
(C) subtract
(D) keep

MAKING NEW WORDS YOUR OWN

Lesson 30 **CONTEXT:** Voices of the United States

Voices at Work

The voice of science is a powerful one. Science has brought about many changes in our lives—in our homes, in our schools, and in our places of work. Even now, changes are occurring that will affect the jobs and careers you will choose.

In the following exercises, you will have the opportunity to expand your vocabulary by reading about some of the differences science has made in the workplace. Below are ten Vocabulary Words that will be used in these exercises.

aeronautics	antibiotics	erosion	parasitic	planetarium
agenda	automaton	hydraulic	photogenic	respiration

EXERCISE 1 *Wordbusting* ✍

Directions. Follow these instructions for this word and the nine words on the next page.
- Figure out the word's meaning by looking at its **context,** its **structure,** and its **sound.** Fill in at least one of the three **CSS** boxes. Alternate which boxes you complete.
- Then, look up the word in a dictionary, read all of its meanings, and write the meaning of the word as it is used in the sentence.
- Follow this same process for each of the Vocabulary Words on the next page. You will need to draw your own map for each word. Use a separate sheet of paper.

1.

(aeronautics) → **Aeronautics** is an interesting field. People have been designing and building airplanes successfully only since the beginning of the twentieth century.

Context:	Structure:	Sound:

Dictionary:

2.
(agenda) → The conference **agenda** covered the most fascinating advances in software design.

3.
(antibiotics) → Think of the lives that have been saved as a result of the discovery of **antibiotics**. Before these medicines were discovered, even simple infections could lead to death.

4.
(automaton) → Thanks to science, much dull and repetitive work that was done by human beings can now be done by robots, or **automatons**.

5.
(erosion) → Studies of the causes of **erosion** have helped us to figure out how to stop land from washing away.

6.
(hydraulic) → My father operates a machine that runs on **hydraulic,** or liquid, pressure.

7.
(parasitic) → Think, too, of the work we have done in eliminating **parasitic** diseases, ailments caused by organisms that feed off host animals.

8.
(photogenic) → There have been many advances in photography, too. Even those of us who are not **photogenic** can be made to look good.

9.
(planetarium) → High-powered telescopes have made a trip to the **planetarium** even more exciting. Now, the projections of the stars and planets show things you never before knew existed!

10.
(respiration) → Thanks to scientists, we know more about everything—from the **respiration,** or breathing processes, of the horned lizard to the first moon of Jupiter.

EXERCISE 2 *Context Clues*

Directions. Scan the definitions in Column A. Then, think about how the boldface words are used in the sentences in Column B. To complete the exercise, match each definition in Column A with the correct Vocabulary Word from Column B. Write the letter of your choice on the line provided. Finally, write the Vocabulary Word on the line before the definition.

COLUMN A	COLUMN B

COLUMN A

____ **11.** word: _____

n. a list of things to be done; things to be dealt with in a business meeting

____ **12.** word: _____

adj. living at the expense of or taking advantage of others; living on an organism and contributing nothing

____ **13.** word: _____

n. the science and practice of aircraft navigation; the engineering of aircraft

____ **14.** word: _____

n. a building with a domed ceiling onto which images of celestial bodies are projected

____ **15.** word: _____

adj. moved or operated by compressing water or some other liquid

____ **16.** word: _____

adj. having qualities that are attractive or suitable for photographing

____ **17.** word: _____

n. infection-fighting substances derived from microorganisms

____ **18.** word: _____

n. a gradual wearing away (as of the earth's surface); deterioration

____ **19.** word: _____

n. a robot; a person acting like a robot

____ **20.** word: _____

n. breathing; a complete breath, including inhaling and exhaling

COLUMN B

(A) If you believe there has been an **erosion** of dedication in the U.S. workplace, consider these voices. They will prove that care and devotion have not deteriorated.

(B) After the doctor examines her patient, she says, "His **respiration** is irregular. Get him on oxygen until he can breathe normally."

(C) "We had better start him on **antibiotics,** too. There is a danger of infection," the doctor adds.

(D) "Has he been anywhere that he might have picked up a parasite? His blood work suggests that some **parasitic** creature may be living in his body."

(E) The foreman calls to a worker, "Get three crates from the warehouse. Use the **hydraulic** lift, but first make sure that it isn't leaking fluid again."

(F) He adds, "Chester, you're beginning to look like an **automaton.** Let's put you to work at a task that will make you feel more like a human and less like a machine."

(G) The director says, "I know he is **photogenic.** The camera loves him, but I want someone who can act. This is a serious film."

(H) The engineer announces, "I have never regretted my decision to go into **aeronautics.** I love designing aircraft."

(I) The architect says, "My favorite project is the **planetarium.** I designed it to produce the best possible model of the heavens."

(J) "Make correcting the errors number one on your **agenda,**" the editor says. "Since thousands of students will be using these books, they need to be perfect!"

EXERCISE 3   *Like Meanings and Opposite Meanings* ✍

Directions. For each item below, circle the letter of the choice that means the same, or about the same, as the boldface word.

21. an interest in **aeronautics**
(A) flying
(B) medicine
(C) astronomy
(D) science

22. the cost of **antibiotics**
(A) cameras
(B) robots
(C) science
(D) medicine

23. with **hydraulic** pressure
(A) decreasing
(B) liquid
(C) great
(D) unfair

24. a view at the **planetarium**
(A) robot for building machinery
(B) expensive spacecraft
(C) room for viewing the stars
(D) factory for making microscopes

25. the rate of **respiration**
(A) eating
(B) breathing
(C) sleeping
(D) working

Directions. For each item below, circle the letter of the choice that means the opposite, or about the opposite, of the boldface word.

26. the **erosion** of hope
(A) end
(B) beginning
(C) wearing away
(D) building up

27. a **parasitic** being
(A) dependent
(B) independent
(C) intelligent
(D) ridiculous

28. a **photogenic** man
(A) creative
(B) unattractive
(C) sick
(D) well-behaved

29. a small **automaton**
(A) robot
(B) free-spirited person
(C) problem
(D) machine-like person

30. a review of the **agenda**
(A) things to be done
(B) things completed
(C) items of business
(D) listed in a series

INTRODUCTION

UNDERSTANDING NEW WORDS AND THEIR USES

Building Your Vocabulary

One way to build your vocabulary is to learn the different meanings of a single word. Another way is to learn how to make new words by using prefixes and suffixes. A third way is to learn about the origins of words. Learning about the origins of words will help you remember the words' meanings. The following exercises will help you build on, and remember, vocabulary.

HOW TO DO EXERCISE 1   *Multimeaning*

Words often have more than one meaning. In a Multimeaning exercise, you will read a boldface Vocabulary Word in a sentence. You will then read four more sentences that use the same Vocabulary Word. Your job is to choose the sentence that uses the Vocabulary Word in the same way as it is used in the first sentence. Here is an example of a Multimeaning exercise:

The fog of nineteenth-century London was, in fact, **foul** air caused by pollution.
- **(A)** Soot from the city's many chimneys would also **foul** the air.
- **(B)** In this setting, Detective Sherlock Holmes tracks down **foul** murderers and other evil-doers.
- **(C)** Nothing keeps Holmes from the chase. He goes out into the streets of London even in a thunderstorm or other **foul** weather.
- **(D)** Waste dumped into London's river Thames had made the waterway **foul**.

In the first sentence, the air was **foul** because of pollution. Pollution makes things dirty or impure. **Foul** is used as an adjective to mean dirty or impure. How does this compare to the uses of the word in choices A, B, C, and D?

- • In choice A, **foul** is a verb meaning to pollute or make dirty.
- • In choice B, **foul** means evil, not dirty.
- • In choice C, **foul** is used to describe weather, and it means unfavorable or stormy.
- • In the correct choice, D, **foul** again describes something made dirty or impure.

HOW TO DO EXERCISE 2   *Word Analysis*

Prefixes and Suffixes

The following items will give you practice in identifying the kinds of prefixes and suffixes that you will run into again and again as you read. In each of these items, you will read two words. Both words will contain the same prefix or suffix. You will be asked to identify the choice that describes the meaning of the prefix or suffix as it is used in both words. Here is an example of a prefix exercise:

readjust   **re**write
(A) after
(B) with
(C) before
(D) again

Hint #1 The second word will usually be a word that you already know well. For example, you probably already know that *rewrite* means "to write again."

Hint #2 The first word or its root (in this case, *adjust*) is a Vocabulary Word in this program. When you remember that *rewrite* means "to write again," you can guess that *readjust* means "to adjust again." That leads you to the correct choice, D.

Note: The tables in the front of this book list some common prefixes and suffixes. These tables will help you to complete the exercises on *Prefixes* and *Suffixes* in the lessons that follow.

Word Origins

Many words in the English language come from Greek, Latin, French, and other languages. Word Origins exercises will give you practice in learning the roots of Vocabulary Words. In these exercises, you will be asked to identify the choice that best completes the sentence.

Here is an example of a Word Origins exercise:

> debt   decrease   definite   descriptive

The Latin word *crescere*, "to grow," combined with the prefix *de–*, "away," gives us the word _____.

Hint #1 Compare the Latin root to the list of words provided above the item. If you remove *de–* from all of the choices, the part of the word left that most resembles the Latin root would be *–crease*, from the word *decrease*.

Hint #2 The choices in Word Origins will be Vocabulary Words you studied in *Making New Words Your Own*. In the introduction to *Making New Words Your Own*, you learned that to decrease means "to grow smaller." *Decrease* is the correct response.

UNDERSTANDING NEW WORDS AND THEIR USES

Lesson 1 | **CONTEXT: The First Americans**

Learning from American Indian Cultures

EXERCISE 1 *Multimeaning*

Directions. Read each numbered sentence below. Then, circle the letter of the choice that uses the boldface word in the same way as it is used in the numbered sentence.

1. American Indians have always believed that it is wrong to **abuse** the land.
   (A) They did not tolerate the **abuse** of animals either.
   (B) They killed animals only when they thought it was necessary. To kill for fun was considered an **abuse**.
   (C) Today many people are involved in the attempt to prevent **abuse** of the environment.
   (D) Many people follow the wisdom of the American Indian elders who teach them not to **abuse** the earth and its residents.

2. At first, the ways of the Europeans seemed to **baffle** American Indians.
   (A) On the other hand, the ways of the American Indians seemed to **baffle,** or confuse, the Europeans.
   (B) As Europeans moved westward, rugged mountains and raging rivers continued to **baffle** their progress.
   (C) The American Indians who occupied the land also **baffled** European settlers' plans for westward movement.
   (D) Some American Indians resisted and temporarily **baffled** the Europeans' settlement of their tribal lands, but ultimately the settlers prevailed.

EXERCISE 2 *Word Analysis*

Prefixes

Directions. Read the numbered pair of words below. Then, circle the letter of the choice that best describes the meaning of the underlined prefix as it is used in each pair.

3. <u>un</u>intentional   <u>un</u>certain
   (A) not
   (B) against
   (C) over
   (D) before

4. <u>im</u>probable   <u>im</u>possible
   (A) not
   (B) against
   (C) over
   (D) before

Suffixes

Directions. Read the numbered pair of words below. Then, circle the letter of the choice that best describes the meaning of the underlined suffix as it is used in each pair.

5. roman*tic*   poe*tic*
   (A) in the direction of
   (B) characteristic of
   (C) state of being
   (D) study of

6. sinceri*ty*   possibili*ty*
   (A) state of being
   (B) study of
   (C) like
   (D) one who does

Word Origins

Directions. Read each of the following sentences. Then, from the vocabulary list below, choose the word that best completes the sentence. Write the word in the blank.

abuse	calamity	folklore	picturesque
appalling	contagious	intentional	probable
baffle	deceive	knoll	romantic
barbarism	eminent	myriad	ruthless
bewilder	epidemic	novelty	sincerity

7. We get a hint of the meaning of the word _____ when we learn that the Middle English word *appallen* means "to grow pale."

8. You may recognize the Greek word *barbaros,* meaning "foreign," in the Modern English word _____.

9. The German word *knollen,* meaning "lump," is closely related to our word _____.

10. You may recognize the Old French word *novel,* meaning "new," in our word _____.

UNDERSTANDING NEW WORDS AND THEIR USES

| Lesson 2 | **CONTEXT:** The First Americans

When Cultures Intermingled

EXERCISE 1 *Multimeaning*

Directions. Read each numbered sentence below. Then, circle the letter of the choice that uses the boldface word in the same way as it is used in the numbered sentence.

1. Many Europeans came to North America seeking **sanctuary** from religious persecution. They hoped to have a place where they were safe to practice their religion.
   (A) Cliff-dwelling Indians built underground chambers called *kivas,* a type of **sanctuary** where they held religious ceremonies.
   (B) Some cliff dwellers lived in caves which provided shelter and **sanctuary** for the families.
   (C) When Europeans first came to America, there was no need for a bird **sanctuary**. Because the land was not heavily populated by humans, a special place did not need to be set aside to protect the birds.
   (D) Some early North American Indians built mounds. A mound could be used for a burial place or as a foundation for a temple, a **sanctuary** for religious ceremonies.

2. American Indians helped the first Europeans **sustain** themselves by showing them how to plant crops.
   (A) Nevertheless, Europeans were to **sustain** many losses during their first years in the new land.
   (B) The American Indians could **sustain** themselves by hunting, fishing, and farming.
   (C) The American Indians would soon **sustain** great losses due to diseases that the Europeans brought.
   (D) Both peoples had to **sustain** many hardships.

EXERCISE 2 *Word Analysis*

Prefixes

Directions. Read the numbered pair of words below. Then, circle the letter of the choice that best describes the meaning of the underlined prefix as it is used in each pair.

3. <u>mis</u>deed   <u>mis</u>understanding
   (A) good
   (B) same, identical
   (C) wrong, bad
   (D) late

4. <u>ad</u>vent   <u>ad</u>mit
   (A) to
   (B) before
   (C) bad
   (D) between

Suffixes

Directions. Read the numbered pair of words below. Then, circle the letter of the choice that best describes the meaning of the underlined suffix as it is used in each pair.

5. eco**logy**   geo**logy**
   (A) one who does
   (B) that which
   (C) study or theory of
   (D) like, resembling

6. pac**ify**   beaut**ify**
   (A) full of
   (B) characteristic of
   (C) to make
   (D) becoming

Word Origins

Directions. Read each of the following sentences. Then, from the vocabulary list below, choose the word that best completes the sentence. Write the word in the blank.

advent	defy	intelligible	pacify
aggressive	ecology	misdeed	sanctuary
alliance	ferocious	motivate	strategy
anthology	inevitable	mystical	sustain
catastrophe	integrity	nourish	valid

7. We get a hint of the meaning of _____ when we learn that the Latin word *sustinēre* means "to hold up."

8. You may recognize the Greek word *katastrophe,* meaning "an overthrowing," in our word _____.

9. The Latin word *ferox,* meaning "wild" or "untamed," is related to our word _____.

10. We get a hint of the meaning of _____ when we learn that the Latin word *intellegere* means "to perceive."

UNDERSTANDING NEW WORDS AND THEIR USES

Lesson 3 | **CONTEXT:** The First Americans

A Culture Rooted in Nature

EXERCISE 1 *Multimeaning*

Directions. Read each numbered sentence below. Then, circle the letter of the choice that uses the boldface word in the same way as it is used in the numbered sentence.

1. Many American Indian stories have animals such as the **badger,** the coyote, and the rabbit for characters.
   (A) European literature is also filled with animal characters, including the bear, the **badger,** and the squirrel.
   (B) In both cultures, children **badger** their parents to tell them stories. The children refuse to sleep until they have heard a bedtime tale.
   (C) In some stories, animals **badger,** or nag, humans into doing the right thing.
   (D) In some stories, the animals behave like humans. For example, the wolf parent might **badger** the wolf cub to behave, just as a human parent might nag a child to be good.

2. The relationships between American Indians and their environments were **harmonious.** American Indians worked with, not against, the environment.
   (A) Many peoples created **harmonious** proportions in their artistic work. This pleasing balance can be seen in a Navajo blanket or in a sand painting.
   (B) Their music was also **harmonious.** Though the music sounded strange to European ears, it was based on an underlying order.
   (C) The relationships between peoples were not always **harmonious.** Groups occasionally went to war against each other.
   (D) Today, elders still teach younger people the **harmonious** songs of their ancestors.

EXERCISE 2 *Word Analysis*

Prefixes

Directions. Read the numbered pair of words below. Then, circle the letter of the choice that best describes the meaning of the underlined prefix as it is used in each pair.

3. <u>inter</u>vene   <u>inter</u>national
   (A) before
   (B) following
   (C) between
   (D) well, good

4. <u>in</u>comparable   <u>in</u>complete
   (A) before
   (B) not
   (C) bad
   (D) with

UNDERSTANDING NEW WORDS AND THEIR USES **129**

Suffixes

Directions. Read the numbered pair of words below. Then, circle the letter of the choice that best describes the meaning of the underlined suffix as it is used in each pair.

5. custom<u>ary</u>   honor<u>ary</u>
   (A) of, relating to
   (B) act of
   (C) part, half
   (D) one who does

6. calculat<u>ion</u>   act<u>ion</u>
   (A) study or theory of
   (B) full of
   (C) act or result of
   (D) to make

Word Origins

Directions. Read each of the following sentences. Then, from the vocabulary list below, choose the word that best completes the sentence. Write the word in the blank.

accessory	calculation	fragile	intervene
adjacent	complement	gallery	multicolored
artisan	convert	glorify	pulverize
attain	customary	harmonious	valor
badger	deceased	incomparable	vitality

7. We get a hint of the meaning of the word _____ when we learn that the Latin word *convertere* means "to turn in character or nature, transform."

8. You may recognize the Latin word *gloria,* meaning "glory," in our word

_____.

9. We get a hint of the meaning of the word _____ when we learn that the Latin word *frangere* means "to break."

10. The Middle English word *deces,* meaning "death," is related to the Modern English word _____.

UNDERSTANDING NEW WORDS AND THEIR USES

Lesson 4 | CONTEXT: The First Americans

An American Indian Woman Today

EXERCISE 1 Multimeaning

Directions. Read each numbered sentence below. Then, circle the letter of the choice that uses the boldface word in the same way as it is used in the numbered sentence.

1. The elders have agreed to **delegate,** or entrust, the responsibility to her.
   (A) She is their chosen **delegate,** or representative.
   (B) She thinks of her ancestor, who was once a **delegate** to the Iroquois federation.
   (C) She remembers when another ancestor was the **delegate** to a convention.
   (D) Before she leaves, she has to **delegate** some of the work to others. She decides to entrust her duties to her brother.

2. She is **descended** from both the Cherokee and the Iroquois people.
   (A) As she **descended** the stairs of the convention hall, all eyes followed her movements down.
   (B) The stairs **descended** in a spiral.
   (C) The crowd **descended** on her as she reached the bottom. Everyone wanted to shake her hand.
   (D) Women played an important role in the Iroquois federation, and she is **descended** from a long line of courageous female ancestors.

EXERCISE 2 Word Analysis

Prefixes

Directions. Read the numbered pair of words below. Then, circle the letter of the choice that best describes the meaning of the underlined prefix as it is used in each pair.

3. <u>fore</u>sight   <u>fore</u>runner
   (A) after
   (B) before
   (C) against
   (D) new

4. <u>con</u>federation   <u>con</u>current
   (A) away from
   (B) first, primary
   (C) against
   (D) with, together

Suffixes

Directions. Read the numbered pair of words below. Then, circle the letter of the choice that best describes the meaning of the underlined suffix as it is used in each pair.

5. isola**tion**   preven**tion**
   - (A) one who does
   - (B) process of
   - (C) tending to
   - (D) result of

6. advantage**ous**   courage**ous**
   - (A) act of
   - (B) full of
   - (C) capable of being
   - (D) suitable for

Word Origins

Directions. Read each of the following sentences. Then, from the vocabulary list below, choose the word that best completes the sentence. Write the word in the blank.

adequate	discord	incite	menagerie
advantageous	enhance	inflexible	mutual
confederation	feline	inherit	phenomenon
delegate	foresight	isolation	posterity
descend	gnarled	menace	revelation

7. We get a hint of the meaning of _____ when we learn that the Latin word *post* means "after."

8. The Middle English word *knore*, meaning "knot," is related to our Modern English word _____.

9. You may recognize the Latin word *flexus*, meaning "to bend," in our word _____.

10. The Greek word *phainomenons*, meaning "appearing," is closely related to our word _____.

UNDERSTANDING NEW WORDS AND THEIR USES

Lesson 5 | **CONTEXT:** The First Americans

Working with the System

EXERCISE 1 *Multimeaning*

Directions. Read each numbered sentence below. Then, circle the letter of the choice that uses the boldface word in the same way as it is used in the numbered sentence.

1. The American Indian group plans to **petition** the United States government to return the land.
   (A) People in neighboring communities have signed a **petition** in support of their cause.
   (B) In the meantime, lawyers plan to **petition** the state courts to reverse an earlier decision.
   (C) If the **petition** fails, the lawyers have another plan.
   (D) The group plans to send a **petition** to both the legislature and the governor. They hope that their earnest request will be taken seriously.

2. The lawyer in charge of the case is aware of **potential,** or possible, problems.
   (A) The group supported him in law school because they believed in his **potential**. In fact, he has turned out to be a superb lawyer.
   (B) He believes the case has the **potential** for appeal even if he loses in the lower courts, but he doesn't want to bank on this possibility.
   (C) He also thinks the attorney general is a **potential** ally. It may be possible to get her support.
   (D) He is relying for help on his assistants, who are all young lawyers with little experience but great **potential**.

EXERCISE 2 *Word Analysis*

Prefixes

Directions. Read the numbered pair of words below. Then, circle the letter of the choice that best describes the meaning of the underlined prefix as it is used in each pair.

3. <u>in</u>soluble <u>in</u>sincere
   (A) away from
   (B) before
   (C) against
   (D) not

4. <u>re</u>store <u>re</u>produce
   (A) back, again
   (B) away from
   (C) through
   (D) into, in

Suffixes

Directions. Read the numbered pair of words below. Then, circle the letter of the choice that best describes the meaning of the underlined suffix as it is used in each pair.

5. durabil**ity**   visibil**ity**
   (A) able to be
   (B) full of
   (C) state of being
   (D) in the direction of

6. creat**ive**   destruct**ive**
   (A) skill
   (B) tending to
   (C) somewhat
   (D) becoming

Word Origins

Directions. Read each of the following sentences. Then, from the vocabulary list below, choose the word that best completes the sentence. Write the word in the blank.

adapt	creative	immense	ordeal
assumption	diction	impel	petition
basis	durable	ingenious	potential
consecutive	feasible	insoluble	primitive
controversy	hilarious	omission	restore

7. You may recognize the Latin word *primus,* meaning "first," in our word

   _____.

8. We get a hint of the meaning of the word _____ when we learn that the Latin word *aptare* means "to fit" and the Latin word *ad* means "at" or "to."

9. The Old French word *faisible,* meaning "possible" is related to our word

   _____.

10. The Latin word *omittere,* meaning "to disregard," is closely related to our word

    _____.

UNDERSTANDING NEW WORDS AND THEIR USES

Lesson 6 | **CONTEXT:** Coming to North America

Leaving the "Old Country"

EXERCISE 1 *Multimeaning*

Directions. Read each numbered sentence below. Then, circle the letter of the choice that uses the boldface word in the same way as it is used in the numbered sentence.

1. Aboard the ship, the **multitude**—from the passengers to the deckhands—cheered as the Statue of Liberty came into view.
   (A) A **multitude** of people entered the United States over the past two hundred years.
   (B) They were escaping a **multitude** of problems such as hunger, religious persecution, and overcrowding.
   (C) They brought with them a **multitude** of strengths and talents.
   (D) The immigrant **multitude** helped build the nation. Without these masses the country's history would have taken a very different course.

2. John's grandfather came to the United States after the failure of a **boycott** he had organized.
   (A) He wanted to **boycott** a chain of stores that paid farmers unfairly low prices for their potatoes.
   (B) The owners heard of his plan to **boycott**.
   (C) They were determined that the **boycott** would fail.
   (D) They arranged for every store they owned to **boycott** all the farmers' produce.

EXERCISE 2 *Word Analysis*

Prefixes

Directions. Read the numbered pair of words below. Then, circle the letter of the choice that best describes the meaning of the underlined prefix as it is used in each pair.

3. <u>mal</u>nutrition   <u>mal</u>function
   (A) before
   (B) against
   (C) wrong, bad
   (D) like, of

4. <u>ir</u>resolute   <u>ir</u>responsible
   (A) over
   (B) all
   (C) after
   (D) not

Suffixes

Directions. Read the numbered pair of words below. Then, circle the letter of the choice that best describes the meaning of the underlined suffix as it is used in each pair.

5. censor**ship**   owner**ship**
   - (A) study or theory of
   - (B) resembling
   - (C) belief
   - (D) state of being

6. optim**ism**   hero**ism**
   - (A) state of being
   - (B) act or result of
   - (C) wrong, bad
   - (D) suitable for

Word Origins

Directions. Read each of the following sentences. Then, from the vocabulary list below, choose the word that best completes the sentence. Write the word in the blank.

anxiety	decade	morale	predicament
aristocrat	deport	multitude	propaganda
boycott	emigrate	nationality	refuge
burly	famine	naturalization	resolute
censorship	malnutrition	optimism	urban

7. The Middle English word *burlich,* meaning "strong," became our word

   _____.

8. We get a hint of the meaning of the word _____ when we learn that the Latin word *urbs* means "city."

9. The Latin word *natio,* meaning "born," is related to our word _____.

10. The English word _____ comes from an incident in nineteenth-century Ireland, in which tenants refused to pay the high rents charged by a land agent named Charles C. Boycott.

UNDERSTANDING NEW WORDS AND THEIR USES

Lesson 7 | CONTEXT: Coming to North America

Freedom and Equality

EXERCISE 1 *Multimeaning*

Directions. Read each numbered sentence below. Then, circle the letter of the choice that uses the boldface word in the same way as it is used in the numbered sentence.

1. Most immigrants felt that it was a **privilege** to come to the United States; they often felt they were more fortunate than those they left behind.
   (A) Some came from countries in which only people who were born into a position of **privilege** had a chance for success.
   (B) In the "Old Country," the government might **privilege** one group over another.
   (C) Of course, in the United States, the government does not **privilege** particular groups. Rather, the government tries to create a level playing field for all groups.
   (D) This equality makes many people feel **privileged** to live here.

2. Last night I saw the **premiere** of a play about Russian immigrants to the United States. Since it was the first showing ever, the play had a few problems.
   (A) A young actor was to **premiere** last night. However, she became ill and now will have to begin her acting career another night.
   (B) Yesterday was an important date in the history of Russian Jews. That is why the director wanted to **premiere** the play last night.
   (C) Originally, the play was to **premiere** in Brookline, Massachusetts, where many of these immigrants settled. Instead, the play opened at a theater in Boston.
   (D) Many Russian Americans were in the audience. After the **premiere** ended, we all participated in a question-and-answer session.

EXERCISE 2 *Word Analysis*

Prefixes

Directions. Read the numbered pair of words below. Then, circle the letter of the choice that best describes the meaning of the underlined prefix as it is used in each pair.

3. <u>re</u>circulate   <u>re</u>appear
   (A) over, above
   (B) before
   (C) back, again
   (D) under, beneath

4. <u>in</u>hospitable   <u>in</u>complete
   (A) not
   (B) against
   (C) after
   (D) with

Suffixes

Directions. Read the numbered pair of words below. Then, circle the letter of the choice that best describes the meaning of the underlined suffix as it is used in each pair.

5. fraudul**ent**   depend**ent**
(A) wrong, bad
(B) full of
(C) away from
(D) showing

6. accept**ance**   disturb**ance**
(A) act of
(B) becoming
(C) like, resembling
(D) study or theory of

Word Origins

Directions. Read each of the following sentences. Then, from the vocabulary list below, choose the word that best completes the sentence. Write the word in the blank.

acceptance	dilapidated	immigrate	privilege
accessible	exaggeration	impulsive	prosecute
bankrupt	fraudulent	intensity	riotous
boisterous	grieve	jubilation	thrive
circulate	hospitable	premiere	transit

7. You may recognize the Old French word *rihoter*, meaning "to make a disturbance," in the Modern English word _____.

8. The Middle English word *boistous*, meaning "rude," became the Modern English word _____.

9. We get a hint of the meaning of the word _____ when we learn that the Latin word *jubilare* means "to raise a shout of joy."

10. The Latin word *migrare*, meaning "to move," is closely related to our word _____.

UNDERSTANDING NEW WORDS AND THEIR USES

Lesson 8 | **CONTEXT:** Coming to North America

Learning to Speak English

EXERCISE 1 *Multimeaning*

Directions. Read each numbered sentence below. Then, circle the letter of the choice that uses the boldface word in the same way as it is used in the numbered sentence.

1. Most immigrants find that it is **imperative,** or absolutely necessary, to learn the language.
   - (A) English teachers explain the indicative, subjunctive, and **imperative** moods of verbs.
   - (B) The **imperative** sentence is a command.
   - (C) Immigrants soon discover that to learn English, it is **imperative** to use the language every day.
   - (D) The English teacher used an **imperative** tone of voice, but her students liked her anyway.

2. Not learning the language can **hamper** an immigrant's progress.
   - (A) On the other hand, a lack of money could **hamper** an immigrant's opportunity to learn the language.
   - (B) One English teacher brought a **hamper** filled with picnic items.
   - (C) The students ate the food from the **hamper** after they had learned what the items were called.
   - (D) The next day, the teacher brought a **hamper** of clothes to teach the students the English words for different items of clothing.

EXERCISE 2 *Word Analysis*

Prefixes

Directions. Read the numbered pair of words below. Then, circle the letter of the choice that best describes the meaning of the underlined prefix as it is used in each pair.

3. <u>de</u>pose   <u>de</u>crease
   - (A) undo
   - (B) repeat
   - (C) all
   - (D) toward

4. <u>im</u>pose   <u>im</u>polite
   - (A) into; not
   - (B) against
   - (C) away from
   - (D) for

Suffixes

Directions. Read the numbered pair of words below. Then, circle the letter of the choice that best describes the meaning of the underlined suffix as it is used in each pair.

5. spac<u>ious</u>   luxur<u>ious</u>
   (A) state of being
   (B) able to be
   (C) full of
   (D) away from

6. neglig<u>ent</u>   intellig<u>ent</u>
   (A) part, half
   (B) one who does
   (C) showing
   (D) study or theory of

Word Origins

Directions. Read each of the following sentences. Then, from the vocabulary list below, choose the word that best completes the sentence. Write the word in the blank.

dedicate	hamper	inconsiderate	presume
depose	haven	intercept	recuperate
dispense	humidity	liable	restrain
dissect	imperative	memento	spacious
exertion	impose	negligent	tumult

7. The Old English word *haefen,* meaning "port," became our word _____.

8. We get a hint of the meaning of our word _____ when we learn that the Latin word *humidus* means "moist."

9. The Latin word *recuperare,* meaning "to recover," is closely related to our word

_____.

10. The Latin word *dispendere,* meaning "to weigh out," carries over into Modern English as the word _____.

UNDERSTANDING NEW WORDS AND THEIR USES

Lesson 9 | CONTEXT: Coming to North America

A Day in the Life

EXERCISE 1 *Multimeaning*

Directions. Read each numbered sentence below. Then, circle the letter of the choice that uses the boldface word in the same way as it is used in the numbered sentence.

1. The family lived in the **capital** city of the old country. Because the government is centered there, many people work in government jobs.
   - (A) They moved to the United States with very little **capital**, or money, to invest.
   - (B) They hoped to visit the U.S. **capital** area of Washington, D.C.
   - (C) The children thought the visit was a **capital** idea. They couldn't wait to go.
   - (D) The grandparents, on the other hand, thought it might be a **capital** mistake.

2. Grandmother's recipe calls for **basting** the tomatoes with oil.
   - (A) Mother is in the living room **basting** together a blouse for Aunt Jennifer.
   - (B) If it fits, she will replace the **basting** with permanent stitches.
   - (C) Grandfather is watching TV and **basting** the coach of the losing team with barbed remarks about his coaching decisions.
   - (D) The next step in the recipe is **basting** the pastry dough with butter.

EXERCISE 2 *Word Analysis* ☞

Prefixes

Directions. Read each numbered pair of words below. Then, circle the letter of the choice that best describes the meaning of the underlined prefix as it is used in each pair.

3. <u>pre</u>arrange   <u>pre</u>paid
   - (A) for
   - (B) against
   - (C) after
   - (D) before

4. <u>dis</u>mantle   <u>dis</u>like
   - (A) opposite
   - (B) before
   - (C) many
   - (D) across

Suffixes

Directions. Read each numbered pair of words below. Then, circle the letter of the choice that best describes the meaning of the underlined suffix as it is used in each pair.

5. grac*ious*   ambit*ious*
   (A) full of
   (B) study of
   (C) becoming
   (D) resembling

6. manage**able**   accept**able**
   (A) resembling
   (B) capable of being
   (C) cause to be
   (D) full of

Word Origins

Directions. Read each of the following sentences. Then, from the vocabulary list below, choose the word that best completes the sentence. Write the word in the blank.

aroma	elegant	manageable	probation
baste	embarrass	monopoly	remote
capital	frequency	occupant	rigid
diminish	gracious	populate	saturate
dismantle	haughty	prearrange	sedate

7. We get a hint of the meaning of the word _____ when we learn that the Middle English word *diminuen* means "to make smaller."

8. The Latin word *saturare,* meaning "to fill up," is closely related to our word

_____.

9. You may recognize the Greek word *monos,* meaning "one," in our word

_____.

10. The Latin word *populus,* meaning "people," is closely related to our word

_____.

UNDERSTANDING NEW WORDS AND THEIR USES

| Lesson 10 | **CONTEXT:** Coming to North America

"Old Country" Cooking

EXERCISE 1 *Multimeaning*

Directions. Read each numbered sentence below. Then, circle the letter of the choice that uses the boldface word in the same way as it is used in the numbered sentence.

1. New immigrants like to have easy **access** to the ingredients they used in their traditional cooking.
   - (A) Today we can **access** information about almost anything from the Internet.
   - (B) Even those who do not yet read English can **access** information by that method.
   - (C) Immigrants who cannot read English might **access** Web pages in their first language.
   - (D) To be sure of **access** to familiar languages, foods, and customs, many immigrants tried to settle in neighborhoods with people from their original countries.

2. Different people consider different foods to be basic, necessary **provisions**.
   - (A) Neighborhood grocery stores made **provision** for their customers' special needs.
   - (B) **Provisions** could be bought within the neighborhood.
   - (C) If the immigrant had to live far away, he or she had to make **provision** for a trip to the grocery store.
   - (D) Often, friends would make **provision** to help each other with the shopping and cooking.

EXERCISE 2 *Word Analysis*

Prefixes

Directions. Read each numbered pair of words below. Then, circle the letter of the choice that best describes the meaning of the underlined prefix as it is used in each pair.

3. <u>dis</u>agreeable   <u>dis</u>pleasure
   - (A) after
   - (B) opposite
   - (C) over
   - (D) before

4. <u>circum</u>navigate   <u>circum</u>ference
   - (A) beneath
   - (B) over
   - (C) around
   - (D) through

Suffixes

Directions. Read each numbered pair of words below. Then, circle the letter of the choice that best describes the meaning of the underlined suffix as it is used in each pair.

5. thrif<u>ty</u>   jealous<u>y</u>
   (A) characterized by
   (B) somewhat
   (C) becoming
   (D) resembling

6. not<u>ify</u>   just<u>ify</u>
   (A) full of
   (B) act of
   (C) to make
   (D) like

Word Origins

Directions. Read each of the following sentences. Then, from the vocabulary list below, choose the word that best completes the sentence. Write the word in the blank.

access	disagreeable	maroon	regime
accommodations	evacuate	notify	remorse
adept	humiliate	persistent	thrifty
circumnavigate	jeopardize	pleasantry	titanic
dingy	liberate	provision	verify

7. We get a hint of the meaning of the word _____ when we learn that the Latin word *liber* means "free."

8. The French word *plaisanterie,* meaning "pleasant remarks," is closely related to our word _____.

9. The Latin word *humiliare,* meaning "to humble," is closely related to our word _____.

10. We get a hint of the meaning of the word _____ when we learn that the Latin word *vacare* means "to make empty."

UNDERSTANDING NEW WORDS AND THEIR USES

Lesson 11 | CONTEXT: Voices of the United States
Reading About United States History

EXERCISE 1 Multimeaning ✍

Directions. Read each numbered sentence below. Then, circle the letter of the choice that uses the boldface word in the same way as it is used in the numbered sentence.

1. The voices that tell the story of history are not always **neutral**.
   (A) Even if a historian is not personally **neutral** about an issue, he or she will usually try not to take sides.
   (B) I just read a book that examines the U.S. attempt to be a **neutral** in the early days of World War II.
   (C) It was interesting, but I have read other books that were so dull that my brain went into **neutral**.
   (D) One of the problems with many books is that they are not eye-catching; they're either black and white, or they use only **neutral** colors. I prefer to look at books with vivid colors.

2. I have read about the **blockade** of Confederate ports by the Union Navy in the Civil War.
   (A) Historians have also written about the attempts of students in the 1960s to **blockade** streets in protest marches.
   (B) I saw an old photograph of a river dammed by a **blockade** of debris.
   (C) Countries have decided to **blockade** various ports throughout history.
   (D) I wonder what the first **blockade** in United States military history was?

EXERCISE 2 Word Analysis ✍

Prefixes

Directions. Read each numbered pair of words below. Then, circle the letter of the choice that best describes the meaning of the underlined prefix as it is used in each pair.

3. <u>re</u>generate   <u>re</u>marry
   (A) before
   (B) across
   (C) through
   (D) again

4. <u>fore</u>word   <u>fore</u>thought
   (A) after
   (B) against
   (C) before
   (D) all

Suffixes

Directions. Read each numbered pair of words below. Then, circle the letter of the choice that best describes the meaning of the underlined suffix as it is used in each pair.

5. diploma**tic**   drama**tic**
    (A) one who
    (B) tending to
    (C) characterized by
    (D) state of being

6. satir**ize**   standard**ize**
    (A) to carry
    (B) to subject to
    (C) study or theory of
    (D) full of

Word Origins

Directions. Read each of the following sentences. Then, from the vocabulary list below, choose the word that best completes the sentence. Write the word in the blank.

aspiration	generate	pewter	sable
blockade	indelible	premier	salutation
confiscate	neutral	pun	satire
diplomat	obituary	quaint	tariff
foreword	obscure	quench	urgent

7. You may recognize the Latin word *obitus,* meaning "death," in our word

    _____.

8. We get a hint of the meaning of the word _____ when we learn that the Italian word *puntiglio* means "verbal hairsplitting."

9. The Latin word *indelibilis,* meaning "not capable of being destroyed," is closely related to our word _____.

10. The Italian word *tariffa,* meaning "rate," is closely related to our word

    _____.

UNDERSTANDING NEW WORDS AND THEIR USES

Lesson 12 | **CONTEXT:** Voices of the United States

Essaying the Essay

EXERCISE 1 *Multimeaning*

Directions. Read each numbered sentence below. Then, circle the letter of the choice that uses the boldface word in the same way as it is used in the numbered sentence.

1. Many professional writers are **apt** to write about topics they know well.
   (A) For instance, **apt** topics may include a hobby or interest, a personal event, or a favorite place.
   (B) Before beginning an article, writers are **apt** to brainstorm many possible topics.
   (C) Writers also consider to whom they are writing when choosing a topic. Knowing the audience helps the writer to make an **apt** choice.
   (D) An **apt** student can use the same strategies as a professional writer to choose a topic.

2. Some essayists write about a local **eccentric**. Neighborhood characters seem to be an endless source of inspiration for writers.
   (A) Essayists need not follow a fixed form. They can take an **eccentric** path.
   (B) Essayists sometimes offer **eccentric** opinions.
   (C) I read an essay on the art of the boomerang that was written by a true **eccentric**.
   (D) Of course, I think it's a bit **eccentric** to read nothing but essays.

EXERCISE 2 *Word Analysis*

Prefixes

Directions. Read the numbered pair of words below. Then, circle the letter of the choice that best describes the meaning of the underlined prefix as it is used in each pair.

3. <u>in</u>variable   <u>in</u>complete
   (A) many
   (B) after
   (C) not
   (D) almost

4. <u>re</u>activate   <u>re</u>appoint
   (A) again
   (B) over
   (C) against
   (D) toward

Suffixes

Directions. Read the numbered pair of words below. Then, circle the letter of the choice that best describes the meaning of the underlined suffix as it is used in each pair.

5. charit**able**   believ**able**
- (A) capable of
- (B) tending to
- (C) becoming
- (D) making

6. deduct**ion**   restrict**ion**
- (A) capable of
- (B) condition of
- (C) pertaining to
- (D) resembling

Word Origins

Directions. Read each of the following sentences. Then, from the vocabulary list below, choose the word that best completes the sentence. Write the word in the blank.

activate	confide	invariable	sarcasm
apt	deduction	irk	successor
charitable	eccentric	petty	summit
clarify	essay	pious	tarnish
colossal	intolerance	proposal	temperament

7. We get a hint of the meaning of the word _____ when we learn that the Latin word *pius* means "dutiful."

8. The Middle English word *petit*, meaning "small," became our Modern English word _____.

9. The Latin word *summus*, meaning "highest," is related to our word _____.

10. The Latin word *succedere*, meaning "to follow after," is closely related to our word _____.

UNDERSTANDING NEW WORDS AND THEIR USES

Lesson 13 | CONTEXT: Voices of the United States
Writing and Publishing

EXERCISE 1 | *Multimeaning*

Directions. Read each numbered sentence below. Then, circle the letter of the choice that uses the boldface word in the same way as it is used in the numbered sentence.

1. Writers know how to **intrigue** the reading public.
   - (A) Some write novels of political **intrigue** that tell of plots against corrupt governments.
   - (B) Some write about lovers engaged in romantic but secret **intrigue**.
   - (C) Some writers **intrigue** us with tales of adventure around the globe.
   - (D) In writing their novels, some writers fulfill their wish for a life of excitement and **intrigue**.

2. Some writers finish their novels with **dispatch** and move on to the next.
   - (A) Some writers **dispatch,** or do away with, the villain in the last chapter.
   - (B) Writers **dispatch** their manuscripts to publishers with either relief or nervousness.
   - (C) Writers always wish editors would read with more **dispatch**. They hate waiting to hear what the editors think.
   - (D) Sometimes a writer will strongly disagree with the **dispatch** he or she receives from an editor, especially if the letter contains a rejection.

EXERCISE 2 | *Word Analysis*

Prefixes

Directions. Read each numbered pair of words below. Then, circle the letter of the choice that best describes the meaning of the underlined prefix as it is used in each pair.

3. <u>con</u>temporary   <u>con</u>tain
   - (A) before
   - (B) through
   - (C) against
   - (D) with

4. <u>non</u>literal   <u>non</u>living
   - (A) many
   - (B) before
   - (C) not
   - (D) after

Suffixes

Directions. Read each numbered pair of words below. Then, circle the letter of the choice that best describes the meaning of the underlined suffix as it is used in each pair.

5. occurr**ence**   confer**ence**
   (A) act or state of
   (B) resembling
   (C) pertaining to
   (D) one who

6. emphas**ize**   computer**ize**
   (A) to study
   (B) to make
   (C) having to do with
   (D) full of

Word Origins

Directions. Read each of the following sentences. Then, from the vocabulary list below, choose the word that best completes the sentence. Write the word in the blank.

anonymous	dictate	falter	intrigue
casual	dilute	famished	literal
climax	dispatch	fictitious	modify
condemn	emphasize	fragment	occurrence
contemporary	endorse	improvise	therapy

7. The Middle English word *modifien,* meaning "to limit," became the Modern English word _____.

8. We get a hint of the meaning of the word _____ when we learn that the Greek word *klimax* means "ladder."

9. The Middle English word *faltren,* meaning "to stagger," became the Modern English word _____.

10. The Latin word *dictare,* meaning "to speak," is closely related to our word _____.

UNDERSTANDING NEW WORDS AND THEIR USES

Lesson 14 | CONTEXT: Voices of the United States

Writing About Experience

EXERCISE 1 | *Multimeaning* ✍

Directions. Read each numbered sentence below. Then, circle the letter of the choice that uses the boldface word in the same way as it is used in the numbered sentence.

1. Reading about others' experiences in the United States can **illuminate,** or make clear, our own lives.
   (A) Some writers **illuminate** or celebrate their past experiences as they retell them.
   (B) Others use their writings as a way to **illuminate** or clarify problems they have had.
   (C) Long ago in the Middle Ages, artists would **illuminate** manuscripts with beautiful colors.
   (D) If they painted at night, these artists had to **illuminate** the manuscripts with candles or oil lamps.

2. Many writers **derive,** or receive, satisfaction from writing about their early experiences in the United States.
   (A) What conclusions might you **derive,** or arrive at by logic, from a study of these writers?
   (B) They seem to **derive** some very similar conclusions about life in a new country.
   (C) Readers **derive** great pleasure from their books.
   (D) Some of my opinions **derive,** or come, from my study of writers from eastern Europe.

EXERCISE 2 | *Word Analysis* ✍

Prefixes

Directions. Read each numbered pair of words below. Then, circle the letter of the choice that best describes the meaning of the underlined prefix as it is used in each pair.

3. <u>super</u>ficial   <u>super</u>visor
   (A) over
   (B) under
   (C) without
   (D) after

4. <u>de</u>tach   <u>de</u>frost
   (A) toward
   (B) together
   (C) undo
   (D) around

Suffixes

Directions. Read each numbered pair of words below. Then, circle the letter of the choice that best describes the meaning of the underlined suffix as it is used in each pair.

5. extens**ive**   expens**ive**
   (A) to make
   (B) relating to
   (C) becoming
   (D) without

6. tang**ible**   collect**ible**
   (A) full of
   (B) familiar with
   (C) similar to
   (D) capable of being

Word Origins

Directions. Read each of the following sentences. Then, from the vocabulary list below, choose the word that best completes the sentence. Write the word in the blank.

articulate	derive	illuminate	superficial
braggart	detach	imply	tangible
category	distraction	inclination	testify
demolish	eligible	miscellaneous	unique
denial	extensive	secluded	upbraid

7. We get a hint of the meaning of the word _____ when we learn that the Latin *de* means "down" and *moliri* means "build."

8. The Latin word *unus*, meaning "one," is related to our word _____.

9. The Middle English word *implien*, meaning "to involve," became the Modern English word _____.

10. The Middle English word *secluden*, meaning "to set apart," became the Modern English word _____.

UNDERSTANDING NEW WORDS AND THEIR USES

Lesson 15 | CONTEXT: Voices of the United States

Reading and Learning

EXERCISE 1 *Multimeaning*

Directions. Read each numbered sentence below. Then, circle the letter of the choice that uses the boldface word in the same way as it is used in the numbered sentence.

1. Here's an article by a writer discussing how many people now **commute** to work.
   (A) Another article discusses whether or not to **commute,** or make less severe, a bank robber's prison sentence.
   (B) This writer discusses how he was able to **commute** an idea for a little feature story into major front-page news.
   (C) Another writer is discussing what it is like to **commute** between the East Coast and the West Coast.
   (D) After hearing the lawyer's argument, the judge decided to **commute** the prisoner's sentence.

2. Another article describes the effect of traffic on our already **congested** highways.
   (A) The writer tells how flash flooding **congested** the river road.
   (B) Here's an article on what to do when you are **congested** from a cold or the flu.
   (C) The writer points out that most of us feel miserable when our heads are **congested** from allergies, which usually are not serious.
   (D) My head is as **congested** as a highway at rush hour; it's crowded with too many facts about traffic and head colds.

EXERCISE 2 *Word Analysis*

Prefixes

Directions. Read each numbered pair of words below. Then, circle the letter of the choice that best describes the meaning of the underlined prefix as it is used in each pair.

3. <u>anti</u>biotics   <u>anti</u>freeze
   (A) across
   (B) two
   (C) good
   (D) against

4. <u>mal</u>function   <u>mal</u>formation
   (A) single
   (B) bad; wrong
   (C) new
   (D) near

Suffixes

Directions. Read each numbered pair of words below. Then, circle the letter of the choice that best describes the meaning of the underlined suffix as it is used in each pair.

5. synthet**ic**   volcan**ic**
   (A) characteristic of
   (B) against
   (C) capable of
   (D) without

6. techno**logy**   bio**logy**
   (A) study of
   (B) having the nature
   (C) in the direction of
   (D) state of being

Word Origins

Directions. Read each of the following sentences. Then, from the vocabulary list below, choose the word that best completes the sentence. Write the word in the blank.

aeronautics	commute	hypothesis	rebate
agenda	congest	malfunction	respiration
antibiotics	considerate	parasitic	synthetic
arrogant	erosion	photogenic	technology
automaton	hydraulic	planetarium	warranty

7. We get a hint of the meaning of the word _____ when we learn that the Greek word *hupothesis* means "to suppose."

8. The Latin word *erodere,* meaning "to gnaw off," is related to our word _____.

9. We get a hint of the meaning of the word _____ when we learn that the Greek word *hydraulis* means "a water organ."

10. You may recognize the Greek words *para*, meaning "beside," and *sitos*, meaning "food," in our English word _____.

Why We Practice Analogies

Practice with analogies builds logic skills. To answer analogy questions correctly, you think about two words and discover the relationship between them. Then you match that relationship with one shared by another pair of words. In addition, when you study analogies, you think about the precise meanings of words and fix these definitions in your memory.

Understanding Word Analogies

A word analogy is a comparison between two pairs of words. Here is how word analogies are written:

Example 1   FIND : LOCATE :: lose : misplace

The colon (:) stands for the phrase "is related to." Here is how to read the relationships in Example 1:

> FIND [is related to] LOCATE
> lose [is related to] misplace

The double colon [::] between the two pairs of words stands for the phrase "in the same way that." Here is how to read the complete analogy:

> FIND [is related to] LOCATE
> [in the same way that]
> lose [is related to] misplace

Here is another way:

> FIND is to LOCATE as lose is to misplace.

A properly constructed analogy, then, tells us that the relationship between the first pair of words is the same as the relationship between the second pair of words. In Example 1, *find* and *locate* are synonyms, just as *lose* and *misplace* are synonyms.

Let's look at another example:

Example 2   GIFT : JOY :: grief : tears

What is the relationship here? A *gift* causes *joy*, just as *grief* causes *tears*. These two pairs of words have the same relationship, a cause-and-effect relationship. The chart on page 156 will help you to identify analogy relationships. No chart could list all possible relationships between words, but the twelve relationships on the chart are the ones most often used. Also, they are the only relationships used in the analogy lessons.

TYPES OF ANALOGIES

RELATIONSHIP	EXAMPLE	EXPLANATION
Synonym	DRY : ARID :: find : locate	*Dry* is similar in meaning to *arid*, just as *find* is similar in meaning to *locate*.
Antonym	KIND : CRUEL :: find : lose	A *kind* action is the opposite of a *cruel* action, just as to *find* something is the opposite of to *lose* it.
Cause and Effect	GIFT : JOY :: rain : flood	A *gift* can cause *joy*, just as *rain* can cause a *flood*.
Part and Whole	CHAPTER : BOOK :: fender : automobile	A *chapter* is a part of a *book*, just as a *fender* is a part of an *automobile*.
Classification	POLKA : DANCE :: frog : amphibian	A *polka* may be classified as a *dance*, just as a *frog* may be classified as an *amphibian*.
Characteristic Quality	PUPPIES : FURRY :: fish : slippery	*Puppies* are *furry*, just as *fish* are *slippery*.
Degree	CHUCKLE : LAUGH :: whimper : cry	A *chuckle* is a little *laugh*, just as a *whimper* is a little *cry*.
Function	KNIFE : CUT :: pen : write	The function of a *knife* is to *cut*, just as the function of a *pen* is to *write*.
Performer and Action	AUTHOR : WRITE :: chef : cook	You expect an *author* to *write*, just as you expect a *chef* to *cook*.
Performer and Object	CASHIER : CASH :: plumber : pipe	A *cashier* works with *cash*, just as a *plumber* works with *pipe*.
Action and Object	BOIL : EGG :: throw : ball	You *boil* an *egg*, just as you *throw* a *ball*.
Location	FISH : SEA :: moose : forest	A *fish* can be found in the *sea*, just as a *moose* can be found in a *forest*.

A Process for Solving Analogies

Your job in solving multiple-choice analogy questions is to identify the relationship between the first two words and then to find the pair of words that has the most similar relationship. Keep in mind that a word pair has the same relationship no matter in which order the two words appear. For example, both CHAPTER : BOOK and BOOK : CHAPTER have a part-and-whole relationship. Here is a hint for identifying relationships. Try using word pairs in the explanation sentences on the chart. When a word pair makes sense in the explanation sentence for a particular relationship, you have found the relationship that the two words have to each other.

Here is a process that will help you with analogy questions:

Answering Analogy Questions: A 4-Step Method

1. Identify the relationship between the capitalized pair of words.
2. Identify the relationship between the pair of words in each possible answer.
3. Eliminate answer choices that have relationships that do not match the relationship between the capitalized words.
4. Choose the remaining possible answer. This answer will have the same relationship as the capitalized pair.

Let's apply this pattern to a sample question.

Example 3

WRITE : PEN :: __F__   [*Function*]

(A)	toe : foot __PW__	[*Part and Whole*—does not match]
(B)	toss : salad __AO__	[*Action and Object*—does not match]
(C)	gymnast : mat __PO__	[*Performer and Object*—does not match]
(D)	sky : blue __CQ__	[*Characteristic Quality*—does not match]
(E)	shine : sun __F__	[*Function*—does match]

None of relationships (A) through (D) match that of the capitalized pair. They can be eliminated. Choice E must be the correct answer. Notice that the words make sense in the explanation sentence: The function of a *pen* is to *write* just as the function of the *sun* is to *shine*.

A Final Word

Analogies are easier and more fun if you tackle them with a sense of adventure. Allow yourself to discover the relationship between the first pair of words and to explore the relationships between the words in the answer choices. Keep in mind that some words can represent more than one part of speech and that many words have several meanings. Remember, these little verbal puzzles call for flexibility as well as logic.

CONNECTING NEW WORDS AND PATTERNS

Lesson 1 ANALOGIES

Directions. On each line, write the letter or letters that describe the type of relationship the words have to each other. Choose from the following types:

S synonym	A antonym	PW part and whole	PA performer and action
F function	L location	CE cause and effect	PO performer and object
D degree	C classification	CQ characteristic quality	AO action and object

Circle the letter of the pair of words that has the same relationship as the capitalized words. Each relationship is used no more than once in each numbered item.

1. ABUSE : CRUEL :: _____
   (A) valuable : priceless _____
   (B) eraser : erase _____
   (C) bake : potato _____
   (D) shutter : camera _____
   (E) celebration : joyful _____

2. APPALLING : UPSETTING :: _____
   (A) sculptor : statue _____
   (B) fascinating : interesting _____
   (C) pineapple : fruit _____
   (D) criticism : disappointment _____
   (E) iceberg : sea _____

3. BAFFLE : CONFUSE :: _____
   (A) sweat : exercise _____
   (B) instrument : tuba _____
   (C) green : grass _____
   (D) attempt : try _____
   (E) pitcher : team _____

4. CALAMITY : DISTRESS :: _____
   (A) banker : money _____
   (B) orange : pumpkin _____
   (C) winning : happiness _____
   (D) grocer : sell _____
   (E) lawn : mow _____

5. DECEIVE : LIAR :: _____
   (A) speeding : dangerous _____
   (B) bound : free _____
   (C) coin : quarter _____
   (D) rescue : hero _____
   (E) pitch : throw _____

6. EPIDEMIC : FEAR :: _____
   (A) puzzle : confusion _____
   (B) baker : bread _____
   (C) rub : scrub _____
   (D) tool : hammer _____
   (E) slumber : sleep _____

7. KNOLL : MOUNTAIN :: _____
   (A) brook : fish _____
   (B) point : pen _____
   (C) ditch : canyon _____
   (D) disk : flat _____
   (E) bushes : trim _____

8. NOVELTY : INVENTOR :: _____
   (A) symphony : composer _____
   (B) space : satellite _____
   (C) programmer : type _____
   (D) oven : rack _____
   (E) improvement : practice _____

9. PROBABLE : UNLIKELY :: _____
   (A) bat : cave _____
   (B) thermometer : nurse _____
   (C) join : stapler _____
   (D) fruit : grape _____
   (E) sad : happy _____

10. RUTHLESS : MERCILESS :: _____
    (A) rule : king _____
    (B) famous : well-known _____
    (C) soft : pillow _____
    (D) rich : poor _____
    (E) praise : pride _____

Name _____ Date _____ Class _____

Lesson 2 | ANALOGIES

Directions. On each line, write the letter or letters that describe the type of relationship the words have to each other. Choose from the following types:

S synonym	A antonym	PW part and whole	PA performer and action
F function	L location	CE cause and effect	PO performer and object
D degree	C classification	CQ characteristic quality	AO action and object

Circle the letter of the pair of words that has the same relationship as the capitalized words. Each relationship is used no more than once in each numbered item.

1. ADVENT : ARRIVAL :: _____
   (A) old : ancient _____
   (B) compass : direct _____
   (C) football : sport _____
   (D) faithfulness : loyalty _____
   (E) lemon : yellow _____

2. AGGRESSIVE : BULLY :: _____
   (A) clip : cut _____
   (B) crime : fear _____
   (C) enrage : annoy _____
   (D) confident : expert _____
   (E) shelf : bookcase _____

3. CATASTROPHE : CONFUSION :: _____
   (A) potter : clay _____
   (B) death : sorrow _____
   (C) clear : cluttered _____
   (D) sleeve : dress _____
   (E) insect : ant _____

4. ECOLOGY : SCIENCE :: _____
   (A) canoe : lake _____
   (B) beverage : quench _____
   (C) gymnast : athletic _____
   (D) actor : script _____
   (E) algebra : mathematics _____

5. FEROCIOUS : GENTLE :: _____
   (A) pleased : dissatisfied _____
   (B) clerk : receipt _____
   (C) toss : ring _____
   (D) sprint : jog _____
   (E) dolphin : sea _____

6. MOTIVATE : DISCOURAGE :: _____
   (A) mix : blender _____
   (B) silk : smooth _____
   (C) puck : hockey player _____
   (D) warn : caution _____
   (E) tarnished : polished _____

7. NOURISH : FOOD :: _____
   (A) guitar : strum _____
   (B) surprised : shocked _____
   (C) instrument : guitar _____
   (D) protect : raincoat _____
   (E) receiver : telephone _____

8. PACIFY : PROVOKE :: _____
   (A) dog : poodle _____
   (B) producer : script _____
   (C) juggler : circus tent _____
   (D) warm : hot _____
   (E) refuse : accept _____

9. SANCTUARY : CHURCH :: _____
   (A) past : previous _____
   (B) hammer : pound _____
   (C) axle : truck _____
   (D) actor : perform _____
   (E) lilac : fragrant _____

10. STRATEGY : METHOD :: _____
    (A) boredom : yawning _____
    (B) intention : purpose _____
    (C) rehearse : actor _____
    (D) gem : emerald _____
    (E) snout : dog _____

CONNECTING NEW WORDS AND PATTERNS

Lesson 3 ANALOGIES

Directions. On each line, write the letter or letters that describe the type of relationship the words have to each other. Choose from the following types:

S synonym	A antonym	PW part and whole	PA performer and action
F function	L location	CE cause and effect	PO performer and object
D degree	C classification	CQ characteristic quality	AO action and object

Circle the letter of the pair of words that has the same relationship as the capitalized words. Each relationship is used no more than once in each numbered item.

1. ACCESSORY : BELT :: _____
   (A) shine : shoes _____
   (B) large : roomy _____
   (C) comedian : entertain _____
   (D) jewelry : bracelet _____
   (E) disagreement : tension _____

2. ARTISAN : POTTERY :: _____
   (A) square : shape _____
   (B) gain : lose _____
   (C) dampness : dew _____
   (D) trim : lawn _____
   (E) architect : blueprint _____

3. BADGER : ANIMAL :: _____
   (A) penguin : Antarctica _____
   (B) striped : zebra _____
   (C) honk : goose _____
   (D) granite : rock _____
   (E) conductor : baton _____

4. CALCULATION : MATH WHIZ :: _____
   (A) comment : remark _____
   (B) formula : chemist _____
   (C) mane : lion _____
   (D) breezy : windy _____
   (E) pride : praise _____

5. CUSTOMARY : UNUSUAL :: _____
   (A) hands : clock _____
   (B) thoughtful : inconsiderate _____
   (C) cut : scissors _____
   (D) fiddler : violin _____
   (E) ostrich : bird _____

6. FRAGILE : EGG :: _____
   (A) birth : celebration _____
   (B) release : capture _____
   (C) invent : create _____
   (D) accountant : calculator _____
   (E) dry : desert _____

7. GALLERY : PAINTING :: _____
   (A) blade : lawn mower _____
   (B) fan : breeze _____
   (C) tiny : small _____
   (D) studio : easel _____
   (E) flannel : warm _____

8. GLORIFY : DEGRADE :: _____
   (A) gold : shiny _____
   (B) desert : cactus _____
   (C) succeed : fail _____
   (D) derby : hat _____
   (E) heat : stove _____

9. MULTICOLORED : RAINBOW :: _____
   (A) shallow : deep _____
   (B) coal : underground _____
   (C) eyes : see _____
   (D) soft : pillow _____
   (E) horse : neigh _____

10. VITALITY : ENERGY :: _____
    (A) colorful : plaid _____
    (B) escape : prisoner _____
    (C) picture : take _____
    (D) beak : bird _____
    (E) sadness : sorrow _____

CONNECTING NEW WORDS AND PATTERNS

Lesson 4 · ANALOGIES

Directions. On each line, write the letter or letters that describe the type of relationship the words have to each other. Choose from the following types:

S synonym	A antonym	PW part and whole	PA performer and action
F function	L location	CE cause and effect	PO performer and object
D degree	C classification	CQ characteristic quality	AO action and object

Circle the letter of the pair of words that has the same relationship as the capitalized words. Each relationship is used no more than once in each numbered item.

1. ADEQUATE : EXCELLENT :: _____
   - (A) gap : opening _____
   - (B) artist : draw _____
   - (C) year : month _____
   - (D) paint : enamel _____
   - (E) tired : frazzled _____

2. DELEGATE : REPRESENT :: _____
   - (A) dog : fox terrier _____
   - (B) moment : brief _____
   - (C) actor : perform _____
   - (D) fence : separate _____
   - (E) exist : live _____

3. DESCEND : RISE :: _____
   - (A) clown : makeup _____
   - (B) delicate : flower _____
   - (C) tell : brag _____
   - (D) shove : pull _____
   - (E) minute : hour _____

4. DISCORD : HARMONY :: _____
   - (A) wheelchair : mobile _____
   - (B) mixer : stir _____
   - (C) war : peace _____
   - (D) boat : canoe _____
   - (E) apple : stem _____

5. ENHANCE : DECORATION :: _____
   - (A) ginger : spice _____
   - (B) deliver : mail _____
   - (C) enrich : fertilizer _____
   - (D) frantic : upset _____
   - (E) foul : penalty _____

6. FELINE : WHISKERS :: _____
   - (A) announcer : microphone _____
   - (B) sincere : honest _____
   - (C) kitten : paw _____
   - (D) telephone : answer _____
   - (E) metal : silver _____

7. INHERIT : HEIRESS :: _____
   - (A) beaten : defeated _____
   - (B) steal : thief _____
   - (C) shell : beach _____
   - (D) game : rules _____
   - (E) vinegar : sour _____

8. ISOLATION : LONELINESS :: _____
   - (A) captain : lead _____
   - (B) experience : confidence _____
   - (C) trunk : tree _____
   - (D) traffic light : street corner _____
   - (E) sailor : compass _____

9. MENACE : FRIGHTENING :: _____
   - (A) assist : help _____
   - (B) crime : offensive _____
   - (C) scold : praise _____
   - (D) blow : fan _____
   - (E) racket : tennis player _____

10. MENAGERIE : CAGED :: _____
    - (A) apart : separate _____
    - (B) crime : illegal _____
    - (C) wick : candle _____
    - (D) singer : tenor _____
    - (E) match : strike _____

CONNECTING NEW WORDS AND PATTERNS

Lesson 5 ANALOGIES

Directions. On each line, write the letter or letters that describe the type of relationship the words have to each other. Choose from the following types:

S synonym	A antonym	PW part and whole	PA performer and action
F function	L location	CE cause and effect	PO performer and object
D degree	C classification	CQ characteristic quality	AO action and object

Circle the letter of the pair of words that has the same relationship as the capitalized words. Each relationship is used no more than once in each numbered item.

1. ADAPT : MODIFY :: _____
   (A) thoughtful : considerate _____
   (B) library : quiet _____
   (C) pencil : sharpen _____
   (D) writer : notebook _____
   (E) drowsiness : nap _____

2. BASIS : FOUNDATION :: _____
   (A) slippers : comfortable _____
   (B) automobile : transport _____
   (C) door : cabinet _____
   (D) delay : prevent _____
   (E) sign : indication _____

3. CONSECUTIVE : INTERRUPTED :: _____
   (A) skim : read _____
   (B) slack : loose _____
   (C) teeth : crocodile _____
   (D) lamp : living room _____
   (E) fresh : stale _____

4. CONTROVERSY : DISPUTE :: _____
   (A) sleeper : snore _____
   (B) soft : cushion _____
   (C) compose : song _____
   (D) promise : pledge _____
   (E) turtle : reptile _____

5. CREATIVE : ARTIST :: _____
   (A) dentist : teeth _____
   (B) germ : illness _____
   (C) idle : inactive _____
   (D) scientific : chemist _____
   (E) palm : tropics _____

6. DURABLE : LEATHER :: _____
   (A) brim : hat _____
   (B) hear : ears _____
   (C) keep : secret _____
   (D) ocean : octopus _____
   (E) gritty : sand _____

7. HILARIOUS : FUNNY :: _____
   (A) police officer : arrest _____
   (B) lighthearted : gloomy _____
   (C) toes : feet _____
   (D) nasty : unpleasant _____
   (E) pain : sunburn _____

8. IMMENSE : LARGE :: _____
   (A) architect : blueprint _____
   (B) snake : hole _____
   (C) frantic : nervous _____
   (D) awkward : clumsy _____
   (E) eagle : bird _____

9. INGENIOUS : INVENTOR :: _____
   (A) lampshade : lamp _____
   (B) artist : draw _____
   (C) antlers : protect _____
   (D) curious : monkey _____
   (E) microscope : biologist _____

10. PRIMITIVE : CRUDE :: _____
   (A) bell : telephone _____
   (B) orchid : jungle _____
   (C) guitarist : strum _____
   (D) complex : complicated _____
   (E) skunk : animal _____

CONNECTING NEW WORDS AND PATTERNS

Lesson 6 | ANALOGIES

Directions. On each line, write the letter or letters that describe the type of relationship the words have to each other. Choose from the following types:

S synonym	A antonym	PW part and whole	PA performer and action
F function	L location	CE cause and effect	PO performer and object
D degree	C classification	CQ characteristic quality	AO action and object

Circle the letter of the pair of words that has the same relationship as the capitalized words. Each relationship is used no more than once in each numbered item.

1. ARISTOCRAT : PRINCESS :: _____
   (A) unlock : door _____
   (B) outdoors : inside _____
   (C) pilot : fly _____
   (D) vessel : sailboat _____
   (E) stick : lollipop _____

2. BURLY : FOOTBALL PLAYER :: _____
   (A) graceful : ballet dancer _____
   (B) plead : beg _____
   (C) science : forestry _____
   (D) trot : horse _____
   (E) entertain : movie _____

3. DECADE : YEAR :: _____
   (A) house : roof _____
   (B) partially : entirely _____
   (C) loneliness : sadness _____
   (D) sandals : footwear _____
   (E) instructor : explain _____

4. FAMINE : WAR :: _____
   (A) forbid : allow _____
   (B) colorful : parrot _____
   (C) sculpture : museum _____
   (D) destruction : hurricane _____
   (E) tap : push _____

5. MALNUTRITION : DEATH :: _____
   (A) bore : hole _____
   (B) kitchen : kettle _____
   (C) monarch : rule _____
   (D) fever : sweating _____
   (E) hold : release _____

6. MULTITUDE : CROWD :: _____
   (A) turn : key _____
   (B) chef : pan _____
   (C) ceremony : service _____
   (D) metal : iron _____
   (E) genius : intelligent _____

7. PROPAGANDA : PERSUADE :: _____
   (A) plow : tool _____
   (B) outburst : attention _____
   (C) knee : leg _____
   (D) computer : office _____
   (E) newspaper : inform _____

8. REFUGE : SAFE :: _____
   (A) anchor : heavy _____
   (B) sack : bag _____
   (C) weave : loom _____
   (D) fountain : park _____
   (E) drizzle : downpour _____

9. RESOLUTE : DETERMINED :: _____
   (A) fat : thin _____
   (B) fruit : plum _____
   (C) playwright : script _____
   (D) steady : regular _____
   (E) irrigate : soil _____

10. URBAN : RURAL :: _____
    (A) hive : bee _____
    (B) child : tricycle _____
    (C) firm : unsteady _____
    (D) game : baseball _____
    (E) claws : defend _____

CONNECTING NEW WORDS AND PATTERNS

Lesson 7 | ANALOGIES

Directions. On each line, write the letter or letters that describe the type of relationship the words have to each other. Choose from the following types:

S synonym   A antonym   PW part and whole   PA performer and action
F function   L location   CE cause and effect   PO performer and object
D degree   C classification   CQ characteristic quality   AO action and object

Circle the letter of the pair of words that has the same relationship as the capitalized words. Each relationship is used no more than once in each numbered item.

1. ACCESSIBLE : UNOBTAINABLE :: _____
    (A) cat : pounce _____
    (B) mast : sailboat _____
    (C) shout : whisper _____
    (D) ball : juggler _____
    (E) lieutenant : officer _____

2. BANKRUPT : RICH :: _____
    (A) torn : mended _____
    (B) luxurious : comfortable _____
    (C) limestone : rock _____
    (D) supermarket : groceries _____
    (E) puddle : muddy _____

3. BOISTEROUS : CALM:: _____
    (A) violent : peaceful _____
    (B) thief : steal _____
    (C) mix : cement _____
    (D) hour : second _____
    (E) sculptor : clay _____

4. DILAPIDATED : OLD RUINS :: _____
    (A) parking lot : car _____
    (B) glee : sadness _____
    (C) harmonica : instrument _____
    (D) towel : absorb _____
    (E) dangerous : parachuting _____

5. FRAUDULENT : EMBEZZLER :: _____
    (A) post office : letter _____
    (B) stingy : miser _____
    (C) buzz : bee _____
    (D) comrade : enemy _____
    (E) tag : game _____

6. GRIEVE : MOURN :: _____
    (A) haul : carry _____
    (B) cyclone : damage _____
    (C) party : celebrate _____
    (D) brush : hair _____
    (E) vitamins : healthful _____

7. HOSPITABLE : CIVIL :: _____
    (A) search : peek _____
    (B) dishonest : burglar _____
    (C) sport : bowling _____
    (D) worry : stress _____
    (E) air : breathe _____

8. JUBILATION : VICTORY :: _____
    (A) needle : tailor _____
    (B) scream : yell _____
    (C) leap : deer _____
    (D) sadness : loss _____
    (E) train : transport _____

9. RIOTOUS : LIVELY :: _____
    (A) veterinarian : vaccine _____
    (B) unhappiness : pouting _____
    (C) shudder : quiver _____
    (D) duck : migrate _____
    (E) greeting : farewell _____

10. TRANSIT : PASSAGE :: _____
    (A) winner : boast _____
    (B) faithful : disloyal _____
    (C) ripe : mature _____
    (D) looking : glaring _____
    (E) cliff : steep _____

CONNECTING NEW WORDS AND PATTERNS

Lesson 8 | ANALOGIES

Directions. On each line, write the letter or letters that describe the type of relationship the words have to each other. Choose from the following types:

S synonym	A antonym	PW part and whole	PA performer and action
F function	L location	CE cause and effect	PO performer and object
D degree	C classification	CQ characteristic quality	AO action and object

Circle the letter of the pair of words that has the same relationship as the capitalized words. Each relationship is used no more than once in each numbered item.

1. DISSECT : BIOLOGIST :: ____
   (A) teach : professor ____
   (B) exercise : strengthen ____
   (C) honest : truthful ____
   (D) dribble : basketball ____
   (E) success : jealousy ____

2. HAVEN : SAFE :: ____
   (A) leg : chair ____
   (B) love : hate ____
   (C) delighted : satisfied ____
   (D) farmer : tractor ____
   (E) treasure : valuable ____

3. HAMPER : HELP :: ____
   (A) England : country ____
   (B) moose : Canada ____
   (C) ignore : disregard ____
   (D) criticize : praise ____
   (E) dog : howl ____

4. HUMIDITY : DAMP :: ____
   (A) cold : cool ____
   (B) wagonload : haul ____
   (C) sleet : cold ____
   (D) desk : office ____
   (E) flour : cake ____

5. INCONSIDERATE : SELFISH :: ____
   (A) fasting : hunger ____
   (B) evil : wicked ____
   (C) vegetable : carrot ____
   (D) keyboard : computer ____
   (E) feathered : duck ____

6. MEMENTO : REMIND :: ____
   (A) helicopter : police officer ____
   (B) heel : foot ____
   (C) pouring : dripping ____
   (D) exploration : discover ____
   (E) heavy : rhinoceros ____

7. RECUPERATE : PATIENT :: ____
   (A) lobster : shellfish ____
   (B) examine : physician ____
   (C) evil : bad ____
   (D) petal : flower ____
   (E) boredom : restlessness ____

8. RESTRAIN : SEAT BELT :: ____
   (A) clutch : hold ____
   (B) lend : borrow ____
   (C) limb : tree ____
   (D) hold : reservoir ____
   (E) loafer : lazy ____

9. SPACIOUS : MANSION :: ____
   (A) bake : bread ____
   (B) salty : sea ____
   (C) train : locomotive ____
   (D) strong : powerful ____
   (E) chef : chop ____

10. TUMULT : UPROAR :: ____
    (A) trunk : attic ____
    (B) tanned : sunburned ____
    (C) feather : light ____
    (D) locker : store ____
    (E) confusion : disorder ____

CONNECTING NEW WORDS AND PATTERNS

Lesson 9 | ANALOGIES

Directions. On each line, write the letter or letters that describe the type of relationship the words have to each other. Choose from the following types:

S synonym	A antonym	PW part and whole	PA performer and action
F function	L location	CE cause and effect	PO performer and object
D degree	C classification	CQ characteristic quality	AO action and object

Circle the letter of the pair of words that has the same relationship as the capitalized words. Each relationship is used no more than once in each numbered item.

1. AROMA : BAKING :: _____
   - (A) wash : dishes _____
   - (B) hat : protect _____
   - (C) accident : speeding _____
   - (D) chef : recipe _____
   - (E) car : vehicle _____

2. BASTE : TURKEY :: _____
   - (A) soldier : defend _____
   - (B) trim : tree _____
   - (C) cruelty : suffering _____
   - (D) forest : owl _____
   - (E) black : crow _____

3. CAPITAL : INVESTOR :: _____
   - (A) fishing : sport _____
   - (B) thirst : salty food _____
   - (C) land : realtor _____
   - (D) underground : oil _____
   - (E) teeth : saw _____

4. ELEGANT : CRUDE :: _____
   - (A) exchange : trade _____
   - (B) publication : magazine _____
   - (C) pond : turtle _____
   - (D) engine : carburetor _____
   - (E) serious : amusing _____

5. HAUGHTY : FRIENDLY :: _____
   - (A) pouring : drizzling _____
   - (B) transport : airplane _____
   - (C) paint : mix _____
   - (D) wealthy : poor _____
   - (E) striped : skunk _____

6. OCCUPANT : RESIDENT :: _____
   - (A) poem : line _____
   - (B) nail : join _____
   - (C) flower : daisy _____
   - (D) scrape : gash _____
   - (E) shrub : bush _____

7. REMOTE : DISTANT :: _____
   - (A) hard : difficult _____
   - (B) reptile : snake _____
   - (C) clean : scour _____
   - (D) driver : license _____
   - (E) egg : nest _____

8. RIGID : FLEXIBLE :: _____
   - (A) baby : bottle _____
   - (B) damaged : repaired _____
   - (C) water : seedling _____
   - (D) advisor : suggest _____
   - (E) song : concert _____

9. SEDATE : ROWDY :: _____
   - (A) protect : endanger _____
   - (B) automobile : horn _____
   - (C) delays : impatience _____
   - (D) lunch : meal _____
   - (E) sprint : run _____

10. SATURATE : MOISTEN :: _____
    - (A) wool : warm _____
    - (B) elephant : jungle _____
    - (C) pour : sprinkle _____
    - (D) bass : fish _____
    - (E) marry : wed _____

CONNECTING NEW WORDS AND PATTERNS

Lesson 10 ANALOGIES

Directions. On each line, write the letter or letters that describe the type of relationship the words have to each other. Choose from the following types:

S synonym   A antonym   PW part and whole   PA performer and action
F function   L location   CE cause and effect   PO performer and object
D degree   C classification   CQ characteristic quality   AO action and object

Circle the letter of the pair of words that has the same relationship as the capitalized words. Each relationship is used no more than once in each numbered item.

1. DINGY : SHABBY :: _____
   (A) chess : game _____
   (B) blame : forgive _____
   (C) joke : amuse _____
   (D) private : personal _____
   (E) wall : fort _____

2. DISAGREEABLE : HORRIBLE :: _____
   (A) repair expert : fix _____
   (B) entrance : exit _____
   (C) difficult : impossible _____
   (D) sticky : tape _____
   (E) window : house _____

3. EVACUATE : BUILDING :: _____
   (A) hasty : speedy _____
   (B) separate : join _____
   (C) entertain : crowd _____
   (D) otter : lake _____
   (E) millionaire : wealthy _____

4. HUMILIATE : FLATTER :: _____
   (A) quail : prairie _____
   (B) criticize : compliment _____
   (C) introduction : essay _____
   (D) swimmer : goggles _____
   (E) hurt : harm _____

5. LIBERATE : CAPTURE :: _____
   (A) feed : starve _____
   (B) burn : heat _____
   (C) marshy : swampy _____
   (D) answer : telephone _____
   (E) tusk : elephant _____

6. MAROON : COLOR :: _____
   (A) fly : kite _____
   (B) alarm clock : wake _____
   (C) pigeon : plaza _____
   (D) diamond : gem _____
   (E) knuckle : finger _____

7. NOTIFY : INFORM :: _____
   (A) scarf : outfit _____
   (B) unhappy : miserable _____
   (C) pupil : eraser _____
   (D) misconduct : punishment _____
   (E) fasten : attach _____

8. REMORSE : WRONGDOING :: _____
   (A) scarecrow : frighten _____
   (B) toss : ball _____
   (C) forgiveness : apology _____
   (D) cuff : shirt _____
   (E) refugee : flee _____

9. THRIFTY : MISERLY :: _____
   (A) wipe : napkin _____
   (B) pink : flamingo _____
   (C) joke : laughter _____
   (D) mischievous : wicked _____
   (E) sport : diving _____

10. VERIFY : WITNESS :: _____
    (A) athlete : play _____
    (B) salt : white _____
    (C) breakfast : meal _____
    (D) note : melody _____
    (E) hay : stable _____

CONNECTING NEW WORDS AND PATTERNS

Lesson 11 ANALOGIES

Directions. On each line, write the letter or letters that describe the type of relationship the words have to each other. Choose from the following types:

S synonym	A antonym	PW part and whole	PA performer and action
F function	L location	CE cause and effect	PO performer and object
D degree	C classification	CQ characteristic quality	AO action and object

Circle the letter of the pair of words that has the same relationship as the capitalized words. Each relationship is used no more than once in each numbered item.

1. ASPIRATION : AMBITION :: _____
   - (A) letter : communicate _____
   - (B) wish : desire _____
   - (C) whistle : shrill _____
   - (D) attack : fort _____
   - (E) cricket : insect _____

2. CONFISCATE : WEAPON :: _____
   - (A) rob : bank _____
   - (B) car : fender _____
   - (C) counselor : advise _____
   - (D) cave : dark _____
   - (E) tree frog : jungle _____

3. DIPLOMAT : REPRESENT :: _____
   - (A) gap : opening _____
   - (B) captain : lead _____
   - (C) tuba player : band _____
   - (D) octagon : shape _____
   - (E) enter : invade _____

4. FOREWORD : INTRODUCE :: _____
   - (A) conclusion : summarize _____
   - (B) light : dark _____
   - (C) inch : foot _____
   - (D) sea : shrimp _____
   - (E) punctuate : sentence _____

5. GENERATE : PRODUCE :: _____
   - (A) firefly : wings _____
   - (B) illustrator : draw _____
   - (C) sick : healthy _____
   - (D) dalmatian : spotted _____
   - (E) contribute : give _____

6. OBSCURE : CLEAR :: _____
   - (A) bagpipes : Scotland _____
   - (B) cyclone : storm _____
   - (C) private : public _____
   - (D) polite : courteous _____
   - (E) dentist : cavity _____

7. PEWTER : GRAY :: _____
   - (A) allergy : sneeze _____
   - (B) lemon : sour _____
   - (C) folks : people _____
   - (D) following : leading _____
   - (E) money : bank teller _____

8. QUENCH : BEVERAGE :: _____
   - (A) absorb : sponge _____
   - (B) spinach : vegetable _____
   - (C) dainty : lace _____
   - (D) painter : ladder _____
   - (E) dessert : meal _____

9. SABLE : MAMMAL :: _____
   - (A) shy : bashful _____
   - (B) infection : fever _____
   - (C) write : book _____
   - (D) maple : tree _____
   - (E) bird : sing _____

10. SALUTATION : LETTER :: _____
    - (A) trunk : tree _____
    - (B) deed : act _____
    - (C) optometrist : glasses _____
    - (D) striped : zebra _____
    - (E) take : seize _____

CONNECTING NEW WORDS AND PATTERNS

Lesson 12 ANALOGIES

Directions. On each line, write the letter or letters that describe the type of relationship the words have to each other. Choose from the following types:

S synonym	A antonym	PW part and whole	PA performer and action
F function	L location	CE cause and effect	PO performer and object
D degree	C classification	CQ characteristic quality	AO action and object

Circle the letter of the pair of words that has the same relationship as the capitalized words. Each relationship is used no more than once in each numbered item.

1. CHARITABLE : STINGY :: _____
   (A) stubborn : flexible _____
   (B) lean : thin _____
   (C) mirror : breakable _____
   (D) scale : weigh _____
   (E) city : village _____

2. COLOSSAL : LARGE :: _____
   (A) roaming : wandering _____
   (B) senator : politician _____
   (C) pound : nail _____
   (D) surgeon : gloves _____
   (E) demand : suggest _____

3. CONFIDE : SECRET :: _____
   (A) measure : ruler _____
   (B) cups : cupboard _____
   (C) watermelon : pink _____
   (D) tell : tale _____
   (E) shade : lamp _____

4. ESSAY : CONCLUSION :: _____
   (A) spider : spin _____
   (B) quartz : rock _____
   (C) textbook : chapter _____
   (D) wrinkled : smooth _____
   (E) wobbly : unsteady _____

5. IRK : IRRITATE :: _____
   (A) satin : fabric _____
   (B) build : construct _____
   (C) effort : accomplishment _____
   (D) cluttered : tidy _____
   (E) win : lottery _____

6. PETTY : IMPORTANT :: _____
   (A) bee : wax _____
   (B) pattern : design _____
   (C) grapes : vineyard _____
   (D) innocent : guilty _____
   (E) snail : slow _____

7. PIOUS : BELIEVER :: _____
   (A) student : lunch box _____
   (B) pond : goldfish _____
   (C) looking glass : mirror _____
   (D) carry : books _____
   (E) talented : artist _____

8. SUMMIT : MOUNTAIN :: _____
   (A) watchdog : bark _____
   (B) swings : park _____
   (C) mouth : river _____
   (D) whole : broken _____
   (E) weaver : cloth _____

9. TARNISH : DISGRACE :: _____
   (A) need : require _____
   (B) perspiration : exercise _____
   (C) instrument : cello _____
   (D) florist : vase _____
   (E) leg : body _____

10. TEMPERAMENT : MANNER :: _____
    (A) athlete : train _____
    (B) region : area _____
    (C) eel : slippery _____
    (D) prehistoric : old _____
    (E) flower : bouquet _____

CONNECTING NEW WORDS AND PATTERNS

Lesson 13 ANALOGIES

Directions. On each line, write the letter or letters that describe the type of relationship the words have to each other. Choose from the following types:

S synonym   A antonym   PW part and whole   PA performer and action
F function   L location   CE cause and effect   PO performer and object
D degree   C classification   CQ characteristic quality   AO action and object

Circle the letter of the pair of words that has the same relationship as the capitalized words. Each relationship is used no more than once in each numbered item.

1. CASUAL : INFORMAL :: _____
   (A) tunnel : dark _____
   (B) photographer : lens _____
   (C) regular : ordinary _____
   (D) water filter : purify _____
   (E) damaged : ruined _____

2. CONDEMN : BUILDING :: _____
   (A) sign : contract _____
   (B) spin : twirl _____
   (C) minnow : fish _____
   (D) hen : cluck _____
   (E) fade : brighten _____

3. DISPATCH : AMBULANCE :: _____
   (A) anger : argument _____
   (B) hurry : rush _____
   (C) comet : space _____
   (D) piece : pie _____
   (E) send : telegram _____

4. EMPHASIZE : STRESS :: _____
   (A) almond : nut _____
   (B) dolphin : swim _____
   (C) tall : ostrich _____
   (D) mice : barn _____
   (E) realize : understand _____

5. ENDORSE : CHECK :: _____
   (A) teacher : faculty _____
   (B) child : pretend _____
   (C) gelatin : wobbly _____
   (D) raise : taxes _____
   (E) mean : merciless _____

6. FAMISHED : HUNGRY :: _____
   (A) skinny : slim _____
   (B) yellow : daffodil _____
   (C) juror : courtroom _____
   (D) helicopter : aircraft _____
   (E) always : never _____

7. FICTITIOUS : REAL :: _____
   (A) quarterback : team _____
   (B) florist : deliver _____
   (C) shake : hand _____
   (D) taste : eat _____
   (E) worried : unconcerned _____

8. FRAGMENT : INCOMPLETE :: _____
   (A) reckless : careful _____
   (B) load : camera _____
   (C) crumb : cookie _____
   (D) chrome : shiny _____
   (E) tension : headache _____

9. IMPROVISE : ACTOR :: _____
   (A) alligator : swamp _____
   (B) recite : poet _____
   (C) instructions : directions _____
   (D) lullaby : song _____
   (E) nozzle : hose _____

10. MODIFY : ALTER :: _____
    (A) car : roller coaster _____
    (B) teacher : computer _____
    (C) earn : medal _____
    (D) copy : imitate _____
    (E) chilly : freezing _____

CONNECTING NEW WORDS AND PATTERNS

Lesson 14 | ANALOGIES

Directions. On each line, write the letter or letters that describe the type of relationship the words have to each other. Choose from the following types:

S synonym	A antonym	PW part and whole	PA performer and action
F function	L location	CE cause and effect	PO performer and object
D degree	C classification	CQ characteristic quality	AO action and object

Circle the letter of the pair of words that has the same relationship as the capitalized words. Each relationship is used no more than once in each numbered item.

1. BRAGGART : BOAST :: ____
   (A) insect : ant ____
   (B) perform : musician ____
   (C) clothing : closet ____
   (D) rose : fragrant ____
   (E) suggest : insist ____

2. DEMOLISH : DAMAGE :: ____
   (A) attorney : courtroom ____
   (B) trespassing : illegal ____
   (C) accomplishment : satisfaction ____
   (D) wing : bird ____
   (E) recover : improve ____

3. DENIAL : ACCEPTANCE :: ____
   (A) helmet : protect ____
   (B) strut : rooster ____
   (C) encouragement : disapproval ____
   (D) stinger : wasp ____
   (E) convict : prison ____

4. DETACH : DISCONNECT :: ____
   (A) dripping : streaming ____
   (B) conductor : ticket ____
   (C) pajamas : comfortable ____
   (D) mend : repair ____
   (E) law : profession ____

5. ELIGIBLE : QUALIFIED :: ____
   (A) ready : prepared ____
   (B) disgusted : delighted ____
   (C) toys : nursery ____
   (D) enraged : annoyed ____
   (E) strawberry : fruit ____

6. ILLUMINATE : LANTERN :: ____
   (A) stub : toe ____
   (B) chill : refrigerator ____
   (C) strict : lenient ____
   (D) eye : iris ____
   (E) ice : slippery ____

7. SECLUDED : PUBLIC :: ____
   (A) inspector : examine ____
   (B) star : night sky ____
   (C) dig : spade ____
   (D) mask : diver ____
   (E) deserted : crowded ____

8. SUPERFICIAL : SCRAPE :: ____
   (A) deep : gash ____
   (B) ship : ocean ____
   (C) handle : tea kettle ____
   (D) frog : croak ____
   (E) snapshot : remind ____

9. TANGIBLE : TOUCHABLE :: ____
   (A) tourist : luggage ____
   (B) odd : strange ____
   (C) crisis : stress ____
   (D) operate : surgeon ____
   (E) open : package ____

10. TESTIFY : WITNESS :: ____
    (A) sticky : glue ____
    (B) spend : shopper ____
    (C) orchard : cultivate ____
    (D) tap : pound ____
    (E) flute : instrument ____

Name _____ Date _____ Class _____

CONNECTING NEW WORDS AND PATTERNS

Lesson 15 ANALOGIES

Directions. On each line, write the letter or letters that describe the type of relationship the words have to each other. Choose from the following types:

S synonym	A antonym	PW part and whole	PA performer and action
F function	L location	CE cause and effect	PO performer and object
D degree	C classification	CQ characteristic quality	AO action and object

Circle the letter of the pair of words that has the same relationship as the capitalized words. Each relationship is used no more than once in each numbered item.

1. ANTIBIOTICS : FIGHT :: _____
   (A) waiting : impatience _____
   (B) stretcher : rescuer _____
   (C) ordinary : unusual _____
   (D) red : strawberry _____
   (E) vaccinations : protect _____

2. AUTOMATON : ROBOT :: _____
   (A) bureau : dresser _____
   (B) kickstand : support _____
   (C) signer : signature _____
   (D) robin : bird _____
   (E) page : book _____

3. CONGEST : CLOG :: _____
   (A) genuine : fake _____
   (B) employ : hire _____
   (C) grove : forest _____
   (D) old : antiques _____
   (E) member : organization _____

4. HYPOTHESIS : UNPROVEN :: _____
   (A) horse : hay _____
   (B) sloppy : neat _____
   (C) nostril : nose _____
   (D) lie : untrue _____
   (E) direct : administrator _____

5. PARASITIC : INDEPENDENT :: _____
   (A) sea : starfish _____
   (B) kill : insecticide _____
   (C) damaged : perfect _____
   (D) alley : narrow _____
   (E) strayed : wandered _____

6. PHOTOGENIC :
   FASHION MODEL :: _____
   (A) journalist : newspaper _____
   (B) limb : body _____
   (C) climb : ladder _____
   (D) strong : steel _____
   (E) sight : sense _____

7. PLANETARIUM : BUILDING :: _____
   (A) mound : hill _____
   (B) orange : fruit _____
   (C) baker : bread _____
   (D) yellow : lemon _____
   (E) headboard : bed _____

8. RESPIRATION : BREATHING :: _____
   (A) count : teller _____
   (B) movie : theater _____
   (C) sharp : nail _____
   (D) clean : wound _____
   (E) exchange : trade _____

9. SYNTHETIC : NATURAL :: _____
   (A) commentator : speak _____
   (B) ill : healthy _____
   (C) metal : gold _____
   (D) fire : carelessness _____
   (E) wing : airplane _____

10. WARRANTY : ASSURE :: _____
    (A) investigation : solve _____
    (B) pouch : bag _____
    (C) squirrel : scamper _____
    (D) wrap : gift _____
    (E) soothing : breeze _____

READING NEW WORDS IN CONTEXT

Why We Read Strategically

Reading is active. As you read, you step into the writer's world. When you come across a new idea, you usually look for a clue to help you determine the writer's meaning. You move ahead to see if the idea is explained, or you retrace your steps to look for any signs you missed.

You can use these same strategies to build your vocabulary. If you do not know the meaning of a word, you should look in the passage surrounding the word for hints. These hints are called context clues. The more you practice hunting for context clues, the better you become at reading new words, and the larger your vocabulary will grow. Remember, strengthening your vocabulary skills will help you to score higher on standardized vocabulary tests.

The following reading selection shows the kinds of context clues you will find in the Reading New Words in Context lessons.

Strategic Reading: An Example

Long, long ago, long before there were humans on Earth—much less humans who could record history—dinosaurs walked the earth. During these **prehistoric** times, strange and wonderful creatures ruled the entire earth. All in all, *this* **reign** lasted 135 million years.

The dinosaur was one **descendant** of the thecodonts, mighty reptiles whose *later generations* also included many other reptiles, as well as all of today's birds. One of these relatives was a huge flying reptile. Another was a creature with a body like that of a turtle but with a 25-foot-long neck. Like the dinosaurs, these unusual *and* **extraordinary** creatures became extinct. Any of these creatures has the power to *stun,* **astonish,** *and amaze* us, but it is the dinosaurs that most people find especially fascinating.

Some dinosaurs were **mammoth** creatures. *The euhelopus, for example, was 60 feet tall and weighed 50,000 pounds.* In contrast, the 20-foot, 7,000-pound stegosaurus seems almost small. Although enormous size *was* a **characteristic** of many dinosaurs, others were much, much smaller, no bigger than a chicken or a duck. Some of these smaller ones looked much like either the iguana or the komodo dragon, two reptiles that inhabit Earth today.

Note that a *summary* indicates the meaning of **prehistoric**.

A *pronoun* (*this*) refers us to the meaning of **reign**.
The meaning of **descendant** is made clear through *restatement,* that is, through saying the same thing in a different way.

A *coordinating conjunction* (*and*) provides a clue to the meaning of **extraordinary**. The words *but, or,* and *nor* are other coordinating conjunctions.
Note that a clue to the meaning of **astonish** is provided by using the word in a *series* of words that have similar meanings.
An *example* provides the key to understanding **mammoth**.

A form of the verb *to be* (*was*) links an example of a quality to the word **characteristic**.

Some of the dinosaurs were fierce, meat-eating creatures. Often, other *milder and gentler dinosaurs were unable to defend themselves from the more savage ones and thus became their* **victims**. Even the vegetarian dinosaurs who roamed about peacefully snacking on plants could be quite frightening to other species that shared the planet. A 55-ton brachiosaurus lumbering across the countryside would have presented a real **threat,** *a clear danger,* to any unsuspecting creature who got in its way. The huge Triceratops had frightening horns on its nose and over both of its eyes. The sight of this 10-ton animal bounding along at 30 miles per hour certainly scared the newly emerging mammals that had to scurry out of its way. Nevertheless, it was also a threat to any other dinosaur that tried to attack it.

Although groups of dinosaurs might be in **competition** with each other, *cooperation within a group was also common.* Members of a species might travel in a herd, eat and nest together, share responsibility for the young, and present a united defense against enemies.

Scientists are still debating about why the dinosaurs disappeared. We do not know for sure. All we know is that **twilight** *arrived for these creatures at the same time all across the earth. Then, in a twinkling, it was night,* and the dinosaurs were gone.

In a *cause-and-effect* relationship, one thing causes another thing to happen. The meaning of **victims** is established through a cause-and-effect relationship. *Thus* is a cause-and-effect clue word.

An *appositive phrase* contains a noun or pronoun that explains the noun or pronoun beside it. An appositive phrase indicates the meaning of **threat**.

Note that the meaning of **competition** is established through *contrast,* the placement of opposites near each other to point out their difference. The word *although* indicates contrast.

The meaning of **twilight** is established through *figurative language.* Figurative language is language that imaginatively describes one thing by comparing it to something else.

A Final Note

How can you learn strategic reading? Practice is a great way to improve your skill. The following lessons will help you learn the different context clues a writer uses. As you complete each lesson, you will become a more effective reader.

READING NEW WORDS IN CONTEXT

Lesson 1 **CONTEXT:** Coming to the United States

Introduction. We know with certainty that Columbus came to North America in 1492. We also know that the Vikings first came to North America on or around A.D. 1000. However, the date that the very first people set foot on the North American continent is hotly debated. Guesses differ by as much as sixty thousand years. What we do know is that the first Americans arrived a very long time ago.

The following article gives you an opportunity to read about the first Americans and their encounters with Europeans. It also gives you an opportunity to expand your vocabulary. Below are twenty Vocabulary Words that are used in the article and in the exercise that follows it.

abuse	bewilder	eminent	knoll	probable
appalling	calamity	epidemic	myriad	romantic
baffle	contagious	folklore	novelty	ruthless
barbarism	deceive	intentional	picturesque	sincerity

North America Meets Europe

Some scientists believe that human beings first began to call North America home twelve thousand years ago. Others believe that twenty-five thousand years is a more likely guess. Still others say that it is most **probable** (1) that people began to arrive here thirty thousand years ago. In any case, the continent has been home to **myriad** (2) groups of people for thousands of years. No one knows for sure exactly how many different groups lived here before the Europeans came five hundred years ago, but the groups numbered well into the hundreds.

Some of the First Americans
Long before Europeans began to arrive, people in the Arctic reaches of the continent traveled by dog sled and kayak. Far to the south, the Anasazi built multilevel cliff dwellings and irrigated their crops. In the southeast, the Choctaw made textiles and buried their dead in elaborate mounds. Many of these **knolls** (3)

are still visible today. In the northeast, the Hurons built stockades and farmed the land. In the continent's heartland, the peoples of the plains grew crops, traded, and hunted bison.

The idea that Christopher Columbus or the Vikings somehow discovered a new world **baffles** (4) many people. Such a one-sided view of history confuses them. Today, we realize that people had discovered the Americas thousands and thousands of years before either the Vikings' or Columbus's arrival.

Some of the First Americans
The original inhabitants were sometimes confused and **bewildered** (5) by the Europeans' strange ways, but they could not know that the arrival of the Europeans would be a **calamity** (6) for them. European weapons and diseases soon began to destroy the native people. Thousands were killed by violence and disease, and entire cultures were

wiped out. The **abuse** (7) began almost as soon as Columbus set foot in the Americas.

Destructive Policies

Throughout the Americas, the original inhabitants were the victims of **ruthless** (8) policies. They were forced into slavery; they were killed if they did not convert to Christianity; and they lost their lives in wars. These terrible events are **appalling** (9) to historians.

Not all of the suffering caused by the Europeans was **intentional** (10). Some of it was accidental. For example, many American Indians died as a result of **contagious** (11) diseases. They had never been exposed to mumps or measles or other illnesses that the Europeans brought with them. As a result, some diseases reached **epidemic** (12) proportions, wiping out entire communities.

Unfortunately, Europeans often approached American Indians without **sincerity** (13), or good faith. Too often, acts of friendship were designed to **deceive** (14). The European Americans often gained the American Indians' trust in order to betray it. In fact, the story of the relationship between European Americans and American Indians is one of the saddest in U.S. history. The **folklore** (15) that North America's native peoples have passed down from generation to generation reflects this fact. Many American Indians tell tales of the conquerors who came from across the sea and changed forever the native peoples' way of life.

Understanding Cultural Differences

While some Europeans respected the cultures they encountered, many did not. They thought that anyone who did not live the way they did must be a savage. As a result, they considered customs of the American Indians to be **barbarisms** (16).

Of course, not all Europeans were so blind. Many respected the native cultures. Some were simply curious about a culture they thought was **picturesque** (17). They were interested in a way of life that seemed charming and pleasant. Others were interested in **novelty** (18), in exploring what was, to them, strange, different, and new. These Europeans had a **romantic** (19) notion of American Indians. They weren't really interested in the realities or difficulties of their daily lives. However, some Europeans understood American Indian cultures' **eminent** (20) worth. They recognized these cultures as remarkable and noteworthy.

EXERCISE *Reading Strategically* 👉

Directions. Answer each of the following items by circling the letter of the correct answer. You may need to refer to the selection as you answer the items. The numbers of the items are the same as the numbers of the boldface Vocabulary Words in the selection.

1. Some people think that it is **probable** that human beings have lived in North America for more than seventy-five thousand years. Here, **probable** means
   (A) likely
   (B) possible
   (C) unlikely
   (D) interesting

2. The writer gives us a clue to the meaning of **myriad**. What is the clue?
   (A) Human beings have lived on the continent for thousands of years.
   (B) Many different groups lived in North America before the Europeans arrived.
   (C) The Europeans came to North America five hundred years ago.
   (D) Scientists disagree about when human beings first lived in North America.

3. You can tell from the article that **knolls** means
   - (A) visible
   - (B) mounds
   - (C) stockades
   - (D) textiles

4. The writer states, "The idea that Columbus or the Vikings somehow discovered a new world **baffles** many people." Here, **baffles** means
   - (A) disturbs
   - (B) confuses
   - (C) crosses
   - (D) ignores

5. You can tell from the article that **bewildered** means
   - (A) frequently
   - (B) strange
   - (C) entertained
   - (D) confused

6. How does the writer let us know that a **calamity** is an event that causes great misery and distress?
   - (A) The writer tells us that the Europeans arrived.
   - (B) The writer tells us that the Europeans brought both weapons and disease.
   - (C) The writer tells us that thousands died and that entire cultures disappeared.
   - (D) The writer tells us that the Europeans had strange ways.

7. The writer states, "The **abuse** began almost as soon as Columbus set foot in the Americas." Here, **abuse** means
   - (A) disease
   - (B) greeting
   - (C) mistreatment
   - (D) culture

8. All of the following are good definitions of **ruthless** *except*
   - (A) cruel
   - (B) hardhearted
   - (C) without mercy
   - (D) unbelievable

9. The writer says that historians today find the actions **appalling**. Here, **appalling** means
   - (A) deadly
   - (B) historic
   - (C) horrifying
   - (D) warlike

10. How does the writer let us know that **intentional** means deliberate?
    - (A) The writer lets us know that diseases are only severe if they are deliberate.
    - (B) The writer contrasts **intentional** with the word *accidental*.
    - (C) The writer tells us that the Europeans brought the diseases.
    - (D) The writer says that Europeans destroyed American Indians.

11. According to the article, _____ is an example of something **contagious**.
    - (A) European Americans
    - (B) starvation
    - (C) measles
    - (D) a result

12. How does the writer let us know that **epidemic** means widespread?
    - (A) The writer tells us that diseases wiped out whole communities.
    - (B) The writer tells us that the diseases were severe.
    - (C) The writer tells us that the Europeans brought the diseases.
    - (D) The writer tells us that no one was exposed to the diseases.

13. The writer says that many Europeans did not approach American Indians with **sincerity,** or good faith. Here, **sincerity** means
- (A) actions
- (B) friendliness
- (C) value
- (D) honesty

14. How does the writer let us know that **deceive** means to mislead?
- (A) The writer tells us that friends deceive one another.
- (B) The writer implies we should trust our own judgment.
- (C) The writer says that some European Americans gained American Indians' trust in order to betray it.
- (D) The writer makes it clear that the relationship between American Indians and European Americans has occasionally been good.

15. The writer mentions that **folklore** has been passed down through generations. Here, **folklore** means
- (A) fact
- (B) traditional stories
- (C) sadness
- (D) historical relationships

16. The writer tells us that many Europeans considered American Indian customs to be **barbarisms.** Here, **barbarisms** means
- (A) historical realities
- (B) uncivilized activities
- (C) un-American actions
- (D) cultural customs

17. The writer states, "Some were simply curious about a culture they thought was **picturesque.**" Here **picturesque** means
- (A) charming
- (B) artistic
- (C) interesting
- (D) honest

18. The writer states, "Others were interested in **novelty,** in exploring what was, to them, strange, different, and new." Here, **novelty** means
- (A) cultures
- (B) something new and unusual
- (C) exploration
- (D) something charming and pleasant

19. The writer of this article gives a clue to the meaning of **romantic.** What is the clue?
- (A) The writer lets us know that the Europeans had notions about American Indians that were different from reality.
- (B) The writer makes it clear that daily life is difficult.
- (C) The writer tells us that some of the Europeans weren't interested in the realities of daily life.
- (D) The writer reminds us that some Europeans continued to explore American Indian cultures.

20. In this article, **eminent** means
- (A) useful
- (B) visible
- (C) wealthy
- (D) noteworthy

READING NEW WORDS IN CONTEXT

Lesson 2   CONTEXT: The First Americans

Introduction. The American Indian people called the Dakotas were not a single, close-knit group. They were divided into several subgroups. Some Dakotas called themselves Mdewakanto, or Spirit Lake People. Others were Sisseton, or People of the Boggy Ground. In all, there were fourteen Dakota groups living in North America.

The following article gives you an opportunity to learn more about the Dakota culture and to expand your vocabulary. Below are twenty Vocabulary Words that are used in the article and in the exercise that follows it.

advent	catastrophe	inevitable	motivate	sanctuary
aggressive	defy	integrity	mystical	strategy
alliance	ecology	intelligible	nourish	sustain
anthology	ferocious	misdeed	pacify	valid

The Dakotas

Some of the knowledge we have of the Dakota people comes from collections of myths and legends found in **anthologies** (1). Most of it, however, is from well-documented research. For example, it is known that before the Europeans came, before the **advent** (2) of the French in Canada and the British in New England, the Dakotas made their homes in areas of what is now the United States and Canada. The several different groups that together are called the Dakotas formed an **alliance** (3), an agreement between nations with a common cause, to govern and protect themselves from enemies. One of the enemies was the Ojibwa people, with whom the Dakotas warred from time to time. A typical Dakota might scorn the Ojibwa for believing they could threaten the Dakotas' security. However, an even more powerful threat to the Dakotas was on its way.

The Beginning of Trouble

The Dakotas first began to encounter Europeans in the 1600s. In the summers, many Dakotas lived in what is now Minnesota, where they found an abundant supply of wild rice, fruits, and vegetables to **nourish** (4) themselves and their children. In the fall, they broke into smaller bands and hunted for game to **sustain** (5) them through the winter.

The Europeans were friendly to the Dakotas, but they were even friendlier to the Dakotas' enemies, the Ojibwas—to whom they sold guns. The Dakotas were concerned that the armed Ojibwas might become **aggressive** (6) and attack them, so the Dakotas moved. By 1750, they established new territory that stretched from the upper Mississippi Valley into the Black Hills. They continued their defensive **strategy** (7) of keeping lodges of soldiers to protect them from any invaders.

Life on the Plains

Like most American Indian peoples, the Dakotas considered the earth as having **mystical** (8) qualities. They thought of it in a spiritual way and, therefore, they respected earth's **ecology** (9), the complex relationship among living things. They never destroyed anything for which they did not have a **valid** (10) use. An animal for which they had a real need was the bison. The Dakotas depended upon the bison for survival. They used the flesh for food; the hides became clothing and shelter; the horns were made into spoons and cups; the muscle tendon was used to make bowstrings and thread. No part of the bison was wasted.

For almost a hundred years the Dakotas lived in relative peace. They traded with the few white merchants who lived near them. They did not know that the presence of trading posts meant that **catastrophe** (11) was **inevitable** (12). They did not know that once a few white people came, wave after wave of land-hungry settlers would follow, demanding the Dakotas' land. They did not know that white hunters would slaughter all the bison. Perhaps they would not have believed it possible. The concept of wasteful slaughter might not have been **intelligible** (13) to a people who used their resources wisely, wasting nothing. The Dakota must have wondered what would **motivate** (14) someone to act so irresponsibly. Soon the Dakotas would have to wage a fierce, sometimes **ferocious** (15) battle in defense of their homeland.

The Coming of the Settlers

By 1850, the number of white settlers pouring west began to alarm the Dakotas. The United States government hoped to **pacify** (16) the Dakotas and avoid war with them by signing three treaties.

The Dakotas gave up more than ten million acres of land in Minnesota and Iowa. In return, they were promised yearly payments. They were also promised that the land along the upper Minnesota River would remain Dakota land. The Dakotas thought of the land as a **sanctuary** (17), a place of shelter that the whites would not enter. Peace, however, was not assured.

In 1854, the first in a long series of battles between the United States and the Dakotas took place near Fort Laramie in Wyoming. A white settler claimed that the Dakotas had stolen one of his cows. He wanted the Dakotas to pay for this **misdeed** (18). When the U.S. troops arrived at the camp to demand payment, the Dakotas chose to **defy** (19) them. They attacked the troops. It was the beginning of almost forty years of struggle.

For several years, the proud Dakotas struggled to maintain the **integrity** (20) of their culture, to keep it whole against overwhelming odds. By 1880, however, most of the Dakotas had been disarmed. Their horses had been taken from them, they were confined to reservation land, and they were dependent on the U.S. government for food and clothing. Today, the Sioux tribes, to which the Dakotas belong, continue to discuss with the federal government the possibilities of a settlement for the lands that were taken from them.

EXERCISE *Reading Strategically* ✍

Directions. Answer each of the following items by circling the letter of the correct answer. You may need to refer to the selection as you answer the items. The numbers of the items are the same as the numbers of the boldface Vocabulary Words in the selection.

1. You can tell from the article that **anthologies** means
   (A) research
   (B) a collection
   (C) legends
   (D) bound books

2. The writer uses **advent** when discussing the French and British. Here, **advent** means
   (A) settling
   (B) push
   (C) arrival
   (D) delivery

3. The writer says that the Dakotas formed an **alliance**. Here, **alliance** means
   (A) an agreement between nations with a common cause
   (B) a group of peoples living in the same general area
   (C) an enemy that threatens a number of different groups
   (D) a declaration of war between two groups that share a region

4. How does the writer let us know that **nourish** means to feed with healthful substances?
   (A) The writer tells us the Dakotas spent summers in what is now Minnesota.
   (B) The writer says Dakota children gathered the food.
   (C) The writer says that fruits and vegetables were in short supply.
   (D) The writer says that the Dakotas found wild rice, fruits, and vegetables.

5. In this article, **sustain** means
   (A) hunt
   (B) search and destroy
   (C) support
   (D) divide

6. All of the following are good definitions of **aggressive** *except*
   (A) hostile
   (B) quick to attack
   (C) ready to fight
   (D) willing to trade

7. The writer of this article gives us a clue to the meaning of **strategy**. What is the clue?
   (A) The Dakotas established new territory.
   (B) The Dakotas moved to the upper Mississippi Valley.
   (C) The Dakotas were concerned by the Ojibwa threat.
   (D) The Dakotas maintained lodges of soldiers to protect them from attackers.

8. The writer says that the Dakotas considered the earth as having **mystical** qualities. Here, **mystical** means
   (A) occult
   (B) mysterious
   (C) secret
   (D) spiritual

9. You can tell from the article that **ecology** means
   (A) the complex relationship among living things
   (B) American Indian cultures
   (C) a kind of religion
   (D) the use of nature for survival

10. In this article, **valid** means
    (A) reasonable
    (B) valuable
    (C) independent
    (D) ordinary

11. _____ is an example of a **catastrophe** that is mentioned in the article.
    (A) The efficient use of bison
    (B) The slaughter of the bison
    (C) A hundred years of peace
    (D) Dakota land

12. How does the writer let us know that **inevitable** means certain to happen?
    (A) The writer tells us that land-hungry settlers demanded Dakota land.
    (B) The writer says that once a few white people came, wave after wave would surely follow.
    (C) The Dakotas would not have believed what would happen.
    (D) The writer refers to trading posts and merchants as **catastrophes**.

13. The writer suggests that the concept of wasteful slaughter might not have been **intelligible** to the Dakotas. Here, **intelligible** means
    (A) understandable
    (B) interesting
    (C) available
    (D) useful

14. The writer says that the Dakota would wonder "what would **motivate** someone to act so irresponsibly." Here, **motivate** means

(A) cause
(B) advise
(C) suggest
(D) join

15. You can tell from the article that **ferocious** means

(A) defensive
(B) very fierce
(C) always better
(D) skillful

16. The writer of this article gives us a clue to the meaning of **pacify**. What is the clue?

(A) The number of settlers alarmed the Dakotas.
(B) No matter how well armed one might be, it is impossible to defeat the United States Army.
(C) The U.S. government signed treaties with the Dakotas to avoid war.
(D) The Dakotas were a powerful military force.

17. The writer tells us that the Dakotas thought of the land as a **sanctuary**. Here, **sanctuary** means

(A) church
(B) gift
(C) long-lasting peace
(D) place of shelter

18. The writer states, "He wanted the Dakotas to pay for this **misdeed**." Here, **misdeed** means

(A) payment
(B) claim
(C) cow
(D) wrongdoing

19. The writer states, "When the U.S. troops arrived at the camp to demand payment, the Dakotas chose to **defy** them." Here, **defy** means

(A) resist
(B) answer
(C) ignore
(D) claim

20. In the last paragraph, **integrity** means

(A) loyalty
(B) wholeness
(C) resistance
(D) bitterness

READING NEW WORDS IN CONTEXT

Lesson 3 | **CONTEXT:** The First Americans

Introduction. Four Corners is the name given to the point where Arizona, Colorado, New Mexico, and Utah meet. For many centuries the area has been home to several groups of American Indians. Among these groups are the various Pueblo peoples, the Navajos, and the Apaches.

The following essay gives you an opportunity to read about the people who live at Four Corners. It also enables you to expand your vocabulary. Below are twenty Vocabulary Words that are used in the essay and in the exercise that follows it.

accessory	badger	customary	glorify	multicolored
adjacent	calculation	deceased	harmonious	pulverize
artisan	complement	fragile	incomparable	valor
attain	convert	gallery	intervene	vitality

Cultures of Four Corners

Much land in the Four Corners area, particularly in New Mexico and Arizona, is reservation land. Some reservations are **adjacent** (1) to each other. For example, the Zuni reservation borders on the Navajo reservation, and the Hopi reservation is actually surrounded by the Navajo land. The area also includes reservations for Apaches and Utes. The Hopis and Zunis of the Pueblo peoples, however, have lived there the longest.

If you visit the Four Corners area, you are sure to get a sense of how old life there is. It's easy to imagine people there a thousand years ago grinding corn, **pulverizing** (2) the grain to make flour. You might imagine a basket weaver at work or a priest preparing for a ceremony. The peoples who have lived there have shown an amazing ability to endure and survive. The **vitality** (3) of these cultures is admired throughout the world.

The Pueblos of the Four Corners Area: Hopis and Zunis

Pueblo was the name the Spanish gave to the nineteen different groups of American Indians who lived in villages in New Mexico and northeastern Arizona. Although these are separate peoples, they have much in common. For example, each group is made up of clans. Each clan may be named after an animal such as the deer or the **badger** (4). Each clan has its own role within the tribe. For example, a clan may perform a particular ceremony. Although many Pueblos became Christians, some chose not to **convert** (5) to Christianity, and each clan plays an important role in traditional religious ceremonies.

Life in a Pueblo culture is **harmonious** (6). The Pueblos do not approve of disagreement within the group. Although they are capable of fighting, and they honor war gods, they do not glorify (7) war. They honor the values of peace and harmony. Perhaps they are able to live together so easily because they participate in a ceremony sometimes called the rites of rebellion. During this ceremony, it is **customary** (8), or usual, for priests to dress as clowns, sometimes called Mudheads, and to pretend to engage in behavior that is normally forbidden. This ceremony helps relieve tension that might lead to disagreements.

The Pueblos have many other ceremonies. One ceremony honors the **deceased** (9) by paying tribute to the souls of the dead. At these ceremonies, dancers may wear **multicolored** (10) costumes, each color having a special meaning.

Neighboring Navajos

The **calculations** (11) of anthropologists and archaeologists indicate that the Pueblos have lived in the Four Corners region for thousands of years. However, scientists figure that the Navajos arrived in the Southwest much more recently, about five or six hundred years ago.

Although the Pueblos probably did not try to **intervene** (12) directly in the affairs of their new neighbors, over the centuries the Navajos have felt the influence of the Pueblo cultures. The Pueblos have, to some extent, been influenced by the Navajos, as well. Each group seems to have selected what would **complement** (13), or add to, their own culture. Yet they are distinctly different peoples.

The Navajos believe the world is **fragile** (14) and that people must treat it with love and care.

They believe that evil is a real presence on the earth and that people must guard against it to remain pure. The Navajos work to achieve *hohzo*. *Hohzo* is a difficult concept for a non-Navajo to understand. It includes beauty, happiness, harmony, and goodness. *Hohzo* is the goal all Navajos reach for, but it is difficult to **attain** (15).

Today, the Navajo nation is the largest American Indian group within the United States, including more than 200,000 people. They have played a major role in twentieth-century history. Many demonstrated their **valor** (16) by bravely serving as soldiers in World War II. The "Code Talkers" were of special importance. They used the Navajo language as a code to prevent the enemy from understanding American radio messages.

American Art

Anyone who is familiar with American Indian art is familiar with the art of the cultures of the Four Corners region. The area has long been home to **artisans** (17) of **incomparable** (18) skill who create rugs, pottery, statuary, and sand paintings of matchless beauty. A **gallery** (19) of this art would include not only these items but also bracelets, necklaces, and other jewelry too beautiful to be worn simply as **accessories** (20). The rich artistic tradition of the Four Corners area is an important part of the fascinating cultures that live in this historic region.

EXERCISE *Reading Strategically* 👉

Directions. Answer each of the following items by circling the letter of the correct answer. You may need to refer to the selection as you answer the items. The numbers of the items are the same as the numbers of the boldface Vocabulary Words in the selection.

1. The writer gives a clue to the meaning of **adjacent**. What is the clue?
   (A) New Mexico and Arizona are home to many reservations.
   (B) The Zuni reservation borders the Navajo reservation.
   (C) There are several reservations.
   (D) The people who have lived there the longest are the Pueblos.

2. The writer says that it's easy to imagine someone grinding corn, **pulverizing** it to make flour. Here, **pulverizing** means
   (A) imagining
   (B) cooking
   (C) borrowing
   (D) grinding

3. The writer of this essay gives a clue to the meaning of **vitality**. What is the clue?
   - (A) The peoples of the Four Corners area have an amazing ability to endure and survive.
   - (B) The cultures are admired throughout the world.
   - (C) You can imagine a basket weaver at work or a priest preparing for a ceremony.
   - (D) A visitor to the Four Corners area can sense how old life is there.

4. In the passage, **badger** means
   - (A) a deer
   - (B) to pester
   - (C) an animal
   - (D) to imagine

5. According to the writer, "Although many Pueblos became Christians, some chose not to **convert** to Christianity." Here, **convert** means
   - (A) change
   - (B) build
   - (C) complain
   - (D) dislike

6. How does the writer let us know that **harmonious** means showing agreement in attitudes and feelings?
   - (A) The writer comments that the Pueblos are capable of fighting.
   - (B) The writer implies that the Pueblo culture is religious.
   - (C) The writer notes that the Pueblos disapprove of disagreement within the community.
   - (D) The writer shows how the Pueblos honor war gods.

7. You can tell from the essay that to **glorify** means
   - (A) to apologize for
   - (B) to go to
   - (C) to give honor to
   - (D) to fight in

8. The writer indicates that at special times it is **customary** for priests to dress as clowns. Here, **customary** means
   - (A) usual
   - (B) ceremonial
   - (C) honorable
   - (D) understandable

9. The writer states, "One ceremony honors the **deceased**. . . ." Here, **deceased** means
   - (A) forbidden
   - (B) things
   - (C) dead
   - (D) dancers

10. The writer states, "At these ceremonies, dancers may wear **multicolored** costumes, each color having a special meaning." Here, **multicolored** means
    - (A) black and white only
    - (B) having different colors
    - (C) honorable
    - (D) having special colors

11. The writer gives a clue to the meaning of **calculations**. What is the clue?
    - (A) Scientists figure that the Navajos arrived five or six hundred years ago.
    - (B) The Pueblos live in the Four Corners region.
    - (C) The writer hints that no one has lived in the region longer than the Pueblos have.
    - (D) The **calculations** are made by anthropologists and archaeologists.

12. You can tell from the essay that **intervene** means
    - (A) control
    - (B) interfere
    - (C) overlook
    - (D) live

13. The writer says that each group se-
lected what would **complement** their
own culture. Here, **complement**
means to
(A) take away from
(B) add to
(C) differ from
(D) contest

14. All of the following are good defini-
tions of **fragile** *except*
(A) frail
(B) easily damaged
(C) delicate
(D) broken

15. All of the following are good defini-
tions of **attain** *except*
(A) to achieve
(B) to reach
(C) to avoid
(D) to gain

16. The writer states, "Many demon-
strated their **valor** by serving as sol-
diers in World War II." Here, **valor**
means
(A) worth
(B) service
(C) wisdom
(D) courage

17. In this essay, **artisans** means people
(A) of the Four Corners region
(B) who are the best
(C) with special abilities
(D) who create hand-made art

18. Another word that means about the
same thing as **incomparable** is
(A) unfriendly
(B) useful
(C) incomplete
(D) matchless

19. You can tell from the essay that a
gallery is
(A) rugs, pottery, statuary, and sand
paintings
(B) American Indian art
(C) a place where art is displayed
(D) a large amount

20. Which of the following are examples
of **accessories**?
(A) artistic traditions
(B) bracelets
(C) beautiful things
(D) sand paintings

READING NEW WORDS IN CONTEXT

Lesson 4 CONTEXT: The First Americans

Introduction. Long before the United States formed Congress, the several groups that made up the Iroquois nations had formed the League of Five Nations. The league was founded in the early 1600s, and each member group had elected representatives. The council was not intended to be a strong, centralized authority, but it was a model of representative government.

The following article gives you an opportunity to learn more about the Iroquois nations. The article also enables you to expand your vocabulary. Below are twenty Vocabulary Words that are used in the article and in the exercise that follows it.

adequate	descend	foresight	inherit	mutual
advantageous	discord	gnarled	isolation	phenomenon
confederation	enhance	incite	menace	posterity
delegate	feline	inflexible	menagerie	revelation

The Five Nations

East of the Great Lakes, in country that is now partly in Canada and partly in the United States, the woods once swarmed with animals. There were moose and beavers and bears—creatures that many of us no longer see except in wildlife parks or caged in **menageries** (1). The lakes and rivers were filled with fish, and the air was alive with the songs of birds. Here, five nations of the Iroquois—the Mohawk, the Seneca, the Oneida, the Cayuga, and the Ondaga—made their homes.

Here, in the sixteenth century, the prophet Deganwidah dreamed of a huge evergreen tree. He understood the dream to be a **revelation** (2), a dramatic sign showing him a path the Iroquois should follow. The roots of the tree were the many groups that formed the Iroquois nation, and the tree itself was the sisterhood of the Iroquois women. The Iroquois nations had lived in **discord** (3), often quarreling with one another. Deganwidah interpreted the dream to mean that the nations should end their differences and band together for support.

Achieving the Dream

It was Hiawatha who made Deganwidah's dream of a **confederation** (4) a reality. From village to village he traveled, encouraging the Iroquois to form a league. He convinced five groups of Iroquois that it would be **advantageous** (5) to adopt the plan. They saw that the league would be to their benefit. In 1570, the League of the Five Nations was formed.

Rules for the league were established, and the Iroquois passed a law saying that **delegates** (6) from each nation had to meet every fifth summer to discuss the needs of the people. The men chosen to represent the people were called sachem, and they were selected by the women. The rule about meeting every five years was **inflexible** (7). In addition to the fixed five-year schedule, however, delegates could meet at other times as they saw fit.

For the most part, the league was **adequate** (8) for the needs of the five nations. The Iroquois were able to settle most of their differences. However, the council did not put an end to war.

The Iroquois and Their Neighbors

From time to time, a group of Iroquois **descended** (9) on another tribe, like a hawk coming down on its prey, and engaged in a quick battle. They did this for glory and to capture prisoners. The prisoners were used as laborers or were adopted into families as replacements for family members who had died.

These attacks were usually brief but violent. Europeans said that the Iroquois, like wild cats, sneaked up on their victims quietly and then attacked and fought ferociously. Stories of this **feline** (10) stealth and ferocity spread throughout European and American Indian communities. The mere thought of the **menace** (11) of an Iroquois raiding party was enough to **incite** (12) fear and terror in the hearts of many.

The Iroquois were among the first people European settlers encountered in North America. The two groups wondered about the other's customs. This **mutual** (13) curiosity led the two groups to have extensive contact with each other.

The Iroquois Heritage

Iroquois culture was impressive in many ways. For example, the Iroquois interpreted dreams with great skill and wisdom, and they used dreams to **enhance** (14), or improve upon, their understanding of themselves and others. In addition, the Iroquois people had the **foresight** (15) to look ahead and plan for future generations. This planning for **posterity** (16) was based on a basic principle of American Indian wisdom: Always consider how any decision you make will affect the seventh generation following you.

Women played a major role in the Iroquois nation. In addition to choosing delegates to the meetings of the League of Five Nations, women owned all the property, and daughters **inherited** (17) it from their mothers. Almost everything in the culture was passed from one generation of women to the next.

The basic social unit of the Iroquois was the *owachiras,* which consisted of a woman and her children. The Iroquois family never experienced the sense of **isolation** (18) that contemporary families may feel. Several families lived together in one long house. They may have been crowded by our standards, but they were never lonely, and parents always had help in caring for their children.

The Iroquois believed that the spirit world revealed itself in the physical world. In other words, the spiritual was not separate from the physical, but was a **phenomenon** (19) that could be sensed in the material world. For example, the face of a spirit might reveal itself in the trunk of a **gnarled** (20) and twisted tree. Thus, the world of the Iroquois—rich in natural and cultural beauty— was also a magical place.

EXERCISE   *Reading Strategically*

Directions. Answer each of the following items by circling the letter of the correct answer. You may need to refer to the selection as you answer the items. The numbers of the items are the same as the numbers of the boldface Vocabulary Words in the selection.

1. The writer says that some animals are now seen only in **menageries**. Here **menageries** means
 (A) collections of caged animals
 (B) areas east of the Great Lakes
 (C) the Iroquois nation
 (D) lakes and rivers

2. In the second paragraph, **revelation** means
 (A) a dramatic disclosure or sign
 (B) a clear view of the past
 (C) a plan to cooperate with the enemy
 (D) a dream of a beautiful garden

3. The writer gives us a clue to the meaning of **discord**. What is the clue?
   (A) Deganwidah interpreted the dreams.
   (B) The groups often quarreled with one another.
   (C) No one can live in peace.
   (D) The nations should band together for support.

4. You can tell from the article that **confederation** means
   (A) reality
   (B) a league
   (C) a dream
   (D) travel

5. All of the following are good definitions of **advantageous** *except*
   (A) favorable
   (B) useful
   (C) profitable
   (D) convincing

6. The writer indicates that the **delegates** were to meet every five years. Here, **delegates** means
   (A) meetings
   (B) people
   (C) representatives
   (D) membership dues

7. You can tell from the article that **inflexible** means
   (A) not enforced
   (B) unworkable
   (C) unchangeable
   (D) not broken

8. The writer of the article gives a clue to the meaning of **adequate**. What is the clue?
   (A) There were only five nations.
   (B) The league was effective most of the time.
   (C) The sachem were required to abide by a strict, five-year meeting schedule.
   (D) The Iroquois attacked other groups.

9. The writer says that the way the Iroquois **descended** on another tribe was most like
   (A) a quick battle
   (B) an occasional burst of aggression
   (C) a hawk coming down on its prey
   (D) adopting a new family member

10. The writer uses **feline** when talking about how the Iroquois attacked their enemies. Here, **feline** means
    (A) polite
    (B) clumsy
    (C) catlike
    (D) fearful

11. The writer shows that **menace** means a threat by saying that
    (A) the mere thought of an Iroquois raiding party caused fear and terror
    (B) the Europeans and other American Indians thought of the Iroquois as ferocious fighters
    (C) the attacks from the Iroquois were usually brief but violent
    (D) the Iroquois were among the first people European settlers encountered in North America

12. The writer tells us that the mere thought of an Iroquois raiding party was enough to **incite** fear and terror in many people. Here, **incite** means
    (A) arouse
    (B) drown out
    (C) think about
    (D) include

13. The writer says that the two groups had **mutual** curiosity. Here, **mutual** means
    (A) normal
    (B) shared
    (C) cultural
    (D) strange

14. The writer states, "They used dreams to **enhance,** or improve upon, their understanding of themselves and others." Here, **enhance** means
  (A) to improve
  (B) to create
  (C) to remove
  (D) to interpret

15. The writer states, "In addition, the Iroquois people had the **foresight** to look ahead and plan for future generations." Here, **foresight** means
  (A) intense desire
  (B) concern for the future
  (C) plan of government
  (D) affection for their relatives

16. In this article, **posterity** means
  (A) wisdom
  (B) American Indians
  (C) future generations
  (D) decisions

17. The writer of the article gives a clue to the meaning of **inherited**. What is the clue?
  (A) Women owned property.
  (B) Women chose sachems.
  (C) The *owachiras* was the basic social unit of the Iroquois people.
  (D) Things were passed from one generation of women to the next.

18. Which of the following is the most likely reason that families never experienced a sense of **isolation**?
  (A) Women owned virtually all the property.
  (B) The basic family unit consisted of a mother and her child.
  (C) The Iroquois believed that the spirit world was evident in the physical world.
  (D) Several families lived together in a long house.

19. You can tell from the article that a **phenomenon** is
  (A) another way of saying separateness
  (B) the face of a spirit
  (C) something that can be sensed or experienced
  (D) the beliefs of the Iroquois

20. The writer states, "For example, the face of a spirit might reveal itself in the trunk of a **gnarled** and twisted tree." Here, **gnarled** means
  (A) growing
  (B) misshapen
  (C) revealed
  (D) carved

READING NEW WORDS IN CONTEXT

Lesson 5 | CONTEXT: The First Americans

Introduction. The first Americans that Europeans encountered were those who dwelled in the upper reaches of the North American continent. In A.D. 1005, Vikings met the Inuits, perhaps somewhere around Labrador in Canada. The Inuits of Canada and the Inupiats and Yu'piks of Alaska are the major groups of native peoples that live in upper North America, on or near the icy northern coasts of the continent.

The following article gives you an opportunity to learn about Inupiat and Yu'pik peoples of Alaska, the northernmost part of the United States. The article also enables you to expand your vocabulary. Below are twenty Vocabulary Words that are used in the article and in the exercise that follows it.

adapt	controversy	feasible	ingenious	petition
assumption	creative	hilarious	insoluble	potential
basis	diction	immense	omission	primitive
consecutive	durable	impel	ordeal	restore

Far to the North: Native Peoples of Alaska

Together, the Inuits, the Inupiats, the Yu'piks, and the Siberian Yuits make up the group that for decades has been called *Eskimos*. No one is sure where the term *Eskimo* came from. One source says that the term was given to the native people of Labrador by fishermen from the Basque region of France and that it means snowshoe net maker. Another story has it that *Eskimo* is an American Indian word originally used by one group of native people to describe their neighbors. When Europeans first heard the term, their **assumption** (1) was that it was, in fact, the correct name. They simply took it for granted that *Eskimo* was the name by which these people, who were probably Inuits, called themselves.

For several centuries, small settlements of people have been scattered along the Arctic coast, which stretches for more than six thousand miles from Alaska to Greenland—an **immense** (2) territory. Among these early settlers were the Inupiat and the Yu'piks. There is no **controversy** (3) about where the Inupiats and Yu'piks originally came from; the evidence is clear that they migrated to North America from Asia. However, there is some debate about how they came. Perhaps they walked across on a land bridge. Perhaps they came by sea. Regardless, these cultures went through several **consecutive** (4), or successive, stages before evolving into the modern Inupiat and Yu'pik cultures.

Creativity in a Harsh Environment
People from warmer climates look at the frozen world of the Arctic and wonder how it is **feasible** (5), or possible, for people to survive in an environment that is so barren. To people from warmer places, the problems of finding food and shelter appear to be **insoluble** (6), and these difficulties seem to be a terrible **ordeal** (7).

However, the **ingenious** (8) people who live in

the Arctic learned how to make the most of their environment. They are highly resourceful in using what is available to **adapt** (9) themselves to the harsh environment. To travel across the frozen terrain, they invented the dog sled. To survive the long months without light in a land with no wood to burn, they invented oil lamps. To prevent snow blindness, they created goggles.

The Inupiats and the Yu'piks are **creative** (10) in other ways, too. Of course, their clothing has to be warm and waterproof. It has to be **durable** (11) because it is needed year in and year out. They also make their clothing—and their other belongings— beautiful. For these peoples, art is essential to life.

Traditionally, the Inupiats and the Yu'piks live in groups in small villages. Today, most of these people live in modern homes, but some live in traditional dwellings. The traditional summer dwelling for most Eskimos is a tent made of caribou skin and sealskin. In Alaska, the Inupiats and the Yu'piks traditionally spend the winter in houses made of sod. (Only in Canada do some Inuits make their permanent homes in ice houses, or igloos). These sod houses, made of pieces of earth, may seem rough and crude, even **primitive** (12), to those used to a different kind of shelter. Actually, however, they are warm and cozy and a testament to the resourcefulness of people who had to carve a home out of a hostile environment.

The Importance of Cooperation

Farming is impossible in this cold environment, so the Inupiats and Yu'piks are **impelled** (13) to hunt. They have no other choice. Surviving by hunting in the frozen north is difficult at best. Game is scarce, and there is a constant possibility of starvation. As a result, sharing is the **basis** (14) of Eskimo society.

Without a foundation of cooperation and generosity, these people could not survive.

Because the native people of northern Alaska depend on each other for survival, they have to avoid disagreements. For times of conflict, they have developed a clever way to handle **potential** (15) violence and to regain harmony. The two people who disagree engage in a duel of songs. However, this is one performance when **diction** (16), or pronouncing the words clearly, is not important. Here, they sing insults to one another while the rest of the group watches. The insults usually take the form of jokes. As a result, a situation that might have ended in violence often ends in **hilarious** (17) laughter instead, and harmony is **restored** (18).

Spiritual Beliefs

Balance and harmony are important to the Inupiats and the Yu'piks, and this is reflected in their religious beliefs. They have many rules that enable them to maintain this positive balance. Some are rules for duties and activities that must be performed. The **omission** (19) of an act that should be performed could displease the spirits. When the spirits are displeased, a spiritual leader and the sinner take part in a ceremony to **petition** (20) the spirits to forgive the sinner. The villagers also join in the ceremony, entering their pleas for the sinner's forgiveness.

The world of the Inupiats and the Yu'piks is a very different world from the one most of us know. They are not concerned with being on time. They are not concerned with money or shopping or cars. Rather, they focus on their life in their cold world, on cooperating with one another, and on living in harmony with nature.

EXERCISE   *Reading Strategically*

Directions. Answer each of the following items by circling the letter of the correct answer. You may need to refer to the selection as you answer the items. The numbers of the items are the same as the numbers of the boldface Vocabulary Words in the selection.

1. The writer explains that Europeans made the **assumption** that all Arctic peoples were called *Eskimo.* Here, **assumption** means the act of
   (A) correcting an error in translation
   (B) deriving a new word from an old word
   (C) creating a problem with pronunciation
   (D) taking something for granted

2. The writer gives a clue to the meaning of **immense**. What is the clue?
   (A) Inupiats and Yu'piks live in Alaska.
   (B) A meeting between Inuits and Vikings occurred.
   (C) Native peoples have lived on the coast for centuries.
   (D) Inupiat, Yu'pik, and Inuit territory covers thousands of miles.

3. Which of the following is the most likely reason that there is no **controversy** about where people who settled the Arctic coast came from?
   (A) They cover a vast territory along the Arctic coast.
   (B) The evidence is clear that they migrated from Asia.
   (C) No one knows how they came to North America.
   (D) They might have come to North America by sea.

4. The writer states that Arctic cultures went through several **consecutive** stages before evolving into modern cultures. Here, **consecutive** means
   (A) ancient
   (B) successive
   (C) cultural
   (D) modern

5. You can tell from the article that **feasible** means
   (A) livable
   (B) warm enough
   (C) possible
   (D) suitable

6. In the third paragraph, **insoluble** means
   (A) unable to be dissolved
   (B) difficult
   (C) unsolvable
   (D) preventable

7. The writer indicates that finding food and shelter in the Arctic appears to be a terrible **ordeal** to people from warmer climates. Here, **ordeal** means
   (A) an impossible plan
   (B) a barren plot
   (C) a possible starvation
   (D) a difficult situation

8. The writer gives a clue to the meaning of **ingenious** by saying that
   (A) the people of the region are highly resourceful
   (B) it is possible to travel by dog sled
   (C) we should make the most of our environment
   (D) there are long months without light in the Arctic

9. Which of the following is an example of a way the people of the Arctic **adapt** to their environment?
   (A) They found a harsh environment.
   (B) Traveling across frozen terrain was very difficult.
   (C) They created goggles to prevent snow blindness.
   (D) There were long months of darkness and no firelight.

10. The writer states, "The Inupiats and the Yu'piks are **creative** in other ways, too." Here, **creative** means
    (A) waterproof
    (B) warming
    (C) inventive
    (D) hopeful

11. The writer indicates that **durable** means long lasting by saying that clothes have to
    (A) be warm
    (B) be waterproof
    (C) be artistic
    (D) last for years

12. The writer gives a clue to the meaning of **primitive** by saying that sod houses
    (A) are warm and cozy
    (B) seem rough and crude
    (C) are not common today
    (D) are winter homes

13. The writer indicates that the Inupiats and the Yu'piks are **impelled** to hunt. Here, **impelled** means
    (A) born
    (B) forced
    (C) urged
    (D) understood

14. All of the following are good definitions of **basis** *except*
    (A) foundation
    (B) base
    (C) chief support
    (D) culture

15. You can tell from the article that **potential** means
    (A) serious
    (B) possible
    (C) powerful
    (D) unending

16. Which of the following is the most likely reason **diction** is not important when the two people are engaged in a duel of songs?
    (A) The manner of speaking is not the main purpose of the singing.
    (B) The singers are singing insults to amuse one another.
    (C) The insults usually take the form of jokes.
    (D) The main purpose in the singing is not to entertain.

17. Which of the following is the most likely reason that a disagreement between members of the community often ends in **hilarious** laughter?
    (A) Members of the community depend on each other for survival.
    (B) The whole community watches the two people work out their conflict.
    (C) Two people often end a conflict by exchanging joking insults.
    (D) A conflict might end in laughter, or it might end in violence.

18. All of the following are good definitions of **restored** *except*
    (A) removed
    (B) brought back
    (C) regained
    (D) reestablished

19. In this article, **omission** means
    (A) adding to
    (B) observing
    (C) doing
    (D) leaving out

20. The writer says that the spiritual leader and the sinner **petition** the spirits. Here, **petition** means
    (A) to collect enough signatures for
    (B) to argue with
    (C) to make a serious request of
    (D) to prepare for

READING NEW WORDS IN CONTEXT

Lesson 6] CONTEXT: Coming to the United States

Introduction. In the last two hundred years, groups of people from many different countries have come to the shores of the United States. The country has been made stronger and richer by each of them. Between 1820 and 1870, a wave of Irish people, fleeing a food shortage in Ireland, came to the United States. Today, Irish Americans are active in every aspect of public life in the country.

The following article gives you an opportunity to expand your vocabulary. Below are twenty Vocabulary Words that are used in the article and in the exercise that follows it.

anxiety	censorship	famine	nationality	propaganda
aristocrat	decade	malnutrition	naturalization	refuge
boycott	deport	morale	optimism	resolute
burly	emigrate	multitude	predicament	urban

Leaving the Emerald Isle

The History of the Irish

One **nationality** (1) that has greatly helped to shape the United States is the Irish. Historically, the Irish have shown a gift for surviving troubled times and a talent for speaking and writing expressively of their struggles. Many of the world's best playwrights, novelists, and poets have been Irish, including Samuel Beckett, James Joyce, and William Butler Yeats. Irish literature tends to reflect a peculiar mixture of **optimism** (2) and negative thinking. The Irish have the faith and hope of people born to a land that seems almost enchanted, but experience tells them that the worst can and sometimes does happen.

Serious difficulties for the Irish people began in the 1600s. The English drove the Irish **aristocrats** (3) out of their castles and off their estates and replaced them with an English ruling class. The English treated Ireland as a colony, and they restricted the rights of the Irish people. For example, **censorship** (4) was common. Irish newspapers were not allowed to criticize the English government.

The people of Ireland suffered in other ways, as well. In the early 1800s, they experienced a dozen crop failures in three **decades** (5), or thirty years. Toward the end of the 1840s, Ireland suffered a terrible **famine** (6). Within three years, 500,000 people starved to death. Thousands watched their loved ones suffer from **malnutrition** (7) due to the lack of food.

The situation seemed hopeless, and hundreds of thousands fled the country. In this case, they were not **deported** (8) but chose to leave the country in hopes of finding a better life. Some headed for Canada and other destinations, but the vast **multitude** (9) went to the United States.

Life in a New Country

The decision to **emigrate** (10) caused great **anxiety** (11). As bad as life in Ireland had become, it was still difficult to leave home for a new country. On the long ocean voyage, the **emigrants** worried about how they would get along in a new world. The Irish were a rural people. They lived on farms and in small villages. When they came to the United States, however, they settled in **urban** (12) areas in the Northeast, especially New York City, Boston, and Philadelphia. In the cities, they took **refuge** (13) in neighborhoods where other Irish newcomers had already settled, where they felt more secure and comfortable living around people from home.

Like members of other incoming groups, many of the Irish were victims of **propaganda** (14). They had been led to believe that the United States offered unlimited opportunities and that any hard-working person could get rich quickly. Of course, that was not the case.

Life in the United States was difficult. It was hard for even the most **resolute** (15) individuals to maintain their **morale** (16). It took great determination to remain courageous and confident in the face of hardships. New arrivals to the United States were usually offered only the lowest paying, least desirable jobs. Most Irish worked at first as laborers and did backbreaking physical labor. There were so many Irish laborers that the image of the Irish American became linked in many people's minds with the image of the **burly** (17), powerful worker. It is true that Irish American laborers helped build U.S. cities.

The Irish Americans remained connected to their culture. In Irish American neighborhoods, reading rooms sprang up with books, newspapers, and magazines that reminded Irish Americans of their heritage. In addition, they did not forgive the injustices they had suffered at the hands of the English. When the Prince of Wales visited the United States in 1860, the Irish **boycotted** (18) the parade that was held in his honor. They refused to participate in any activities that honored the English prince.

Most Irish Americans chose **naturalization** (19), but, like all recent immigrants, they faced the **predicament** (20) of deciding how to be loyal to their past while becoming citizens of a new country. Like most other new citizens, they eventually found a way to balance old and new, and in doing so, they greatly enriched the United States.

EXERCISE *Reading Strategically*

Directions. Answer each of the following items by circling the letter of the correct answer. You may need to refer to the selection as you answer the items. The numbers of the items are the same as the numbers of the Vocabulary Words in the selection.

1. An example of a **nationality** that is mentioned in the first paragraph of the article is
   (A) expressive writing
   (B) gifts
   (C) survival
   (D) the Irish

2. The writer explains that Irish literature mixes **optimism** and negative thinking. Here, **optimism** means
   (A) the belief that things will work out for the best
   (B) a belief in magic
   (C) a special form of literature
   (D) the belief that the worst is likely to happen

3. You can tell from the article that **aristocrats** means
   - (A) the English
   - (B) the upper class
   - (C) the Irish
   - (D) the castles and estates

4. The writer of this article gives a clue to the meaning of **censorship**. What is the clue?
   - (A) The writer mentions that the English treated Ireland as a colony.
   - (B) The writer notes that Irish newspapers were forbidden to criticize the English government.
   - (C) The writer regrets that the people of Ireland suffered in other ways.
   - (D) The writer explains that the English became the ruling class.

5. The writer indicates that the crops failed twelve times in three **decades**. Here, **decade** means
   - (A) twelve times
   - (B) the 1800s
   - (C) crop failures
   - (D) ten years

6. How does the writer let us know that **famine** means a widespread shortage of food?
   - (A) The writer tells us that the **famine** occurred toward the end of the 1840s.
   - (B) The writer refers to a period of just three years.
   - (C) The writer tells us that 500,000 people starved to death.
   - (D) The writer uses the adjective *terrible*.

7. The most likely reason that **malnutrition** occurred is that
   - (A) there was not enough food
   - (B) the children had to be buried
   - (C) the end of the **decade** arrived
   - (D) people told stories

8. The writer states, "In this case they were not **deported** but chose to leave the country in hopes of finding a better life." Here, **deported** means
   - (A) anxious to leave the country
   - (B) forced to leave the country
   - (C) sent away
   - (D) homeless

9. The writer states that the vast **multitude** fled to the United States. Here, **multitude** means
   - (A) great number of people
   - (B) people who believe the best will happen
   - (C) pessimistic people
   - (D) destination

10. The writer indicates that choosing to **emigrate** can create problems. Here, **emigrate** means
    - (A) to move to the United States
    - (B) to continue to worry beyond a reasonable point
    - (C) to move from one country to another
    - (D) to travel by ship

11. All of the following are good definitions of **anxiety** *except*
    - (A) worry
    - (B) uneasiness
    - (C) stress
    - (D) homesickness

12. The writer states that the Irish people settled in **urban** areas. Here, **urban** means having to do with
(A) villages
(B) cities
(C) the Irish people
(D) farms

13. The writer of this article gives us a clue to the meaning of **refuge**. What is the clue?
(A) that the newly arrived Irish felt safer with people from home
(B) that the cities were unsafe
(C) that cities offered nearly unlimited opportunities to hard-working people
(D) that the newly arrived Irish were generally rural people

14. You can tell that **propaganda** means
(A) hard work
(B) misleading information
(C) mistaken identities
(D) a terrible food shortage

15. All of the following are good definitions of **resolute** *except*
(A) immediate
(B) determined
(C) resolved
(D) purposeful

16. The writer of this article gives a clue to the meaning of **morale**. What is the clue?
(A) that there were no real hardships
(B) that some people might get rich quickly
(C) the phrase "remain courageous and confident"
(D) the word *maintain*

17. The writer uses **burly** when talking about workers. Here, **burly** means
(A) poetic and beautiful
(B) twisted and gnarled
(C) big and strong
(D) small and weak

18. The writer of this article gives a clue to the meaning of **boycotted**. What is the clue?
(A) The Prince of Wales visited the United States.
(B) The Irish remembered their heritage.
(C) The Irish suffered injustices at the hands of the English government.
(D) The Irish refused to participate in honoring the English royalty.

19. In this article, **naturalization** means
(A) a new country
(B) freedom
(C) the act of behaving naturally
(D) the process of becoming a citizen

20. The writer explains that Irish Americans faced a **predicament**. Here, **predicament** means
(A) prediction
(B) problem
(C) option
(D) old saying

READING NEW WORDS IN CONTEXT

Lesson 7 | CONTEXT: Coming to the United States

Introduction. Italians came to the United States before 1870, but only in small numbers, and most of them were from northern Italy. Beginning in 1871, people from southern Italy began to arrive in large numbers. Tens of thousands arrived in the country between 1871 and 1925.

The following article gives you an opportunity to read about the experiences of Italian immigrants and to expand your vocabulary. Below are twenty Vocabulary Words that are used in the article and in the exercise that follows it.

acceptance	circulate	grieve	intensity	prosecute
accessible	dilapidated	hospitable	jubilation	riotous
bankrupt	exaggeration	immigrate	premiere	thrive
boisterous	fraudulent	impulsive	privilege	transit

From Roma, Napoli, and Palermo to Ellis Island

Like most people who came to live in the United States in the late nineteenth and early twentieth centuries, southern Italians **immigrated** (1) by way of Ellis Island in New York Harbor. The familiar image of immigrants arriving after their long **transit** (2) across the Atlantic Ocean is that of men and women gazing in wonder at the New York skyline. The city must have seemed an almost magical place. Many Italians did experience a sense of **jubilation** (3) as the ships drew near the city.

All too often, however, their joy turned into frustration. The streets were not paved with gold as many had been led to believe. Because they found themselves in a strange country where they did not speak the language and where jobs were difficult to find, Italian immigrants sometimes **grieved** (4) over their decision to leave Italy.

Some Reactions

Some U.S. citizens were not **accessible** (5) or even **hospitable** (6) to the Italian immigrants. These people did not welcome the immigrants because of opinions about Italians that were not based in reality. They believed that Italians were too **impulsive** (7), or spontaneous. Further, they did not approve of people who did not speak English. Such prejudice against Italians varied in **intensity** (8). Some people wanted to limit the kinds of jobs Italians could hold. Others wanted to prevent Italians from entering the country altogether. Fortunately, not everyone had such misguided notions. It is hard to imagine the United States today without its Italian heritage.

The new citizens faced other problems as well. Many were the victims of people who hired poor immigrants to work in the United States in order to take advantage of them. Some of these people were involved in **fraudulent** (9) schemes that tricked the newcomers out of their wages. These individuals were morally **bankrupt** (10)—that is, they had no morals and did not care about the harm they did to innocent people. They caught the immigrants in a system of continual debt. It was unfortunate that these actions were rarely, if ever, **prosecuted** (11) in the courts.

Italian Neighborhoods

Italian Americans were usually forced to live in **dilapidated** (12) old apartments in run-down neighborhoods. However, these small neighborhoods preserved something of the flavor of village life in southern Italy and enabled the culture of southern Italy to **thrive** (13) in the United States.

At first, survival was the main goal of the families in these neighborhoods. The rule was loyalty to family above all else. Outsiders were viewed with suspicion. Italian American children might be criticized or even punished if they forgot their loyalties. Such were the ways of families struggling to survive.

Because the Italian Americans lived in crowded apartments, much of life was lived on front stoops and out in the streets, especially in the summertime. On warm days, people opened what windows they had to allow the air to **circulate** (14) through the building. The noisy, lively laughter of **boisterous** (15) children drifted in with the fresh air. There was also **riotous** (16) laughter from the adults as they exchanged jokes and gossip. Life was very hard for these new citizens, but they found joy in their close communities.

Education

Italian American communities began to change when the children began to attend school. At first, some parents saw the schools as a threat to the preservation of their Italian heritage. However, **acceptance** (17) of the public schools soon led to outright enthusiasm for them. The immigrants began to see school as a **privilege** (18), as an honor that would give their children an advantage. Education proved useful in escaping the cycle of poverty in which so many Italian Americans had become trapped.

Today, Italian Americans play significant roles in all aspects of life in the United States. They are lawyers, doctors, journalists, social workers, businesspeople, and politicians. Italian Americans are also artists, writers, singers, and actors. It is hard to imagine the **premiere** (19) of a major motion picture without famous Italian American actors and directors pulling up in limousines to watch the first showing. It is not an **exaggeration** (20) to say that Italian Americans have enriched the United States beyond measure. Their contribution to American society cannot be overstated.

EXERCISE *Reading Strategically*

Directions. Answer each of the following items by circling the letter of the correct answer. You may need to refer to the selection as you answer the items. The numbers of the items are the same as the numbers of the boldface Vocabulary Words in the selection.

1. According to the article, southern Italians **immigrated** to the U.S. by way of New York Harbor. Here, **immigrated** means
   (A) left the United States
   (B) resembled most people
   (C) moved to a country
   (D) visited another country

2. In order to give a clue to the meaning of **transit,** the writer
   (A) refers to a familiar picture
   (B) uses the phrase "across the Atlantic Ocean"
   (C) tells us that men and women gaze
   (D) hints that the New York skyline is impressive

3. In order to let us know that **jubilation** means gladness, the writer
   (A) tells us that the ships drew near the city
   (B) makes it clear that the streets were not paved with gold
   (C) uses the phrase "almost magical"
   (D) tells us that too often joy became frustration

4. Which of the following is a reason mentioned in the article that the Italian immigrants sometimes **grieved** over their decision to leave Italy?
   (A) Jobs were difficult to find.
   (B) They were overjoyed as they drew near Ellis Island.
   (C) The streets were paved with gold.
   (D) They were impressed by the New York skyline.

5. All of the following are good definitions for **accessible** *except*
   (A) obtainable
   (B) understandable
   (C) approachable
   (D) expensive

6. In order to give a clue to the meaning of **hospitable,** the writer
   (A) tells us that the Italians were immigrants
   (B) tells us that some people did not welcome the Italians
   (C) hints that people should not be quick-tempered
   (D) hints that **hospitable** means unwelcoming

7. The writer says that some people believed that Italian immigrants were too **impulsive**. Here, **impulsive** means
   (A) unwilling to make a commitment
   (B) very intelligent and thoughtful
   (C) likely to act on sudden feelings
   (D) easily discouraged

8. The writer states, "Such prejudice against Italians varied in **intensity**." Here, **intensity** means
   (A) kindness
   (B) degree
   (C) stupidity
   (D) cruelty

9. All of the following are good definitions of **fraudulent** *except*
   (A) dishonest
   (B) deceitful
   (C) crooked
   (D) business

10. In order to let us know that **bankrupt** means lacking in some quality, the writer
    (A) tells us that some people were involved in schemes
    (B) implies that employers can be dishonest
    (C) tells us that employers had no feelings for the innocent people they hurt
    (D) says some immigrants could not get out of debt no matter how hard they tried

11. You can tell from the article that **prosecuted** means
    (A) accused
    (B) tried in the courts
    (C) judged
    (D) thought to be illegal

12. You can tell from the article that **dilapidated** means
   (A) run-down
   (B) deserted
   (C) large
   (D) expensive

13. The writer indicates that the culture of southern Italy was allowed to **thrive**. Here, **thrive** means
   (A) to preserve
   (B) to disappear
   (C) to grow
   (D) to cook

14. The writer states, "On warm days, people opened what windows they had to allow the air to **circulate** through the building." Here, **circulate** means
   (A) to heat
   (B) to trap
   (C) to flow
   (D) to escape

15. The writer mentions the noisy laughter of **boisterous** children. Here, **boisterous** means
   (A) rude and hateful
   (B) gentle and kind
   (C) faint and far away
   (D) lively and loud

16. The writer states, "There was also **riotous** laughter from the adults as they exchanged jokes and gossip." Here, **riotous** means
   (A) insincere
   (B) loud
   (C) cruel
   (D) quiet

17. In the article, **acceptance** most nearly means
   (A) threat
   (B) enthusiasm
   (C) importance
   (D) approval

18. Which of the following is the most likely reason that Italian Americans began to see school as a **privilege**?
   (A) The children enjoyed school.
   (B) Education helped them escape poverty.
   (C) The schools were seen as a threat.
   (D) Everyone seemed trapped by poverty.

19. All of the following are good definitions of **premiere** *except*
   (A) awards ceremony
   (B) opening
   (C) first showing
   (D) first exhibition

20. The writer claims "It is not an **exaggeration** to say that Italian Americans have enriched the United States." Here, **exaggeration** means
   (A) possibility
   (B) enrichment
   (C) advantage
   (D) overstatement

READING NEW WORDS IN CONTEXT

Lesson 8 | CONTEXT: Coming to the United States

Introduction. The Statue of Liberty is associated undeniably with the new beginning sought by many immigrants to the United States. This monument to freedom, however, was not always in the New York Harbor and did not always mean the end of a traveler's journey.

The following article gives you an opportunity to expand your vocabulary. Below are twenty Vocabulary Words that are used in the article and in the exercise that follows it.

dedicate	exertion	imperative	liable	recuperate
depose	hamper	impose	memento	restrain
dispense	haven	inconsiderate	negligent	spacious
dissect	humidity	intercept	presume	tumult

The Statue of Liberty and Ellis Island

The image that most people have of immigrants arriving in the United States from Europe includes a picture of the Statue of Liberty. However, the statue was not a part of New York Harbor until 1886. The towering monument was the work of French sculptor Frédéric Auguste Bartholdi (1834–1904). It was a gift of the French people, who **dedicated** (1) it to—that is, presented it in honor of—the people of the United States.

Actually, the statue almost did not make it into the harbor. Completion was **hampered** (2) by a lack of funds, but publisher Joseph Pulitzer launched a campaign to raise the needed money and to speed up the process. The nation's people responded with enough pennies, nickels, and dimes to make the dream a reality.

Today, it is almost impossible to imagine the harbor without the statue. It has become a symbol of the United States as a **haven** (3) for the poor and burdened, as a place where people could be safe and have a chance at a better life. More than 100 million immigrants have sailed past the statue

on their way into the United States.

When the descendants of those immigrants visit New York City, they usually feel it is **imperative** (4) to visit the monument. They feel that the visit is necessary out of respect to their families. Many come away with some sort of souvenir, or **memento** (5), such as a snapshot or a postcard, of their visit. However, most will need nothing to remind them of such a moving experience. The sight of the statue makes a lasting impression on people's minds. The inside of the huge monument is also remarkable. It is large and **spacious** (6), and it houses the American Museum of Immigration. The museum's exhibits tell the story of immigration to the United States. Climbing the stairs to the statue's crown requires great **exertion** (7); visitors must climb 142 steps to reach it, but the wonderful view from the observation windows is worth the effort.

Liberty After All?

When we imagine immigrants seeing the Statue of Liberty for the first time, we **presume** (8) that it was a joyous event. We may suppose that some people could barely **restrain** (9) their joy and relief, especially after a long, hard sea voyage. On the other hand, some immigrants probably held back their emotions because they feared that their escape to the U.S. was not final. Some of those immigrants whom the statue welcomed might not be allowed into the country after all.

From 1892 to 1954, immigrants who passed the Statue of Liberty went straight to Ellis Island, where they were "processed." There, they waited on the second floor of the reception center, referred to as the Tower of Babel. It is easy to imagine the noise and **tumult** (10) of thousands of people speaking many different languages as they awaited their fates. Incoming immigrants were met by officials whose duty was to **intercept** (11), or stop, and turn back those who were in less than perfect health. The immigrants received a complete but very brief physical. The officials **dispensed** (12), or dealt out, white chalk marks that indicated whether the new arrivals could stay or had to go. Some of the examiners were careless and **negligent** (13) at best. Others were downright dangerous. Imagine an official lifting eyelid after eyelid with a buttonhook to check for signs of disease!

It is also easy to imagine the fear of a young couple who have fled their country after taking part in a failed attempt to **depose** (14) a tyrant. Would they pass inspection, or would they be returned to face punishment for the attempted overthrow? The stress caused by being processed at Ellis Island was great. Moreover, immigrants faced this ordeal before they had a chance to **recuperate** (15) after their hard journey aboard a crowded ship. The facilities on Ellis Island made recovery from the hard trip difficult. In the winter, the building was cold and damp. In the muggy days of summer, the heat and **humidity** (16) could be unbearable. Decent sleeping arrangements were nonexistent, and processing could take days.

Once the immigrants passed inspection, they were **liable** (17) —in fact, almost certain—to encounter officials who were rude and **inconsiderate** (18). If their names were difficult for an official to pronounce or to spell, they were likely to come away with a new name **imposed** (19) on them by an official who changed it without a second thought.

Hopes for a Better Life

Despite this treatment, immigrants held on to their dreams of a better life in the United States. More than 100 million of them—the grandparents and great-grandparents and great-great grandparents of more than 40 percent of the citizens of the United States—came through Ellis Island.

Now, when their descendants come to New York for a glimpse of the statue that welcomed them, the descendants can also visit the museum that opened on Ellis Island in 1990 to honor the immigrants. Those who visit say that there is something awesome about simply being there. They also report feeling overwhelmed by emotion. Later, when they **dissect** (20) the feeling and examine its parts, they find that it is part joy, part hope, and part sorrow—but mostly it is love and pride.

EXERCISE   *Reading Strategically*

Directions. Answer each of the following items by circling the letter of the correct answer. You may need to refer to the selection as you answer the items. The numbers of the items are the same as the numbers of the boldface Vocabulary Words in the selection.

1. The writer indicates that the French **dedicated** the statue. Here, **dedicated** means
   (A) made a sculpture of
   (B) presented in honor of
   (C) withheld from
   (D) worked hard on

2. In the second paragraph of the article, **hampered** means
   (A) held up   (C) finished
   (B) in a basket (D) caused

3. In order to give a clue to the meaning of **haven,** the writer
   (A) points out that the statue is a symbol
   (B) notes that the United States is a place where people could be safe
   (C) says that the poor and oppressed saw the statue
   (D) mentions that more than 100 million immigrants came into New York Harbor

4. To let us know that **imperative** means essential or really important, the writer
   (A) tells us that the descendants come to New York
   (B) says that the descendants feel that the visit is necessary
   (C) notes that the ancestors were welcomed
   (D) believes that one should respect one's family

5. _____ is an example mentioned in the article of a **memento** that a visitor might take away from the monument.
   (A) A museum   (C) An experience
   (B) Respect   (D) A postcard

6. You can tell from the article that **spacious** means
   (A) roomy
   (B) historical
   (C) empty
   (D) dramatic

7. Which of the following is the most likely reason that it takes great **exertion** to reach the statue's crown?
   (A) The museum's exhibit tells the story of the immigrants.
   (B) The view from the observation windows is wonderful.
   (C) Visitors must climb 142 steps.
   (D) It is worth the effort.

8. You can tell from the article that **presume** means
   (A) to imagine feelings
   (B) to forget the past
   (C) to remember carefully
   (D) to suppose

9. To give a clue to the meaning of **restrain,** the writer
   (A) suggests that we imagine the joy of seeing the statue for the first time
   (B) tells us that seeing the statue was a joyous event for immigrants
   (C) contrasts immigrants who could not **restrain** their emotions with those who held back their emotions
   (D) says that some immigrants might not be allowed into the United States

10. The writer says that it is easy to imagine the noise and **tumult** at Ellis Island. Here, **tumult** means
    (A) unhappiness
    (B) boredom
    (C) commotion
    (D) language

11. The writer states, "Incoming immigrants were met by officials whose duty was to **intercept** . . . and turn back those who were in less than perfect health." Here, **intercept** means
    (A) to congratulate
    (B) to stop
    (C) to welcome
    (D) to prepare

12. The author writes, "The officials **dispensed,** or dealt out, white chalk marks that indicated whether the new arrivals could stay or go." Here, **dispensed** means
    (A) received
    (B) gave out
    (C) preferred
    (D) ignored

13. You can tell from the article that **negligent** means
    (A) nervous
    (B) professional
    (C) rude
    (D) careless

14. All of the following are good definitions of **depose** *except*
    (A) to create
    (B) to overthrow
    (C) to remove
    (D) to unseat

15. You can tell from the article that to **recuperate** means
    (A) to repeat
    (B) to recover
    (C) to remember
    (D) to relate

16. To let us know that **humidity** means the degree of dampness in the air, the writer
    (A) comments on the terrible conditions at Ellis Island
    (B) mentions the immigrants' hard journey
    (C) links **humidity** to the word *muggy*
    (D) tells us that decent sleeping arrangements were impossible to find

17. To give a clue to the meaning of **liable,** the writer
    (A) tells us that immigrants were almost certain to meet rude officials
    (B) tells us that names could be difficult to spell
    (C) says that processing could take days
    (D) says that officials were encountered

18. Another word that has nearly the same meaning as **inconsiderate** is
    (A) thoughtless
    (B) likely
    (C) difficult
    (D) vicious

19. The writer says that officials sometimes **imposed** a new name on an immigrant. Here, **imposed** means
    (A) called
    (B) repeated
    (C) forced
    (D) created

20. You can tell from the article that **dissect** means
    (A) to examine
    (B) to experience
    (C) to report
    (D) to recall

READING NEW WORDS IN CONTEXT

Lesson 9 | CONTEXT: Coming to the United States

Introduction. In most cases, people came to the United States, bringing with them their culture. But in a few cases, as with American Indians and many Mexican Americans, the United States came to the people.

The following article tells how the United States came to the Mexicans living in Texas. The article gives you an opportunity to expand your vocabulary. Below are twenty Vocabulary Words that are used in the article and in the exercise that follows it.

aroma	dismantle	gracious	occupant	remote
baste	elegant	haughty	populate	rigid
capital	embarrass	manageable	prearrange	saturate
diminish	frequency	monopoly	probation	sedate

When the Country Came to the People: Mexican Americans

People whose ancestors came with John Smith to Virginia or with the Pilgrims to Massachusetts rightfully take pride in their roots. However, those that become **haughty** (1) about their colonial heritage should remember that another group of Europeans settled in the Americas first—the Spanish.

The Spanish frequently intermarried with the American Indian population. The children of Spanish and American Indian parents were called *mestizos.* The settlers in Mexico established forts, missions, and ranches and **populated** (2) villages in what is now the southwestern United States. They settled there long before other settlers pushed westward across the Mississippi River.

Life in the Southwest
Many of these settlements were isolated from one another, and the sprawling ranches could be very **remote** (3) indeed. However, in southern Texas and southern California, there were **elegant** (4) houses with luxurious furnishings and gracious (5), welcoming courtyards. The **occupants** (6) of these houses were wealthy families who had **capital** (7) to invest in the new territory, and they became the aristocrats of the Southwest.

In small villages, people lived by certain social rules. These rules may seem **rigid** (8) by today's standards, but the people who lived by them did not seem to find them too restrictive. For example, **sedate** (9) behavior was expected from young people, and being swept away by emotion was frowned upon. A young woman would not **embarrass** (10) her family by paying obvious attention to a young man. Similarly, no polite young man would make a young woman feel uncomfortable by being overly friendly. That could damage a girl's reputation and **diminish** (11), or lessen, her family's standing in the community.

Ranch life was much more rugged. On the ranches, the vaqueros, or cowboys, herded sturdy, rangy cattle. Such was life in the country, first under Spanish rule and later, after Mexico won its independence from Spain, under Mexican rule.

Settlers from the United States

The United States was pushing westward, and change was coming. In the early 1800s, Mexico began to encourage settlement in one of its northern provinces—what is now Texas. At first, no one group had a **monopoly** (12) on settling the region; people came from everywhere. However, more and more settlers came from the southern United States. Soon these people became anxious to mold the territory in their own image. It seems unlikely that they had **prearranged** (13) a revolution. They did not plan to revolt against Mexican rule. However, it is clear that they never truly thought of themselves as citizens of Mexico.

Settlers arrived from the United States with increasing **frequency** (14). More and more of them moved West, and they soon outnumbered the Mexican population five to one. The government of Mexico found it increasingly difficult to control the large number of people moving to Texas, and they decided to prohibit further immigration in an attempt to make the northern province more **manageable** (15). Their action was too late. The settlers were determined to achieve independence.

The settlers' decision to declare independence presented a problem for the Mexican community in Texas. Most were loyal to the Mexican government. After all, Mexico had only just succeeded in establishing its independence from Spain. Others, however, saw an advantage in establishing a new form of government, so some Mexicans sided with the U.S. citizens in the Texas Revolution.

When the war was over, the Mexicans in Texas had two choices. They could stay in their homes and accept their roles in a new country, or they could abandon their homes and move back across the new border to Mexico, Many Mexicans decided not to make a hasty decision. They wanted to avoid having to **dismantle** (16) their homes, to take apart everything they had worked for. They decided on a period of **probation** (17). They took a wait-and-see attitude. Many eventually decided to accept the change. It was in this manner that many people of Mexican descent became citizens of the United States.

Appreciating the American Southwest

Visitors to the Southwest are often entranced with the harsh beauty of the region. They soak up its culture so that later, back home, they can still see the sweeping plains, the rugged mountains, and the deep canyons. They can still smell the clean, fresh **aroma** (19) of the piñon tree. Their tongues remember the bite of jalapeño peppers and the rich flavor of ears of corn lightly **basted** (20), or moistened, with oil that had been **saturated** (18), or thoroughly soaked, with red pepper, and roasted on the grill. They fall in love with the architecture, with adobe and red tile, with the statues and the cathedrals. Most come away with a new appreciation of Mexican American culture and long to return.

EXERCISE *Reading Strategically*

Directions. Answer each of the following items by circling the letter of the correct answer. You may need to refer to the selection as you answer the items. The numbers of the items are the same as the numbers of the Vocabulary Words in the selection.

1. Another way to say **haughty** is
   (A) overly proud
   (B) thickly settled
   (C) colonial
   (D) forgetful

2. You can tell from the article that **populated** means
   (A) inhabited
   (B) destroyed
   (C) abandoned
   (D) conquered

3. The writer states, "Sprawling ranches could be very **remote** indeed." Here, **remote** means
(A) old
(B) large
(C) isolated
(D) rough

4. The writer states, "However, in southern Texas and southern California, there were **elegant** houses with luxurious furnishings. . . ." Here, **elegant** means
(A) old-fashioned
(B) luxurious
(C) small
(D) ranch style

5. In the article, an example of something **gracious** is a
(A) wealthy family
(B) southern Californian
(C) welcoming courtyard
(D) sprawling ranch

6. The writer uses the term **occupants** when talking about the houses. Here, **occupants** means
(A) the furnishings of the houses
(B) the people who lived in the houses
(C) the visitors to the houses
(D) the houses themselves

7. The writer gives a clue to the meaning of **capital**. What is the clue?
(A) The writer notes that settlements were isolated from one another.
(B) The writer implies that the wealthy families founded their own states.
(C) The writer comments on the beautiful homes of the wealthy families.
(D) The writer indicates that **capital** is what people invest.

8. The writer gives a clue to the meaning of **rigid**. What is the clue?
(A) Young people went for strolls.
(B) People lived in small villages.
(C) Boys did not make girls feel uncomfortable.
(D) People didn't find the rules too restrictive.

9. The writer states, "For example, **sedate** behavior was expected from young people. . . ." Here, **sedate** means
(A) uncomfortable
(B) rapid
(C) calm
(D) frowning

10. The writer says that a young woman would not **embarrass** her family. Here, **embarrass** means
(A) to ignore
(B) to ridicule
(C) to make uncomfortable
(D) to lie to

11. All of the following are good definitions of **diminish** *except*
(A) improve
(B) lessen
(C) reduce
(D) decrease

12. Which of the following is mentioned in the article to explain why, at first, no one group had a **monopoly** on the settlement of Texas?
(A) Most Texas settlers were U.S. citizens.
(B) Settlers from all over came to Texas.
(C) Settlers came from the United States.
(D) Mexico tried to discourage U.S. citizens from settling Texas.

13. You can tell from the article that **prearranged** means
   (A) planned
   (B) spontaneous
   (C) loyal
   (D) revolutionary

14. To let us know that **frequency** means the rate of occurrence, the writer
   (A) mentions that more and more colonists moved to the West
   (B) suggests that the government regretted its decision
   (C) notes that white settlers never truly thought of themselves as citizens of Mexico
   (D) reminds us that the province was in the northern part of Mexico

15. In this article, **manageable** means
   (A) original
   (B) controllable
   (C) small
   (D) similar

16. The writer states that the Mexicans didn't want to **dismantle** their homes. Here, **dismantle** means to
   (A) build a fire in a fireplace
   (B) construct
   (C) take apart
   (D) sell to the highest bidder

17. The writer states, "They decided on a period of **probation**." Here, **probation** means
   (A) punishment
   (B) forgiveness
   (C) problem
   (D) trial

18. To let you know that **saturate** means to soak, the writer
   (A) refers to delicious southwestern food
   (B) indicates that visiting the Southwest is a strange experience
   (C) refers to canyons
   (D) notes that the oil had been soaked with red pepper.

19. The writer uses the word **aroma** when describing the piñion tree. Here, **aroma** means
   (A) sweeping
   (B) freshness
   (C) smell
   (D) cleanliness

20. You can tell from the article that **basted** means
   (A) salted
   (B) moistened
   (C) soaked
   (D) stitched

READING NEW WORDS IN CONTEXT

Lesson 10 CONTEXT: Coming to the United States

Introduction. People immigrate to the United States for a number of reasons. Unhappily, one of the most common reasons for leaving one's country behind is war. In the 1970s and 1980s, many people left their homes and loved ones behind in the war-torn country of Vietnam to make a new home in the United States.

The following article tells you about Vietnamese immigration to the United States and gives you an opportunity to expand your vocabulary. Below are twenty Vocabulary Words that are used in the article and in the exercise that follows it.

access	dingy	jeopardize	persistent	remorse
accommodations	disagreeable	liberate	pleasantry	thrifty
adept	evacuate	maroon	provision	titanic
circumnavigate	humiliate	notify	regime	verify

Leaving Saigon

The country of Vietnam was torn by civil war for years. The United States military played a role in that war for many of those years, but by the early 1970s most U.S. troops had returned home. However, a few Americans remained. It was to these Americans that many Vietnamese turned in 1975 when the North Vietnamese entered Saigon, the capital of South Vietnam.

The North Vietnamese claimed they were freeing the city from a corrupt government, but many South Vietnamese did not feel that they were being **liberated** (1). They were afraid of the actions the new government might take. Many were certain to be imprisoned or executed by the new **regime** (2). The men and women who had worked for the U.S. felt particularly **jeopardized** (3) by the change in power. They knew they were in danger of being marked as traitors.

As the North Vietnamese troops approached Saigon, many South Vietnamese citizens made the decision to flee the city. U.S. citizens were also preparing to **evacuate** (4) their embassy. For many Vietnamese, the embassy seemed to be the only escape. Crowds of people began to make their way there, hoping to be picked up and taken to safety by helicopters. It soon was clear that there would be too many people and not enough helicopters.

There was much confusion in the city. Family members were separated and could not find each other. Some who were leaving did not have time to **notify** (5) their families. They left without having the opportunity to say goodbye. Some felt guilty, as though they were abandoning their families, and this sense of **remorse** (6) would cause them much pain for many years. Eventually, many of these people made homes in the United States. They were the first of several waves of Vietnamese immigrants to this country.

The Boat People

In the late 1970s and early 1980s, many other Vietnamese fled turmoil in their homeland. Most escaped in small fishing boats. These boat people, as they were called, had to be careful, for they would be sent to prison if they were caught. They had to begin gathering their supplies and **provisions** (7) weeks in advance. They might hide cans of gasoline, jars of water, and extra bags of rice in the jungle. It was a **titanic** (8) undertaking, and it took all their strength and courage.

It was also a dangerous journey, for the fishing boats were never intended to sail the high seas. Still, the boat people were willing to **circumnavigate** (9), or sail around, the globe in these boats for a chance for a new life in a free country. However, their goal was the safety of a refugee camp in Thailand, Hong Kong, or the Philippines.

Today, we cannot **verify** (10) the exact number of Vietnamese who left in this way, nor can we confirm how many of them died at sea. We do know that thousands of Vietnamese people, desperate to escape Vietnam, began their journey to the United States in small boats.

The Camps

Those who survived the sea voyage ended up in refugee camps in other Southeast Asian countries. The **accommodations** (11) were terrible; people lived in small tents and flimsy lean-tos. Life in the camps was **disagreeable** (12) at best. For most, it was miserable. The refugees often had to wait long months in the dirty and dangerous camps before they could continue their journey to their new homelands.

In a New Country

Starting life in a new country is always difficult.

Sadly, many U.S. citizens made it even more difficult for Vietnamese immigrants. They demonstrated their prejudice in many ways. They often made rude remarks that caused the immigrants to feel embarrassed and **humiliated** (13).

A dark, **dingy** (14) apartment in a huge city is quite an adjustment for someone used to the rich, tropical lushness of Vietnamese village life. Sometimes refugees would be placed in apartments far from other Vietnamese people. Without telephones, transportation, or any other means of easy **access** (15) to other Vietnamese immigrants, they felt stranded, **marooned** (16). As soon as they could, they moved into one of the city's Vietnamese neighborhoods. There at least life was a bit more familiar. Grocery stores sold the vegetables and ingredients necessary to make Vietnamese food. The pharmacies carried familiar ointments and herbs. In the Vietnamese neighborhoods, immigrants could exchange gossip and **pleasantries** (17).

Life was hard. Yet, the Vietnamese people were **adept** (18) at survival. Years of hardship had made them strong and capable. They were also **persistent** (19). They did not give up in the face of difficulties. Many immigrants coped with their lack of resources by being **thrifty** (20). They lived as cheaply as possible and saved their money. They opened their own businesses and sent their children to college. Today, they have found a place in the United States, the country that they sometimes refer to as the Freedom Land.

EXERCISE *Reading Strategically* ✍

Directions. Answer each of the following items by circling the letter of the correct answer. You may need to refer to the selection as you answer the items. The numbers of the items are the same as the numbers of the boldface Vocabulary Words in the selection.

1. The writer of this article gives a clue to the meaning of **liberated**. What is the clue?
   (A) The South Vietnamese were afraid.
   (B) The new government would take action.
   (C) The North Vietnamese claimed they were freeing the city.
   (D) The South Vietnamese turned to the Americans for help.

2. You can tell from the article that **regime** means
   (A) government
   (B) workers
   (C) action
   (D) prison

3. The writer states, "The men and women who had worked for the U.S. felt particularly **jeopardized** by the change in power." Here, **jeopardized** means
   (A) excited
   (B) threatened
   (C) angered
   (D) criticized

4. In the third paragraph, **evacuate** means
   (A) to destroy
   (B) to overrun
   (C) to withdraw from
   (D) to go to an embassy

5. The writer states, "Some who were leaving did not have time to **notify** their families." Here, **notify** means
   (A) to remember
   (B) to abandon
   (C) to take
   (D) to tell

6. The writer indicates that some who left South Vietnam felt guilty and that the **remorse** caused them pain for many years. Here, **remorse** means
   (A) suffering
   (B) escape
   (C) guilt
   (D) impossibility

7. Which of the following is a way that some South Vietnamese people gathered **provisions** for their departure?
   (A) They knew it was important to be careful.
   (B) Those who were caught would go to prison.
   (C) They stored gasoline, water, and food for their trip.
   (D) They knew that the journey would be dangerous.

8. In this article, **titanic** means
   (A) enormous
   (B) courageous
   (C) important
   (D) special

9. The writer indicates that the Vietnamese were willing to **circumnavigate** the globe to find freedom. Here, **circumnavigate** means
   (A) to go fishing
   (B) to hide from
   (C) to begin again
   (D) to sail around

10. The writer says that we can't **verify** the exact number of Vietnamese who left. Here, **verify** means
    (A) to improve upon
    (B) to argue with
    (C) to confirm
    (D) to imagine

11. You can tell that **accommodations** means
    (A) workload
    (B) camping trip
    (C) housing
    (D) sea voyage

12. The writer states, "Life in the camps was **disagreeable** at best." Here, **disagreeable** means
    (A) tending to argue
    (B) unpleasant
    (C) dull
    (D) eventful

13. Which of the following is a reason mentioned in the article that some Vietnamese immigrants felt **humiliated**?
    (A) Starting life in a new country is a challenging task.
    (B) Some Vietnamese immigrants had never lived in a city.
    (C) Some U.S. citizens made rude comments about them.
    (D) Some Vietnamese immigrants lived far from other Vietnamese communities.

14. All of the following are good definitions of **dingy** *except*
    (A) dirty
    (B) dry
    (C) grimy
    (D) shabby

15. To suggest that **access** means a way to contact, the writer
    (A) says that the Vietnamese did not have telephones or transportation
    (B) mentions that many Vietnamese immigrants did not speak English
    (C) refers to Vietnamese village life
    (D) explains that there were Vietnamese neighborhoods

16. You can tell from the article that **marooned** means
    (A) stranded
    (B) unhappy
    (C) unfriendly
    (D) adventurous

17. The writer indicates that the Vietnamese exchange **pleasantries**. Here, **pleasantries** means
    (A) recipes
    (B) neighborhoods
    (C) small talk
    (D) businesses

18. All of the following are good definitions of **adept** *except*
    (A) skilled
    (B) very able
    (C) expert
    (D) clumsy

19. You can tell from the article that people who are **persistent**
    (A) face hardship
    (B) keep trying
    (C) are immigrants
    (D) live cheaply

20. The writer of this article gives a clue to the meaning of **thrifty**. What is the clue?
    (A) Years of hardship had made Vietnamese immigrants strong.
    (B) Vietnamese immigrants lived as cheaply as possible.
    (C) Vietnamese immigrants did not give up in the face of difficulties.
    (D) Vietnamese immigrants opened their own businesses.

READING NEW WORDS IN CONTEXT

Lesson 11 CONTEXT: Voices of the United States

Introduction. History is not just the memorization of names and dates. The study of history can help us understand who we are, where we come from, and where we are going.

In the following story, a social studies teacher talks about what U.S. history means to him. The story also gives you an opportunity to expand your vocabulary. Below are twenty Vocabulary Words that are used in the story and in the exercise that follows it.

aspiration	foreword	obituary	pun	salutation
blockade	generate	obscure	quaint	satire
confiscate	indelible	pewter	quench	tariff
diplomat	neutral	premier	sable	urgent

A Teacher Speaks

James Matsamura teaches social studies at Washington Middle School. Today he is talking with some of his students about the political heritage of the United States.

"There are many things that I love about this country," he says, "but what moves me the most may be the Constitution of the United States. It reflects the **aspirations** (1), the ambitions, of the nation's people, both when it was written and today. Sometimes I feel as though the words 'We, the people' are a part of me, as if they are permanently written on my heart in **indelible** (2) ink."

Alan raises his hand. "Mr. Matsamura, why should we have to remember all this historical stuff? It happened a long time ago. Why should we remember that guy who made silver trays and **pewter** (3) candlesticks or whatever?"

Mr. Matsamura's tone is **urgent** (4) because he wants his students to mark his words. "The person you refer to, Paul Revere, might have been an **obscure** (5) silversmith, remembered by almost no one. After he died, there would have been nothing much to write in his **obituary** (6) other than the fact that he made nice tea services—if he

hadn't played such an important role in founding this country. The story of his ride is not just a **quaint** (7) little tale—a pleasant, old-fashioned story. It's part of our heritage. What other stories have you heard about the country's founders?"

A Student Discussion

Mr. Matsamura's remarks seem to **generate** (8) some enthusiasm. For a few minutes, the students in the class engage in a noisy discussion of stories. Then they focus on the Boston Tea Party. They discuss the colonists' decision to **confiscate** (9) British tea, to seize it and dump it into the harbor. They talk about the British **blockade** (10) of Boston Harbor following the incident, and they offer ideas about why the British wanted to cut Boston off from the rest of the world. They debate why the colonists resented the taxes, or **tariffs** (11), on imports and exports. It's a lively discussion.

An Explanation

After a while, Mr. Matsamura begins an explanation of why **diplomats** (12) were unable to resolve the differences between the colonists and England.

"Actually," he says, "I suppose **diplomat** is the wrong word, since **diplomacy** usually involves discussions between separate countries. Ben Franklin wasn't an official **diplomat** when he went to England in 1757, but he did represent the colonists. For him, it was of **premier** (13) importance that the British government understand the colonists' concerns. In fact, it was his first and only goal. Some British officials were **neutral** (14), but most were firm in their belief that the colonies should remain colonies. It's fascinating to imagine what the world would be like today if they had listened to the colonists' demands."

"I was wondering," Suni asks, "if you take all this stuff so seriously, why do you let us joke around about it?"

The Importance of Humor

"Remember that almost every one of the founders had a sense of humor," Mr. Matsamura says. "**Satire** (15), a form of writing that attacks faults, was one of their favorite weapons. Most of them loved a good **pun** (16), or play on words, too."

"Actually, this country has almost always had a sense of humor. I once read—I think it was in the foreword (17) to a history of New England—that the Puritans believed that a certain element of fun and playfulness was important to even the most serious issues. I guess not many people have read that introduction because most people believe that the Puritans were a humorless bunch. Anyway, I also believe a sense of humor is very important. Anyone who wants to silence laughter is likely to be a person who wants to **quench** (18) the flame of liberty itself."

A Land of Freedom

Mr. Matsamura adds, "Let me share with you a couple of other things that I admire about this country. I like it when the President addresses us as 'My fellow Americans.' It's a little corny, but that **salutation** (19) says to me that in some way the President is like any other citizen."

"And I like to see people out demonstrating for various causes—people protesting the manufacturing of fur coats from animals like minks and **sables** (20), people protesting the dumping of sewage in our rivers, people protesting the closing of libraries. I don't always agree with their causes, but I love seeing people out there, exercising their constitutional rights. It reminds me that we live in a country that is truly free."

EXERCISE *Reading Strategically*

Directions. Answer each of the following items by circling the letter of the correct answer. You may need to refer to the selection as you answer the items. The numbers of the items are the same as the numbers of the boldface Vocabulary Words in the selection.

1. The writer says the Constitution reflects the **aspirations** of the citizens of the United States. Here, **aspirations** means
   (A) frustrations
   (B) independence
   (C) ambitions
   (D) reflections

2. You can tell from the story that **indelible** means
   (A) permanent
   (B) black
   (C) unforgivable
   (D) interesting

3. You can tell by the story that **pewter** means
   (A) very large
   (B) a kind of metal
   (C) beautiful
   (D) very old

4. Which of the following is a reason mentioned in the story that Mr. Matsamura speaks with an **urgent** tone?
   (A) He wants his students to know that he is joking.
   (B) He wants his students to pay attention to what he says.
   (C) He does not want his students to dwell on Paul Revere.
   (D) He is annoyed by Alan's question.

5. The writer provides a clue to the meaning of **obscure**. What is the clue?
   (A) Paul Revere was a talented silversmith.
   (B) Mr. Matsamura's tone is **urgent**.
   (C) Paul Revere played an important role in the founding of the United States.
   (D) Paul Revere might not have been remembered by anyone.

6. The writer provides a clue to the meaning of **obituary**. What is the clue?
   (A) Paul Revere played an important role in founding the country.
   (B) The writer remembers the story of Revere's ride.
   (C) The writer associates the word with something written after someone dies.
   (D) The writer uses the word *heritage*.

7. You can tell from the story that **quaint** means
   (A) pleasantly old-fashioned
   (B) inherited
   (C) American
   (D) important but subtle

8. How does the writer let us know that **generate** means to cause or create?
   (A) The discussion is over.
   (B) Mr. Matsamura asks a question.
   (C) There's not much enthusiasm over Mr. Matsamura's remarks.
   (D) Mr. Matsamura's remarks start a discussion.

9. The writer states, "They discuss the colonists' decision to **confiscate** British tea, to seize it and dump it into the harbor." Here, **confiscate** means to
   (A) drink
   (B) borrow temporarily
   (C) take away by force
   (D) destroy senselessly

10. The writer of the story gives a clue to the meaning of **blockade**. What is the clue?
    (A) The colonists resented taxes.
    (B) The colonists destroyed British property.
    (C) The British wanted to cut off Boston.
    (D) The British taxed the colonists heavily.

11. The writer uses the word **tariffs** when writing about the colonists. Here, **tariffs** means
    (A) taxes
    (B) trade
    (C) resentments
    (D) punishments

12. You can tell from the article that **diplomats** are
    (A) people from the colonies who went to England
    (B) persons who represent the interests of one country to another
    (C) any members of government
    (D) people who are not from a particular country

13. The writer states, "For him, it was of **premier** importance that the British government understand the colonists' concerns." Here, **premier** means

(A) major
(B) understandable
(C) general
(D) some

14. The writer indicates that some British officials were **neutral**. Here, **neutral** means

(A) not taking sides
(B) patriots
(C) uninterested
(D) not serious

15. The writer indicates that **satire** was a favorite weapon of the country's founders. Here, **satire** means

(A) physical attacks
(B) writing that attacks faults
(C) writing that resists humor
(D) humor that makes a play on words

16. The writer states, "Most of them loved a good **pun**." Here, **pun** means

(A) a word puzzle
(B) writing that attacks faults
(C) a play on words
(D) jokes in a foreign language

17. All of the following are good definitions of **foreword** *except*

(A) introduction
(B) preface
(C) opening remarks
(D) conclusion

18. In the story, Mr. Matsamura compares a person who wants to **quench** the flame of liberty to someone who

(A) drinks water
(B) silences laughter
(C) encourages laughter
(D) writes humorous political sketches

19. An example of a **salutation** that appears in the story is

(A) the President of the United States
(B) a demonstrator
(C) "My fellow Americans"
(D) a corny or trite phrase

20. In the last paragraph, **sable** means

(A) a protestor
(B) an animal
(C) a dark color
(D) a fake fur coat

READING NEW WORDS IN CONTEXT

Lesson 12 | CONTEXT: Voices of the United States

Introduction. One of the greatest compliments we can give someone is to say that he or she has a great sense of humor. It's not much fun being around someone who has lost his or her sense of humor—or who never had one at all.

The following selection gives you an opportunity to read about the role of humor in society. The selection also enables you to expand your vocabulary. Below are twenty Vocabulary Words that are used in the selection and in the exercise that follows it.

activate	colossal	essay	petty	successor
apt	confide	intolerance	pious	summit
charitable	deduction	invariable	proposal	tarnish
clarify	eccentric	irk	sarcasm	temperament

The Sound of Laughter

Most of us find it impossible to believe that someone really doesn't have a sense of humor. We assume that it's in there somewhere, and if we can only push the right button we'll be able to **activate** (1) it, to set it into motion.

Humor: No Laughing Matter
Since we all know that a sense of humor is important, why is it that we refuse to take it seriously? Okay, don't answer that. But think about this. If you started talking about what a great sense of humor people like George Washington and Abigail Adams had, some people might think you were attempting to **tarnish** (2) their reputation. Some people have an **intolerance** (3) for seeing famous people in this light. They would see it as an insult, not as a compliment. In fact, some people act as though our society would fall apart if we laughed at ourselves or our traditions. However, a more likely cause for a society to fall apart would be its inability to laugh at itself.

Cultural Diversity
The truth is that a sense of humor has always been an important part of the **temperament** (4) of the people of the United States. It's part of our national personality. Every group that has contributed to the cultural variety of the United States has contributed to our heritage of humor. American Indian cultures enjoy jokes and pranks. The British are famous for their **eccentric** (5) approach to humor: Few cultures have produced as many odd and offbeat humorists. Of course, the Irish are famous for laughter, and so are Jamaicans. Laughter seems to cut across religious lines, too. Even the most **pious** (6) nun or the most dedicated rabbi can enjoy a good laugh. The point is that laughter is universal and cuts across cultural boundaries.

Types of Humor

Humor in the United States comes in a variety of styles. There is a heritage of humor that is cutting and bitter, like the **sarcasm** (7) of H. L. Mencken (1880–1956). There is also humor that takes a more **charitable** (8) form, like the kindly humor of E. B. White (1899–1985). Some humor is lively and loud; some is quiet and easy to miss.

Another form is the humorous **essay** (9). For example, Benjamin Franklin (1706–1790) wrote short compositions designed not only to make a point but also to make the audience laugh. Today, humorous **essays** still appeal to us. For example, look at the success of newspaper columnist Dave Barry.

Now, humor also takes another form—the stand-up comic. Comedians who are **apt** Twain (10) in this particular style, such as Jerry Seinfeld, are **successors** (11) to Mark (1835–1910), Will Rogers (1879–1935), and numerous others who were famous for their ability to make an audience laugh. People like Seinfeld are following a long tradition. Some of these comics make jokes about politics, fads, and current events. Others seem to **confide** (12) the details of their personal lives. They treat audiences as trusted friends who will laugh with them at their foolish mistakes.

Traditionally, many humorists have focused on everyday things that **irk** (13), irritate, and annoy us, the small, even **petty** (14) details of everyday life. Sometimes they make us laugh by describing the ridiculous series of events that turned a minor mistake, such as wearing mismatched shoes, into a **colossal** (15) disaster, such as a herd of cattle stampeding through the White House Rose Garden during the annual Easter egg hunt.

Many people have tried to create humor by using some sort of logical process, but we can't be funny by using the process of **deduction** (16). It's hard to figure out logically what will make an audience laugh. Humor always seems to lose something when we try to make it clear by asking, "Why exactly is that funny?" When we try to **clarify** (17) the humor of something, the **invariable** (18) result of our attempt is confusion. It seems always to be true that we can't explain why something is funny—we just know humor when we see it or hear it.

As long as humor is not mean-spirited and hateful, it's good for us—as important as vegetables, exercise, rest, and fresh air. In fact, it's a wonder that no one has suggested that world leaders call a **summit** (19), or meeting of the heads of government, to discuss humor on a global scale. Here's my **proposal** (20)—lock them all in a room and don't let them out until they are all laughing.

EXERCISE   *Reading Strategically* 👉

Directions. Answer each of the following items by circling the letter of the correct answer. You may need to refer to the selection as you answer the items. The numbers of the items are the same as the numbers of the Vocabulary Words in the selection.

1. You can tell from the selection that **activate** means
    (A) to push
    (B) to start
    (C) tpend
    (D) to avoid

2. The clue to the meaning of **tarnish** is
    (A) George Washington and Abigail Adams are famous citizens
    (B) We refuse to enjoy humor
    (C) Some would see it as an insult to say great people had a sense of humor
    (D) Great people have a sense of humor

3. The writer states, "Some people have an **intolerance** for seeing famous people in this light." Here, **intolerance** means
   (A) absence of a sense of humor
   (B) quality of seriousness
   (C) closed mind
   (D) inability

4. The writer of this selection gives a clue to the meaning of **temperament**. What is the clue?
   (A) Humor is part of the personality of the U.S.
   (B) A sense of humor has always been important.
   (C) People should be humorous.
   (D) The U.S. has cultural variety.

5. All of the following are good definitions of **eccentric** *except*
   (A) odd
   (B) offbeat
   (C) forgettable
   (D) unusual

6. You can tell from the selection that **pious** means
   (A) poor and humble
   (B) good-natured and humorous
   (C) humorless and serious
   (D) religiously devoted

7. The writer indicates that **sarcasm** plays a role in our heritage of laughter. Here, **sarcasm** means
   (A) cutting and bitter humor
   (B) old-fashioned, gentle humor
   (C) inherited humor
   (D) a variety of humor

8. In this selection, **charitable** means
   (A) loud
   (B) kind
   (C) famous
   (D) funny

9. The writer gives us a clue to the meaning of **essay**. What is the clue?
   (A) **Essays** are a part of the country's heritage.
   (B) **Essays** are written to make audiences laugh.
   (C) Some humor is quiet and easy to miss, and some is loud and lively.
   (D) Ben Franklin wrote short compositions designed to make a point.

10. In this selection, **apt** means
    (A) able
    (B) funny
    (C) unusual
    (D) talkative

11. The writer gives a clue to the meaning of **successors**. What is the clue?
    (A) Stand-up comedy is a form of humor.
    (B) Stand-up comics are following a long tradition.
    (C) Audiences laugh at stand-up comics.
    (D) Stand-up comics make jokes about politics.

12. The writer gives us a clue to the meaning of **confide**. What is the clue?
    (A) Stand-up comics treat the audience as trusted friends.
    (B) Stand-up comics' mistakes are foolish.
    (C) Stand-up comics are following a long tradition.
    (D) Stand-up comics make jokes about current events.

13. In this selection, **irk** means all of the following *except*
    (A) irritate
    (B) annoy
    (C) threaten
    (D) bother

14. The writer states, "Traditionally, many humorists have focused on small, even **petty** details of everyday life." Here, **petty** means

(A) lovely
(B) forgotten
(C) humorous
(D) unimportant

15. The writer indicates that a minor mistake might lead to a **colossal** blunder. Here, **colossal** means

(A) interesting
(B) enormous
(C) public
(D) everyday

16. Which of the following is the most likely reason that, in the writer's words, "We can't be funny by using the process of **deduction**"?

(A) Humor can't be created through a logical process.
(B) The writer is making a bad joke.
(C) Stand-up comics can make humor out of unimportant events.
(D) Some people try to analyze humor through a logical process.

17. The writer indicates that it's difficult to **clarify** our answers to questions about humor. Here, **clarify** means

(A) to laugh during
(B) to confuse
(C) to make clear
(D) to understand

18. In this selection, **invariable** means

(A) constant
(B) important
(C) likely
(D) occasional

19. In the last paragraph, **summit** means

(A) meeting of world leaders
(B) comedy
(C) humor on a global scale
(D) mountain top

20. Which of the following is an example of a **proposal** made by the writer?

(A) Humor is as important to us as vegetables, exercise, and rest.
(B) Lock all the world's leaders in a room until they are all laughing.
(C) Most people know humor when they see it, even if they can't explain it.
(D) Humor that is mean-spirited or hateful is not healthy.

READING NEW WORDS IN CONTEXT

Lesson 13   CONTEXT: Voices of the United States

Introduction. For Chinese Americans, the entryway to the United States between 1910 and 1940 was not New York Harbor and Ellis Island, but San Francisco Bay and Angel Island.

The following article gives you an opportunity to read about Chinese emigrants, people who left China in search of a better life. The article also enables you to expand your vocabulary. Below are twenty Vocabulary Words that are used in the article and in the exercise that follows it.

anonymous	contemporary	emphasize	fictitious	literal
casual	dictate	endorse	fragment	modify
climax	dilute	falter	improvise	occurrence
condemn	dispatch	famished	intrigue	therapy

Poems on the Wall: The Voices of Chinese Americans

When the United States Congress passed the Chinese Exclusion Act of 1882, it became nearly impossible for Chinese emigrants to enter the United States. Congress continued to **endorse** (1) the restrictions in this act or support similar ones for sixty years. The laws did allow for a few exceptions, and some Chinese people entered each year under special circumstances. The laws **dictated** (2) guidelines for entrance and also set the rules for determining who would be admitted to the country. The officials on Angel Island decided who met the requirements and would be allowed to stay.

Waiting on Angel Island

Most Chinese who arrived at Angel Island believed that they would be admitted to the United States right away. They were bitterly disappointed to discover that the **climax** (3) of their long journey was to await their fate for several nerve-wracking weeks on Angel Island. During this time, they were locked up as if they were criminals in prison. During their weeks of imprisonment, it is not surprising that the hope of the would-be immigrants began to **falter** (4) as they realized that they might be turned away. For some, the weeks dragged to months, and they gave in to despair. Some would be **condemned** (5) by circumstances to spend two years on Angel Island.

The Writing on the Wall

With nothing to do but wait, many of the Chinese turned to writing. Perhaps writing served as a kind of emotional **therapy** (6) by helping to heal their frustration and stress. The form they chose was poetry, and they wrote it where they could—on the walls of their prison. These poems were not **fragments** (7) and they were not the **casual** (8) scribblings of graffiti. They were complete and formal works of art.

Not all the poems survived. Some were written in pencil and were eventually painted over, but others were carved into the walls. The poets are **anonymous** (9). They did not sign their work, so no one knows their names. People who read the poems are **intrigued** (10) by the power and the beauty of the poetry, and they become curious about the fates of individuals who wrote them. We don't know for sure, however, which poets were allowed to stay and which were turned away.

Powerful Voices

Translation of poetry can be difficult. Sometimes the translator has to **modify** (11) the poem, making changes that will help the readers understand its meaning. However, translation has not **diluted** (12) the emotional impact of the Angel Island poems. These are words of pain, and they are powerful enough to retain their full effect even in translation.

The poets were **famished** (13) in more ways than one. The food was inedible, but they were also starving for freedom, for respect, and for dignity. Some of their poems read like **dispatches** (14) from a battle front. They are messages from people struggling to survive.

It should be pointed out, and perhaps even **emphasized** (15), that some of the poems are better than others. Some of the poets had clearly been educated in the art of Chinese poetry. Others had to **improvise** (16), to make do with sheer imagination, in the absence of formal training.

The language of the wall poems is the language of poetry. It is often not **literal** (17). The poets used many figures of speech. For example, one poet wrote about his or her willingness to become an ox, just to have the chance to work hard for a living. It is easy to imagine the frustration this poet must have felt as he or she sat idle in the cell.

The poems can also serve as a brief introduction to Chinese history and culture. Some mention historical figures. Others mention **fictitious** (18) characters from Chinese literature and myth. Some poems are about **occurrences** (19) in the daily lives of the poets. For example, a poet might mention the breakfast that day or a conversation with another prisoner.

A Timeless Message

Angel Island was closed in 1940, and the wall poems were lost for almost thirty years until they were rediscovered in 1970. Even though the most recent of these poems was written long ago, they speak to **contemporary** (20) audiences. They remind us today of those the world over who are camped along borders and who are knocking on the doors of free nations asking to be admitted. However, they speak most strongly to the children and grandchildren of the Chinese wall poets. The poems express the voices of people of courage and vision, of people who contributed to the song of liberty and diversity in the United States.

EXERCISE   *Reading Strategically* ☞

Directions. Answer each of the following items by circling the letter of the correct answer. You may need to refer to the selection as you answer the items. The numbers of the items are the same as the numbers of the boldface Vocabulary Words in the selection.

1. The writer states, "Congress continued to **endorse** the restrictions in this act or support similar ones for sixty years." Here, **endorse** means
(A) discourage
(B) approve
(C) leave off
(D) throw out

2. In the article, a clue to the meaning of **dictated** is
(A) that the laws also set the rules for determining entry
(B) that some Chinese were admitted under special circumstances
(C) that there were officials at Angel Island
(D) that the rules were seldom followed

3. The writer uses **climax** when referring to a part of the journey. Here, **climax** means
   (A) a sudden return to the beginning
   (B) the most intense part
   (C) an unlawful imprisonment
   (D) an unplanned detour

4. Which of the following most likely caused the Chinese emigrants' hopes to **falter** when they arrived at Angel Island?
   (A) Some managed to gain entry without much of a wait.
   (B) They realized that they might be turned way.
   (C) They believed that they would gain entry right away.
   (D) They had successfully completed a long journey.

5. You can tell from the article that **condemned** means
   (A) prevented
   (B) encouraged
   (C) bothered
   (D) doomed

6. You can tell from the article that **therapy** means
   (A) treatment for stress or illness
   (B) feelings of anger and frustration
   (C) the tendency to display emotion
   (D) a special form of writing

7. The writer of the article gives a clue to the meaning of **fragments**. What is the clue?
   (A) The writer contrasts **fragments** with complete works.
   (B) The writer associates **fragments** with walls.
   (C) The writer implies that most poems are **fragments**.
   (D) The Chinese chose to write poetry.

8. The writer indicates that the poems were not **casual** scribblings. Here, **casual** means
   (A) confused
   (B) printed
   (C) informal
   (D) bad

9. To show that **anonymous** means unknown, the writer
   (A) tells us that some poems did not survive
   (B) tells us that the surviving poems were carved
   (C) tells us that the poets did not sign their works
   (D) hints that there were many poets

10. The writer states, "People who read the poems are **intrigued** by the power and the beauty of the poetry. . . . " Here, **intrigued** means
    (A) fascinated
    (B) frightened
    (C) confused
    (D) unimpressed

11. The writer says that the translators had to **modify** the poems so that readers would understand them. Here, **modify** means to
    (A) borrow
    (B) change
    (C) destroy
    (D) translate

12. All of the following are good definitions of **diluted** *except*
    (A) lessened
    (B) weakened
    (C) destroyed by
    (D) watered down

13. The writer gives a clue to the meaning of **famished**. What is the clue?
   (A) The poems are messages.
   (B) The Chinese were not allowed to enter the country.
   (C) The poems have a strong impact.
   (D) The poets were starving.

14. The writer states, "Some of their poems read like **dispatches** from a battle front." Here, **dispatches** means
   (A) messages
   (B) bullets
   (C) struggles
   (D) riddles

15. You can tell from the article that **emphasized** means
   (A) noticed
   (B) stressed
   (C) ignored
   (D) encouraged

16. The writer says that some poets had to **improvise**. Here, **improvise** means
   (A) to borrow from
   (B) to study
   (C) to make do
   (D) to forget about

17. The writer states, "The language of the wall poems is the language of poetry. It is often not **literal**." Here, **literal** means
   (A) complex and confusing
   (B) unbelievable, ridiculous
   (C) full of unspoken meaning
   (D) limited to exact meaning

18. The writer states, "Others mention **fictitious** characters from Chinese literature and myth." Here, **fictitious** means
   (A) famous
   (B) realistic
   (C) imaginary
   (D) borrowed

19. An example mentioned in the article of **occurrences** in the daily lives of the Angel Island poets is
   (A) a brief introduction to Chinese history and literature
   (B) a mention of a historical figure
   (C) a mention of a character from Chinese myth
   (D) a conversation with another prisoner

20. Another way to say **contemporary** is
   (A) old-fashioned
   (B) of the present day
   (C) poet
   (D) immigrant

READING NEW WORDS IN CONTEXT

Lesson 14 | CONTEXT: Voices of the United States

Introduction. Storytelling can be used to entertain or simply to pass the time. However, in the hands of people who have been denied the means of directly expressing their feelings, storytelling takes on a much more important role. For enslaved African Americans, whose every action and every word were closely watched, storytelling was a tool for survival.

In the following article, you will learn how African Americans turned to stories for hope and made important contributions to American literature. The article also gives you an opportunity to expand your vocabulary. Below are twenty Vocabulary Words that are used in the article and in the exercise that follows it.

articulate	denial	eligible	inclination	tangible
braggart	derive	extensive	miscellaneous	testify
category	detach	illuminate	secluded	unique
demolish	distraction	imply	superficial	upbraid

African American Folk Tales and Storytellers

The African American experience is **unique** (1) in at least one important way. Almost every other group of immigrants came to the United States by choice. African Americans, however, were forced to make the trip across the ocean in chains.

Unlike other immigrants, they did not have the chance to pack their goods, and, once they landed, they were not allowed to settle in family groups. They arrived in a frightening new world with nothing but their memories and their stories.

It is important to realize that the position of storyteller among most African peoples was an important one. The storyteller was not a **braggart** (2), or know-it-all, but was highly respected in the community. Perhaps that explains why the literature of African Americans is so **extensive** (3). African American culture has produced a vast number of writers and storytellers who work in a wide variety of forms. Many of the stories have roots in African folk tales.

A Word About Folk Tales

Some people don't understand the importance of folk tales. They think of them only as stories that people tell to children. However, folk tales are a very special **category** (4) of literature, a type that is important in itself.

If a folk tale is not read carefully, it may seem to be a **superficial** (5) story, one that lacks depth. A serious look at folk tales will **demolish** (6) that false belief and replace it with a new insight. Folk tales are more than the expression of fantastic events; they actually **articulate** (7) the deepest beliefs of a people.

Hidden Meanings

For the enslaved African Americans, the stories they told were a way of keeping their different cultures alive. They could tell their stories without inviting slaveholders' suspicion, in part because the slaveholders thought the stories were just entertainment, a kind of **distraction** (8). Certainly, they missed the folklore's significance. At any rate, the slaveholders, and whites in general, showed no tendency to take part in the oral literature of the African Americans, nor did they have an **inclination** (9) to examine it closely. If they had looked beyond what the stories said outright to what the stories **implied** (10), they might have been surprised and angered. Very likely, they would have felt the need to **upbraid** (11), or take the African Americans to task, and tried to stamp the stories out.

Anyone who was familiar with the stories could **testify** (12) that they were not just harmless tales told to amuse the children. Such people could also have borne witness to the fact that the stories played an important role in the African American culture, but no one was about to give the secret away.

Storytelling

The African Americans lived separately from the white masters. In the evenings, **secluded** (13) in the slave quarters, they told their stories. Some of the stories were **derived** (14) from African folk tales. For example, many of the animal stories, such as the stories of Brer Fox and Brer Bear, have their source in older, eastern African folk tales.

The stories allowed the African Americans to **detach** (15), or disconnect, themselves from their suffering, and to look at their experiences from a different perspective. The stories that seemed so innocent to the white masters were in fact powerful messages of hope for enslaved people.

Later Folk Tales

It is not true that only stories told long ago are **eligible** (16) to be included in a collection of folk tales. Stories being invented in the streets, homes, and schools today qualify as folk tales, too; people share these stories with each other in a meaningful way just as they have always shared folk tales.

Any collection of **miscellaneous** (17) African American folk tales will include in the assortment stories that were created after the enslaved people were freed. These tales are likely to show an awareness that they were not yet truly free. Such stories often reflect the African Americans' attitudes toward the continued **denial** (18) of their rights. Like a light in the darkness, the stories **illuminate** (19) the feelings of a people who were free and yet still chained.

The folk tales are **tangible** (20) proof of the courage and wisdom of African Americans. Concrete evidence of their influence can be observed in the works of many African American writers, including Zora Neale Hurston (1891–1960), Langston Hughes (1902–1967), Toni Morrison (b. 1931), Alice Walker (b. 1944), Toni Cade Bambara (1939–1995), and Ralph Ellison (1914–1994). African American stories continue to give shape and voice to one more version of the American experience.

EXERCISE *Reading Strategically* ✍

Directions. Answer each of the following items by circling the letter of the correct answer. You may need to refer to the selection as you answer the items. The numbers of the items are the same as the numbers of the boldface Vocabulary Words in the selection.

1. The writer states, "The African American experience is **unique**. . . ." Here, **unique** means
   (A) one of a kind
   (B) similar to others
   (C) an interesting story
   (D) frequently considered

2. You can tell from the article that **braggart** means
   (A) boastful person
   (B) intelligent person
   (C) respected person
   (D) important person

3. According to the article, African American literature is **extensive.** Here, **extensive** means
   (A) important
   (B) vast
   (C) original
   (D) unusual

4. The writer states, "However, folk tales are a very special **category** of literature. . . ." Here, **category** means
   (A) organization
   (B) type
   (C) version
   (D) folk tale

5. You can tell from the article that **superficial** means
   (A) very serious
   (B) out of the ordinary
   (C) confusing
   (D) lacking depth

6. All of the following are good definitions of **demolish** *except*
   (A) to destroy
   (B) to tear down
   (C) to replace
   (D) to smash

7. To give a clue to the meaning of **articulate,** the writer
   (A) lets us know that new insights are possible
   (B) associates **articulate** with the word *depth*
   (C) associates **articulate** with the word *expression*
   (D) lets us know that folk tales are important

8. The writer explains that slaveholders "thought the stories were just entertainment, a kind of **distraction.**" Here, **distraction** means
   (A) stories
   (B) culture
   (C) amusement
   (D) confusion

9. The writer says that the whites had no **inclination** to examine the literature. Here, **inclination** means
   (A) tendency
   (B) understanding
   (C) examination
   (D) time

10. To give a clue to the meaning of **implied,** the writer
    (A) says the slaveholders were not interested in African American stories
    (B) hints that the stories were not just entertainment
    (C) hints that an **implied** meaning is not stated outright
    (D) says that slaveholders did not try to stamp out oral literature

11. All of the following are good definitions for **upbraid** *except*
    (A) criticize
    (B) harm
    (C) scold
    (D) blame

12. You can tell from the article that **testify** means to
    (A) completely understand
    (B) bear witness
    (C) pretend
    (D) fully deny

13. The writer gives us a clue to the meaning of **secluded.** What is the clue?
    (A) African Americans told stories.
    (B) African Americans lived separately.
    (C) Stories were told in the evenings.
    (D) African American storytellers used African folk tales as sources for stories.

14. To let us know that **derived** means taken from, the writer
    (A) gives an example of an African American folk tale that comes from an African source
    (B) says the African Americans were taken from their homes without their consent
    (C) associates **derived** with the term *folk tales*
    (D) tells us that the stories of Brer Fox and Brer Bear are part of America's folklore

15. The writer indicates that the stories allowed African Americans to **detach** themselves from their suffering. Here, **detach** means to
    (A) review
    (B) separate
    (C) reconnect
    (D) understand

16. To let us know that **eligible** means qualified or suitable, the writer
    (A) hints that most folk tales are passed down from generation to generation
    (B) uses the phrase "long ago"
    (C) says that new stories can qualify as folk tales
    (D) uses the word *collection*

17. To let us know that **miscellaneous** means "various kinds of," the writer
    (A) hints that stories are constantly being created
    (B) mentions memories
    (C) refers to the time after the enslavened people were freed
    (D) refers to an assortment of stories

18. The writer states, "Such stories often reflect the African Americans' attitudes toward the continued **denial** of their rights." Here, **denial** means
    (A) extension of
    (B) eventual acceptance of
    (C) decision to advance
    (D) refusal of a request

19. Which of the following items is an example of how folk tales **illuminate** the feelings of African Americans?
    (A) The stories reflect African American values and culture.
    (B) The stories are proof of the courage and wisdom of African Americans.
    (C) The stories continue to give shape and voice to one version of the American experience.
    (D) The stories reveal, like a light in darkness, the feelings of a people.

20. To let us know that **tangible** means "capable of being felt," the writer
    (A) says the old stories are proof of African American courage and wisdom
    (B) restates **tangible** proof as concrete evidence
    (C) mentions several famous authors
    (D) associates **tangible** with the phrase "continue to give shape and voice to"

Name _____ Date _____ Class _____

READING NEW WORDS IN CONTEXT

Lesson 15 CONTEXT: Voices of the United States

Introduction. Many people think of a job as something they do to make money for themselves or their families. However, a job is more than that. Each person's work, whether it is in a science laboratory, on the farm, or in the home, contributes to the country as a whole.

In the following story, an eighth-grade class is talking about the jobs the members of their families do. The story gives you an opportunity to expand your vocabulary. Below are twenty Vocabulary Words that are used in the passage and in the exercise that follows it.

aeronautics	automaton	erosion	parasitic	respiration
agenda	commute	hydraulic	photogenic	synthetic
antibiotics	congest	hypothesis	planetarium	technology
arrogant	considerate	malfunction	rebate	warranty

Building the United States

Mr. Nguyen's students at Quannah Parker Middle School are discussing how members of their families are contributing to today's world.

"My grandfather was always interested in flying," says Mohammed. "That's why he's very pleased that my father is doing research in the field of **aeronautics** (1)."

"My mom does research, too," says Mariante. "She's working on developing a new **antibiotic** (2). It's for people who are allergic to most other **antibiotics**. If she can develop it, it will really help them when they get infections. At least that's her **hypothesis** (3)."

"Excuse me," says Arnold, "but what's a **hypothesis**?"

"An unproven theory," says Mariante. "She thinks that's what will happen, but she hasn't proved it yet."

"That's interesting," Juan Carlos responds. "You know, my brother is thinking about going into research. He's interested in applying scien-

tific knowledge to farming, in the **technology** (4) of farming. He may become a soil scientist. He's especially interested in learning how to prevent soil **erosion** (5)—you know, to prevent the soil from wearing away. He's also interested in plant diseases, especially in **parasitic** (6) ones—the kind that are caused by an organism that draws its life from the plant it lives on."

Silvia remarks, "My grandparents were farmers. They used to grow cotton, but then people started wearing **synthetic** (7) fabrics like polyester, so they tried some other crops. Finally, they decided to just farm part time and to take other jobs."

"There are still farmers in my family," says Kenneth. "I've always loved the farm machinery. When I was a little kid, it seemed enormous. Today I can operate some of that equipment, and someday I'm going to be a farmer."

"Not me," says Meigumi. "I like living in the city. There's always something to do. Last week, one of the things on our **agenda** (8) was to go to

Copyright © by Holt, Rinehart and Winston. All rights reserved.

READING NEW WORDS IN CONTEXT **231**

the **planetarium** (9). We made sure that it was included in our schedule because there was a special show. On the ceiling was a kind of movie of the planets and stars, projected up there like a film."

"That's interesting, Meigumi, but let's try to stay on the topic of careers," says Mr. Nguyen.

Tasha raises her hand. "My sister is a sociologist, and she studies urban life. She says the crime rate in cities is always higher. Of course, there is crime in the country, but not as often."

"What other jobs do your family members have?" asks Mr. Nguyen.

"Well, my sister is very **photogenic** (10). That's why she decided to be a model. I don't mean to sound **arrogant** (11), or conceited, but she's been on the cover of three magazines," Leroi says.

Camilla says, "My mom gives this special kind of treatment at the hospital. The treatment she gives helps people with **respiration** (12), or breathing, problems. She is a **respiratory** specialist. Sometimes a person's lungs will become **congested** (13) because they're filling up with fluid, and my mom works to prevent that from happening."

"My sister works at the electronics factory out in Redbud," say Tanika. "She checks to make sure that a **warranty** (14) is packed in the box with every microwave oven. That's the little piece of paper that guarantees that the microwave will work for at least twelve months. During that time, if it starts overcooking your food or

malfunctions (15) in some other way, you can get it replaced. Sometimes her duties change. Last week, she was checking to make sure there was a **rebate** (16) coupon packed in with every VCR. If you bought a certain brand of videotape, you could get two dollars off with the coupon."

"My dad isn't working right now," says Chris. "He finds ways to stay busy, though. He's a really **considerate** (17) person. One of the nice things he does is to help some of the elderly people in our neighborhood do their shopping and stuff. He says he'd like to get a job doing that."

"You know," adds Estelle, "both my dad and mom were out of work for a while last year. It was pretty tough. Now Mom works at home doing day care, and Dad **commutes** (18) back and forth between here and the auto plant out in Green Springs. His job has something to do with **hydraulic** (19) brakes."

"Hywhatics?"

"**Hydraulic**. You know. Brakes that are operated by the pressure of a liquid forced through the brake lines. The new plant there is really cool— it's totally modern. They have—what do you call them?—**automatons** (20) working on the assembly line. Can you imagine working with a robot?"

"Let's save that question for science. What other jobs have members of your families done?" Mr. Nguyen looks out at the class. Six more hands go up.

EXERCISE *Reading Strategically* ✍

Directions. Answer each of the following items by circling the letter of the correct answer. You may need to refer to the selection as you answer the items. The numbers of the items are the same as the numbers of the Vocabulary Words in the selection.

1. You can tell from the story that **aero-nautics** means
  (A) a contribution to today's world
  (B) an occupation
  (C) a field that needs research
  (D) the science of aircraft

2. The writer provides a clue to the meaning of **antibiotics**. What is the clue?
  (A) Many people are allergic to **antibiotics**.
  (B) Mariante's mother does research on **antibiotics**.
  (C) **Antibiotics** are new.
  (D) **Antibiotics** help people who get infections.

3. You can tell from the story that **hypothesis** means
(A) interesting research
(B) unproven theory
(C) scientific research
(D) scientific proof

4. The writer tells us that Juan Carlos's brother is interested in the scientific aspects, or **technology,** of farming. Here, **technology** means
(A) farm equipment
(B) applied science
(C) soil
(D) information

5. Juan Carlos says, "He's especially interested in learning how to prevent soil **erosion**." Here, **erosion** means
(A) wearing away
(B) disease
(C) technology
(D) a kind of science

6. The writer indicates that Juan Carlos's brother is interested in studying **parasitic** diseases. Here, **parasitic** means
(A) like or of any disease
(B) farming equipment
(C) living off a living thing
(D) the research of plant life and plant diseases

7. The writer indicates that people wear **synthetic** fabrics. Here, **synthetic** means
(A) expensive
(B) cotton or other natural fibers
(C) not of natural origin
(D) anything raised on a farm

8. The writer states, "Last week, one of the things on our **agenda** was to go to the planetarium." Here, **agenda** means
(A) serious thoughts
(B) errands to run
(C) leisure time
(D) list of things to do

9. Meigumi tells us that they went to the **planetarium** last week. **Planetarium** means
(A) something to do
(B) special show
(C) a place that shows a kind of film of the stars
(D) a movie theater that shows science fiction films only

10. The writer gives us a clue to the meaning of **photogenic**. What is the clue?
(A) Leroi has a sister.
(B) Leroi's sister made a decision concerning her career path.
(C) Leroi's sister has a successful career.
(D) Leroi's sister has been on the cover of three magazines.

11. All of the following are good definitions of **arrogant** *except*
(A) haughty
(B) vain
(C) conceited
(D) meek

12. Camilla says that her mother helps people who have **respiration** problems. Here, **respiration** means
(A) having to do with the emotions
(B) having to do with breathing
(C) having to do with hospitals
(D) special

13. Which of the following is the most likely reason that lungs become **congested**?
(A) Camilla's mother helps them.
(B) People have breathing problems.
(C) People are in the hospital.
(D) Lungs fill up with fluid.

14. You can tell from the story that **warranty** means
(A) a package
(B) a guarantee
(C) a little
(D) a microwave oven

15. An example the story mentions of one way a microwave oven **malfunctions** is that
(A) it may come with a little piece of paper
(B) it will work for at least twelve months
(C) it may overcook food
(D) it may be replaced

16. To let us know that a **rebate** is a reduction or discount, the writer
(A) lets us know that the coupon was good for two dollars off
(B) hints that the job is a new one
(C) suggests that a **rebate** should be included in every box
(D) hints that the VCR would not work without a **rebate**

17. In this story, **considerate** means
(A) thoughtful
(B) busy
(C) unemployed
(D) interested only in the elderly

18. Estelle says that her dad **commutes** back and forth between home and a job at an auto plant. Here, **commutes** means
(A) runs a day-care center
(B) runs
(C) travels back and forth
(D) works

19. The writer of the story gives us a clue to the meaning of **hydraulic**. What is the clue?
(A) The brakes are installed at an automobile assembly plant in Green Springs.
(B) Brakes are operated by the pressure of a liquid forced through the brake lines.
(C) The brakes are in automobiles.
(D) Mr. Nguyen doesn't approve of lengthy discussions about **hydraulics**.

20. The writer of this story gives us a clue to the meaning of **automatons.** What is the clue?
(A) The writer mentions the pressure created by a liquid.
(B) The writer links **automatons** to brake lines.
(C) The writer links **automatons** to the word robot.
(D) Mr. Nguyen seems reluctant to spend class time talking about **automatons**.

Vocabulary Words

abuse
acceptance
access
accessible
accessory
accommodations
activate
adapt
adept
adequate
adjacent
advantageous
advent
aeronautics
agenda
aggressive
alliance
anonymous
anthology
antibiotics
anxiety
appalling
apt
aristocrat
aroma
arrogant
articulate
artisan
aspiration
assumption
attain
automaton

badger
baffle
bankrupt
barbarism
basis
baste
bewilder
blockade
boisterous
boycott

braggart
burly

calamity
calculation
capital
casual
catastrophe
category
censorship
charitable
circulate
circumnavigate
clarify
climax
colossal
commute
complement
condemn
confederation
confide
confiscate
congest
consecutive
considerate
contagious
contemporary
controversy
convert
creative
customary

decade
deceased
deceive
dedicate
deduction
defy
delegate
demolish
denial
deport
depose

derive
descend
detach
dictate
diction
dilapidated
dilute
diminish
dingy
diplomat
disagreeable
discord
dismantle
dispatch
dispense
dissect
distraction
durable

eccentric
ecology
elegant
eligible
embarrass
emigrate
eminent
emphasize
endorse
enhance
epidemic
erosion
essay
evacuate
exaggeration
exertion
extensive

falter
famine
famished
feasible
feline
ferocious

fictitious
folklore
foresight
foreword
fragile
fragment
fraudulent
frequency

gallery
generate
glorify
gnarled
gracious
grieve

hamper
harmonious
haughty
haven
hilarious
hospitable
humidity
humiliate
hydraulic
hypothesis

illuminate
immense
immigrate
impel
imperative
imply
impose
improvise
impulsive
incite
inclination
incomparable
inconsiderate
indelible
inevitable
inflexible

Vocabulary Words, *(continued)*

ingenious
inherit
insoluble
integrity
intelligible
intensity
intentional
intercept
intervene
intolerance
intrigue
invariable
irk
isolation

jeopardize
jubilation

knoll

liable
liberate
literal

malfunction
malnutrition
manageable
maroon
memento
menace
menagerie
miscellaneous
misdeed
modify
monopoly
morale
motivate
multicolored
multitude

mutual
myriad
mystical

nationality
naturalization
negligent
neutral
notify
nourish
novelty

obituary
obscure
occupant
occurrence
omission
optimism
ordeal

pacify
parasitic
persistent
petition
petty
pewter
phenomenon
photogenic
picturesque
pious
planetarium
pleasantry
populate
posterity
potential
prearrange
predicament
premier
premiere

presume
primitive
privilege
probable
probation
propaganda
proposal
prosecute
provision
pulverize
pun

quaint
quench

rebate
recuperate
refuge
regime
remorse
remote
resolute
respiration
restore
restrain
revelation
rigid
riotous
romantic
ruthless

sable
salutation
sanctuary
sarcasm
satire
saturate
secluded
sedate

sincerity
spacious
strategy
successor
summit
superficial
sustain
synthetic

tangible
tariff
tarnish
technology
temperament
testify
therapy
thrifty
thrive
titanic
transit
tumult

unique
upbraid
urban
urgent

valid
valor
verify
vitality

warranty

NOTES

NOTES

NOTES

NOTES